THE MAKING OF
MODERN
The Age of Empire to the New Millennium
BRITAIN

THE MAKING OF
MODERN
The Age of Empire to the New Millennium
BRITAIN

JEREMY BLACK

THE HISTORY PRESS

First published in 2001 by Sutton Publishing Limited

This paperback edition first published in 2008 by
The History Press · Cirencester Road · Chalford · Stroud
Gloucestershire GL6 8PE

British Library Cataloguing in Publication Data
A catalogue record for this book is available from the British
Library.

ISBN 978-0-7509-4755-8

Typeset in Galliard.
Typesetting and origination by
Sutton Publishing Limited.
Printed and bound in England.

CONTENTS

JEREMY BLACK MBE is Professor of History at the University of Exeter. His many publications include *War for America* and *Culloden and the '45*.

To Trevor and Liz Phillpot,
good friends

LIST OF ILLUSTRATIONS

PREFACE

In taking the national story to today, covering just over 200 years, this book presented challenging problems of deciding what to include. Not everyone will agree with my choices, but I have been motivated by a desire to focus on big themes, to give due weight to economic, social and cultural developments, to place Britain in its world context, and also to show how developments within Britain affected the individual communities that it comprises.

Similarly, not all readers will agree with the views expressed, but I hope they stimulate thought and debate. With recent history, it is very much the case that we are not calm observers of the passage of time. Instead, being part of the world that is described poses problems for both writer and reader. Furthermore, terms such as overcrowding or radical, conservative or consumerist, have had very different meanings and connotations at different times; and to assume that attitudes and experiences in the past were shared by all is just as mistaken as such a view of the present. Interest as well as opinion varied and vary, and this necessarily affects both author in the choice of what is covered and reader in how it is assessed.

What follows conforms to an understanding of history as contingent, not fixed, as affected by the choices of millions of people, not determined by 'structures' or 'forces'. I am always worried when I read that such an event or change was inevitable as this does violence to the role of people and takes history from them. What is inevitable, though, is change, and the pace and impact of change and changes are central to the account that follows. They join 1776 to today, and us to our future.

The comments of Nigel Aston, Grayson Ditchfield, Stephen Evans, Bill Gibson, Paul Harvey, Harald Kleinschmidt, Murray

Pittock, Nigel Saul, Nick Smart, Henry Summerson, David Taylor, and Andrew Thorpe on an earlier draft of the first edition have been most helpful. I am most grateful for the encouragement and support of Christopher Feeney, Sarah Moore, Sarah Flight and Jim Crawley at Sutton Publishing. Lectures to the Oxford University Department for Continuing Education, the University of Virginia Summer School at Oxford, and the University of Cambridge Summer School have provided opportunities to develop ideas.

This book draws on my own research and on the work of others, particularly the first-rate work published in the numerous local history publications, many of which are unduly neglected. I am also fortunate, as editor of *Archives*, the journal of the British Records Association, from 1989 to 2005, and as general editor of the Macmillan series *British History in Perspective, Social History in Perspective and British Studies*, to have kept in touch with excellent work in many fields. Those who have provided friendship and hospitality during my travels in Britain have been more helpful than they probably appreciate.

ONE

INDUSTRIALISATION AND WAR,
1776–1815

In 1776, Britain's most populous colonies in North America declared independence; Adam Smith, a Glasgow professor, published *The Wealth of Nations*; Edward Gibbon, an enlightened MP, brought out the first volumes of his *Decline and Fall of the Roman Empire;* and, in 1777–9, an iron bridge was erected at Coalbrookdale in Shropshire. Each was an aspect of modernity and all represented change toward a different world.

The American Declaration of Independence made it clear that the revolution that had begun the previous year was intended to lead to a new state that would destroy the unity of the British Empire. It also asserted a set of principles that suggested a radically different political system and culture, one in which inherited privilege and power were replaced by a fairer society that was open to talent. *The Wealth of Nations* provided the basis for modern economic theory and argued the case for the free trade that was to become the ideology of the nineteenth-century British state, and the cause of much prosperity, as well as much hardship. In place of a cyclical theory of history, Gibbon's *Decline and Fall* suggested that progress was possible, and indicated it was not inevitable that a fresh wave of barbarians would destroy Britain and British civilisation, as it had done Rome.

The Coalbrookdale bridge, designed in 1775 by Thomas Farnolls Pritchard, showed progress in action. It had a 120-foot span, and carried the road on arched ribs springing from the bases of two vertical iron uprights. The construction details were worked out by experienced iron-founders.

Change was certainly coming from a series of developments that are collectively known as the Industrial Revolution. The development of industry and trade, agricultural improvement, and the construction of canals and better roads, led to a growth in national wealth and a gradually emerging new economy. Population growth produced rising demand. The percentage of the male labour force employed in industry rose from 19 in 1700 to 30 in 1800, while, because agricultural productivity increased, that in agriculture fell from 60 to 40. The British economy developed powerful advantages in trade and manufacturing compared to foreign states and greatly impressed informed foreign visitors.

A sense of economic change and the possibilities of progress was widely experienced in the later eighteenth century and can be glimpsed in depictions of industrial scenes, such as Coalbrookdale. Heroic paintings were produced in praise of scientific discovery and technological advance, for example by Joseph Wright of Derby. In the Frog Service that Josiah Wedgwood designed for Catherine the Great of Russia each piece of china was painted with a different British scene. These included not only aristocratic landscapes, such as Stowe, Buckinghamshire, but also the Prescot glassworks on Merseyside. From the 1730s and 1740s the majority of British commentators argued that modern achievements were superior to those of former times, especially the ancient world. A culture of improvement lay at the heart of much innovation and the diffusion of new techniques and machinery, although art, architecture, furniture, and other aspects of the cultural world, all used classical designs.

Progress took many forms, but the most important was a belief in the prospect and attraction of change. From 1759, there was a marked increase in the number of patents, testimony to an interest in the profitable possibilities of change.

Industrial development led to more specialisation, as well as a greater division of labour and the growth of capital. In parts of the economy, there were important changes in the experience and intensity of work, the organisation of labour, and in material conditions. There was a greater emphasis on the need for constant and regular work. New working practices and technology required a more disciplined workforce. The Derby clock- and instrument-maker John Whitehurst designed the first factory time-clocks, although most workers never saw or heard one, and time remained an indistinct concept until railways and factory buildings incorporated clocks in the nineteenth century. The cumulative impact of often slow and uneven progress was impressive by the end of the century, and, by then, the rate of industrial growth had risen markedly. Although by the end of the eighteenth century fewer than 2,500 steam engines had been produced, they each represented a decision for change.

This meant more than it does today, because the background was not one of a world of machines. Instead, for 1775 it is necessary to think of a country where distance kept most people for most of the time in their own neighbourhoods, where travel, especially by land, was difficult, and where the dark, the damp and the cold pressed hard on people. It is necessary to think of an age when injuries and illnesses that we now regard as posing few problems, instead were killers.

For rapid industrial growth, the essentials were capital, transport, markets and coal. Coal, a readily transportable and controllable fuel, was useful in the preparatory stages of traditional manufacturing methods, such as soap-boiling, and, of course, in new processes and in factories. Wood, with its greater bulk for calorific value and less readily controllable heat, was, in contrast, a poor basis for many industrial processes. Coal had to be mined and transported, and both these requirements acted as spurs for innovation and activity, especially the construction of canals and railways, along which horses pulled barges and wagons respectively. Without transport, coal was of scant value, but coal with transport could serve as the basis for the creation of buoyant mixed-industrial regions with large pools of labour and demand, and also specialist services. Faced by the costs of moving coal 3 miles by packhorse and barge from his colliery at Middleton to Leeds, in 1758 Charles Brandling secured an Act of Parliament 'for laying down a Wagon-way, in order for the better supplying the Town and neighbourhood of Leeds . . . with coals', the first Act to authorise the construction of a railway. In 1780, a

Newcomen steam engine was installed at Middleton, and, by the close of the century, the pit's average annual output was 78,500 tons. In 1776, Brandling had installed a steam engine at his pit in Felling, east of Gateshead, following up with the opening of a deep pit.

Steam engines were the icons of the new age. Thomas Jefferson, the future US president, visited the Albion Mill, a steam-powered corn mill, when he went to London in 1785. Although most power generation at the end of the century was still by traditional methods, steam engines offered an alternative source. They were best suited to enterprises where substantial quantities of energy were required for long periods, such as pumping water out of mines. Steam engines were also used for winding and, by the end of the century, for driving machinery. Continual change and the search for improvement were important parts of the process of the Industrial Revolution, and the Newcomen engine was improved as the casting and boring of cylinders developed, particularly thanks to the new boring machines produced by John Wilkinson in 1774 and 1781. These developments enabled the steam engine to become more efficient in its fuel use and more regular in its operation. In 1769, James Watt, the first to perfect the separate condenser for the steam engine, patented an improved machine that was more energy-efficient and therefore less expensive to run, although more expensive to buy. In 1782, Watt patented the double-acting rotative engine, which gave a comparative uniformity of rotary motion, and thus improved the capacity of steam engines to drive industrial machinery which required a reasonably smooth engine. In 1779, James Pickard, a Birmingham button-manufacturer, had fitted a crank and flywheel to his Newcomen engine in order to use its power to drive a mill that could grind metals. This innovation greatly enlarged the market for steam engines which was exploited by the partnership of Watt and the Birmingham industrialist Matthew Boulton. In 1802, Richard Trevithick patented beam engines powered by high-pressure steam, such as those near Redruth, Cornwall. They were used for pumping water out of mines and for winding men and ore.

There were also important developments in metallurgy. Coke replaced charcoal for smelting iron and steel. Henry Cort's method of puddling and rolling, invented in 1784, but not adopted until the 1790s, used coal to produce malleable iron more cheaply than the charcoal forge and refinery.

Combined with the application of steam power to coal mining, blast furnaces, and the new rolling and slitting mills, these changes led to a new geography of economic activity. Steam power freed industries from having to locate near riverine sites where water power could be obtained. Instead, industry was increasingly attracted to the coalfields. This was true, for example, of South Staffordshire, and also of South Wales, which also attracted copper smelting. Coastal shipping and canals helped overcome communication problems. The copper works in the lower Swansea valley depended on sea-borne supplies and used Cornish, Irish and Welsh copper. The valley dominated the non-ferrous smelting industry in Britain.

Demand for iron helped stimulate mining. The national production of the metal rose from an annual average of about 27,000 tons in 1720–4 and 1745–9, to 80,000 in 1789, while the production of coal rose from about 3 million tons in 1700 to 5.2 in 1750, 8.8 in 1755 and 15 by 1800, with the rate of growth accelerating from mid-century. Coal also became more important to the national economy as mining developed outside North-East England, which had been the most important coalfield in 1700 and continued growing. From mid-century there was also major growth in South Lancashire, South Wales, Cumberland and South Staffordshire.

Demand for coal, copper and iron helped to bring great wealth to landowners, and helped to drive the growth of the canal system. The Sankey Brook Navigation of 1755 carried coal from St Helens to Liverpool, and stimulated both the development of coal-consuming industries on Merseyside and the expansion of Cheshire's salt industry which depended on coal-fired salt pans. James Brindley, who was to become a great canal engineer, planned the canal by which, from 1761, Francis, 3rd Duke of Bridgewater moved coal from his Worsley mines to nearby Manchester. By 1792 freight traffic on the canal was worth £80,000 a year. Bridgewater's role is an instance of the cooperation between the landed order and commerce, as was the work of Sir Roger Newdigate in Warwickshire. He sought to link the coal mines developed by his father to Coventry by canal, and also actively promoted the Oxford Canal and the Coventry to Leicester turnpike road.

The pace of change was impressive. The building of the Staffordshire and Worcestershire Canal between 1766 and 1770 enabled the movement of Staffordshire coal and iron to the River Severn, and thence to the sea. The new town of Stourport was built at the junction of the canal and the river. The first coal barge arrived in Birmingham on the new Birmingham Canal in 1772. The Trent and Mersey Canal, known as the Grand Trunk and Brindley's most important canal, was completed three years later. The Coventry Canal carried coal from the 1780s, and the opening of the Monkland Canal in 1793 stimulated the development of the Lanarkshire coalfield in order to serve the rapidly growing Glasgow market. Delayed, in part, by the need to build many locks, the Birmingham to Worcester Canal was finished in 1815.

Canals were not separate from the process of industrial change, but integral to it. The location of new mine shafts, factories and wharves responded to the possibilities of canal transport. When the Britannia Foundry was established in Derby in 1818 to produce quality cast-iron products, it was sited on the banks of the River Derwent, and linked, via that and the Derby Canal, to the Midlands' canal system and the sea. *Smart's Trade Directory* for 1827 noted that from Pickfords' canal wharf in Wolverhampton, a leading centre for the manufacture of iron products, goods could be sent direct to seventy-three towns including Bristol, Liverpool, London and Manchester. The Exeter Canal was lengthened (and its banks raised) in 1825 to 1827, enabling ships of up to 400 tons to sail up to Exeter where a basin was opened in 1830.

Canals made it easier to transport bulk goods, although only on a wharf-to-wharf basis. Unless the water froze, they had a particular advantage over roads in the winter, as many of the latter were then impassable. This was especially true of routes across the Midland clays. Canals were also more predictable than coastal shipping.

Today these waterways are noted for leisure activities. It is a little difficult to visualise the major changes that they brought. In practice there was a new geography, as landlocked counties, such as Derbyshire and Staffordshire, found their relative position transformed. Totally new links were created. Isolation was lessened. This was not only true of industrial and mining areas. Agricultural regions were also affected. The opening of the canal between Aberdeen and Inverurie in 1805 made it easier for the Leith Hall estate to sell and deliver goods.

It is appropriate that the eighteenth century is known for canals, as the nineteenth is for railways, and the twentieth for roads. Each transport system was the product of the socio-political systems of the age, and each was central to economic transformation and to shifts in attitude. Each also led to geographical change, as new nodes emerged, although, unlike rail and road, canal was crucial to freight but not passenger traffic. The centre of passenger traffic, London, was not central to the canal system. Instead, thanks to the mutually stimulating interaction of waterways and industry, the West Midlands, South Lancashire and South Yorkshire became more important to communications.

In some regions, such as Cumbria, mountainous terrain limited the development of waterways, although in 1819 the Lancaster Canal linked Kendal to Preston. Carlisle was linked to the sea by a route maintained by the largest beam engine pump in the country. However, these regions were better served by the development of the turnpike system. Turnpike trusts were bodies authorised by parliament to raise capital in order to repair and build roads and to charge travellers to these ends. By 1800, there was a good system and, thereafter, a series of often quite small-scale changes greatly improved the network. Thus in Devon, the Honiton and Ilminster Turnpike Trust constructed a new road from Yarde to near Ilminster in 1807–12 and the Cullompton Turnpike Trust another from near Broadclyst to near Cullompton in 1813–16. There were also improvements to existing roads. In the 1820s and early 1830s, the worst routes of the Exeter Turnpike Trust were replaced. The use of macadam, for example on the Exeter to Exmouth turnpike in 1819, greatly helped with durability.

All these small developments led to smoother and more level roads, and thus to an ability to pull heavier loads. Road transport of freight had improved with the introduction in the 1760s of fly wagons. By changing teams of horses, these could travel day and night, covering 40 miles every twenty-four hours. The canals also encouraged related road transport. Thus, after the opening of Samuel Greg's cotton mill at Quarry Bank in Cheshire south of Manchester in 1784, wagons carried his raw cotton and spun yarn to and from his warehouse on the Bridgewater Canal.

There was also some important bridge-building. Cheshire's were improved in the 1770s, with bridges repaired and a new one constructed across the River Bollin. The iron Wear Bridge, built by Rowland Burdon in 1796, was the new lowest crossing point on the river and the first bridge in Sunderland. It was crucial to the development of the town and was regarded as a great achievement of the age. In London, Westminster Bridge in 1750 was followed by new bridges across the Thames at Blackfriars (1769), Vauxhall (1816), Waterloo (1817) and Southwark (1819).

At sea, storms claimed many lives. In addition, there were too few lighthouses or other helps to navigators. In the Bristol Channel, many ships were lost on Lundy's reefs, and the construction of the Old Light on Lundy, a major lighthouse completed in 1820, was long overdue.

Coal and canals were vital to the industrialising regions of Britain, but there were also other important changes. This was particularly, but not only, true of textiles, an industry that benefited from the growing consumerism of the period. In the cloth trade a series of technological changes attracted and attract attention because they dramatically altered what individual workers could achieve and transformed the organisational basis of industry. John Kay's flying shuttle of 1733 increased the productivity of handloom weavers by making it possible both to produce double-width cloths and to weave more speedily, although it was half a century before it came into general use. Woollen textile manufacturing was greatly changed by the early machinery that raised the productivity of labour, such as James Hargreaves' hand-powered spinning jenny of 1764. The same period also saw developments that produced machine-spun cotton yarn strong enough to permit all-cotton cloth. These included Richard Arkwright's water frame of 1768, which applied the principle of spinning by rollers, and Samuel Crompton's mule of 1779 with its spindle carriage. In 1773, Arkwright produced a cloth solely of cotton, and two years later he patented a process enabling yarn manufacture on one machine.

Machine-produced yarn was smoother and more even than hand-spun cotton. This encouraged the transfer of spinning from home to factory production. From 1771, Arkwright and his partners built a number of water-powered cotton mills in Lancashire and the Midlands that displayed the characteristics of the factory system, including the precise division of labour and the continual cooperation of workers in the different manufacturing processes. The first worsted spinning mill was constructed in 1784, and in 1790 Arkwright erected a Boulton and Watt steam engine in his Nottingham mill. The cylinder printing machine invented in 1783 transformed the basis of the calico printing industry. The potential for industrial development was not only a product of new technology. In addition, agricultural developments and population growth both led to a larger workforce available for work in industry, while rising population and prosperity increased demand.

While it is important not to exaggerate the scale of economic change, especially the number of factories, it was, nevertheless, more extensive in Britain than elsewhere in Europe or the world. Furthermore, a new economic geography of Britain, of expansion and decline, winners and losers, was being created. By the 1790s, industrial change had a clear regional pattern that was reflected in indicators such as expenditure on poor relief by head of population. Seasonally unemployed labourers, many of whom worked in farming, were a major call on poor relief, although the elderly poor also required aid. In 1801 the average figure per head for England and Wales was 9s 1d (45p), but in the industrial counties it was far lower – 4s 4d in Lancashire and 6s 7d in the West Riding of Yorkshire – while counties with hardly any industry, such as Sussex, or with declining industries, such as Essex, Norfolk and Suffolk, had to pay far more than the average.

There was a general crisis of industry in southern England from the late eighteenth century, as coal-based manufacturing, factories, and less restrictive working practices encouraged developments in Lancashire and Yorkshire, where labour was cheaper. For example, from the 1780s, the woollen textile industry of the West Riding of Yorkshire acquired a price advantage over competitors such as those in Devon. Exeter, a major centre for the export of serges, a type of cloth, exported 390,000 pieces in 1777 but only 8,126 in 1800.

In 1787, John Rolle MP proposed a radical response to the issue of poor relief. 'At the express desire of his constituents' and in response to 'the very heavy and increasing [poor] rates', Rolle suggested a national fund provided by progressive taxation and compulsory national insurance. Nothing came of this.

Slumps that hit manufacturing and mining in expanding or buoyant areas, however, could lead to severe conditions, especially given the limited nature of social welfare. In March 1800, William Jenkin, land agent at Lanhydrock in Cornwall, reported that the local copper miners had been hard hit: 'There are a great number of families in this neighbourhood who never provide themselves with any kind of food but Barley Bread, Potatoes and Salt Pilchards from one week to another, with which they sip what they call Tea, little better than warm water without milk or sugar.'

Industry became especially significant in Central Scotland, in the North and the Midlands of England, and in South Wales; in all cases in or near coalfields. The population rose rapidly in such areas: in County Durham from about 70,000 in 1700 to 150,000 by 1801. In addition, urban manufacturing was very important, with towns such as Derby, Newcastle, Nottingham and Stockport becoming major centres of activity. The national population shot up, and especially in such centres – in the borough of Liverpool from 83,250 in 1801 to 375,955 in 1851, and in Stockport in Lancashire from 3,144 in 1754 to 4,975 in 1779 and 14,830 in 1801. The relationship between urbanisation and industrialisation became closer, with the growing cities closely associated with manufacturing or with related commerce and services.

Political changes encouraged this process. The reopening of the crucial export trade to America in 1783 encouraged a boom that was particularly important for cotton production. War with France from 1793 led to far greater demand for metallurgical products and greatly encouraged the development of iron production, especially in South Wales. Further north, John Wilkinson produced cannon, mortars and shells in his iron works at Bersham near Wrexham and Broseley near Bridgnorth.

Living Conditions

Yet economic development produced stresses. The environmental damage was little recognised and, therefore, rarely mentioned, but it was considerable. Slag and pit heaps expanded across the landscape. Jabez Fisher, a visiting American Quaker, commented in 1776 on the Forest Copper works at Morriston in the Swansea valley: they 'vomit out vast columns of thick smoak, which, curling as this rise, mount up to clouds'. Illustrations of industrial sites from the period made much of smoke. This was true, for example, of those of the Shropshire ironworks in Coalbrookdale, which Fisher described as representing 'all the horrors that Pandemonium could show . . . an immense Theatre lighted only by the streams of light which rise from the Furnaces . . . the Craters of the burning Mountains'.

Industrial fumes must also have been considerable, as, too, the pollution of rivers caused by untreated industrial effluent. Trace elements in the domestic water supply, much of which was taken direct from rivers, would have increased. The chemical factories along the Tyne, such as the alkali plant at Low Walker, produced noxious gases. In 1829, Newcastle Corporation sued Doubleday & Easterly because of the pollution produced by their soapworks. Even leisure resorts were affected. The colliers that unloaded coal until 1830 on the beach at the newly fashionable resort of Brighton produced floating coal dust that covered swimmers.

Such conditions hit life expectancy. Lancashire had high marriage and birth rates, but also high death rates, higher than those in other counties in the 1830s and 1840s. Living conditions were generally grim. At the birthplace of the railway engineer George Stephenson, a stone tenement in the Tyne valley at Wylam, the Stephensons had only two rooms. They had to share the building with three other families. George's father was a coal miner, and George himself started work at the age of ten.

Working conditions deteriorated for many. The poet John Keats wrote in 'Isabella' (1830):

> . . . many a weary hand did swelt
> In torched mines and noisy factories.

The pauper children from the workhouses who made up about a third of the workforce at Quarry Bank Mill worked twelve hours a day for six days a week, and were sent to praise God twice on Sundays. Child labour is considered especially deplorable today, but the difference between rich and poor counties in the early nineteenth century was largely the result of job opportunities (or their absence) for all family members. Child labour was not new in Britain, although the conditions in which it now took place were awful.

Individual working processes were frequently harmful. Needle-manufacture, which was concentrated in Warwickshire and Worcestershire, involved scouring and sharpening the needles, and this produced harmful dust. A Somerset miners' song of about 1800 included the verse:

> Sometimes the staunce air makes us tremble for fear,
> When candles blaze high and burn blue,
> The flame from the snuff-flash like lightning goes off,
> Whence fatal effect do ensue, my brave boys,
> And lives have been lost not a few.

The imperial economic system also depended in part on the harsh practice of slavery and on the brutal slave trade. The British had played the leading role in the slave trade, but abolitionist sentiment, pushed hard by evangelicals, led to the Abolition Act of 1807 which banned the importation of slaves into British colonies. Slavery itself was abolished in 1833.

Within Britain there was concern about the effects of new machinery on traditional working practices. Charles Whetstone's *Truths No. 1, or the Memoirs of Charles Whetstone, or an Exposition of the Oppression and Cruelty Exercised in the Trades and Manufactures of Great Britain* (1807), one of the earliest working-class autobiographies produced during the Industrial Revolution, referred to himself as born 'without any other birthright than that of being impelled along the common beaten-road of life, by the stern and unrelenting commands of Poverty and Labour'. Whetstone condemned the employment of child-labour in the Derby silk mills, and the nature of factory employment. Some took violent action. James Hargreaves' spinning jennies were destroyed by rioters in Blackburn in 1768-9. Hargreaves fled to Nottinghamshire. In 1779, Arkwright's new factory at Birkacre near Chorley in Lancashire was burnt down by 3,000-4,000 rioters angered by the offer of work at lower rates. Over 100 machines were destroyed in the Lancashire riots of that year, but troops reimposed order and Parliament refused to condemn the new machines. In Leicester there were riots in 1773 and 1787 against improved stocking frames, and in Shepton Mallet spinning jennies were smashed.

Industrial relations were not always violent, and it was possible to win a measure of agreement for change. Dialogue, albeit not from a position of equality, between employers and workers facilitated industrialisation in the West Riding and in Malmesbury. Yet economic change could focus social tension, and this in the context of an increasing amount of rivalry between different social groups after 1760. The press was generally unsympathetic to rioters. The *Salisbury and Winchester Journal* of 23 May 1791 commented on a recent riot against new machinery at Bradford, Wiltshire, a textile centre, in which a carding machine was 'tried' and ceremoniously burnt: 'Eighteen or twenty years experience in Yorkshire has shown that all machinery in manufactures does not lessen but increases the ability and means of employing the poor.' There were also protests in other centres in and near Wiltshire, including Trowbridge, Frome and Chippenham. The protests delayed the adoption of new machines in the area and this contributed to a slower growth rate than in Yorkshire.

Anxiety about popular economic discontent climaxed during the Luddite riots of 1812, which drew their name from the mythical Ned Ludd. Numerous attacks on new knitting frames in Nottinghamshire led the government to send 2,000 troops to the county, and more than 12,000 were deployed across the Midlands and the North to deal with popular unrest. In Yorkshire, the assaults were on new machines in the woollen industry, while in Lancashire pressures in the cotton industry led to food riots and attacks on equipment.

On the land, rising demand for food benefited landlords and tenant farmers, and not the landless poor. Agricultural wages remained low. Social tensions in rural areas can be seen with poaching. The Game Laws were widely regarded as unfair, while the gentry viewed challenges to them as theft and as threats to the preservation of the social order. From the late eighteenth century, game preserves came to be protected by spring (automatic) guns and man traps.

Political Developments

This was a major problem for a state then engaged in a life and death struggle with Napoleonic France, but there was no linkage between machine-breaking and the war. In general, after the American War of Independence (1775–83), in which the Revolutionaries had successfully sought French help, there was only a tenuous relationship between domestic and foreign challenges to the British state. There was no equivalent in England, Scotland or Wales to the Irish rising of 1798, which was both a very major insurrection and one that sought, and received, foreign, in this case French, help. This revival, in a different cause, of the earlier geopolitics of Jacobitism – the conflation of French enmity and security problems in the Celtic kingdoms – was crushed, and not matched by comparable domestic problems nor by foreign intervention in England or Scotland. In Scotland, the United Scotsmen did work in close concert with the United Irishmen but their importance was far less. Scotland (as later in 1820) was not totally stable, but, by European or Irish standards, it was relatively quiet.

With the very important exception of Ireland, it proved possible to redefine Britishness without civil conflict. Britishness had been outlined in the terms of the established Protestant churches, but, after the defeat of Jacobitism in 1746, awareness of Britain's position as a great power, competing with others both in Europe and for an expanding overseas empire, ensured a re-evaluation of attitudes to the religiously heterodox. By the 1770s political elites were contemplating Catholic emancipation. The American War of Independence and the broad European alliance against Britain during that conflict forced consideration of ways to allow the mass of the Irish population and also Scots Highlanders to be recruited into the armed forces, and directed attention to the penal religious legislation which prevented this. Relief Acts in England and Ireland followed in 1778, and were proposed for Scotland, before anti-Catholic rioting caused the authorities to back off.

The process of extending civil rights to non-Anglicans was difficult, and old prejudices did not disappear. Nevertheless, the role of religion in defining and expressing political allegiance declined. This was crucially important during the Napoleonic Wars. Irish recruiting in the fifteen years before Waterloo exceeded 90,000.

From the crushing defeat of Scottish Jacobitism at Culloden in 1746 until the 1790s, Britain was essentially politically stable, certainly in comparison with the decades of Jacobite challenge. An emphasis on Jacobitism and a reconsideration of the nature of stability, so that attention is focused on viable challenges to the established structure of authority rather than on opposition to particular ministries, offers a different chronology of eighteenth-century stability to the customary one. It can be

seen that the seriousness of the challenge offered to George III
(1760–1820) and his ministries by opposition agitation in the
first three decades of his reign, especially by John Wilkes in the
1760s, was in fact limited, particularly in so far as England was
concerned. Political stability in the late eighteenth century did
not preclude serious constitutional disputes, as in the 1760s,
1782–4 and 1788–9, and extra-parliamentary action, some of
it radical, but discord was compatible with a stable political
system. However, a degree of ambivalence (albeit diminished
compared to the past) towards the notion of a loyal opposition
and legitimate opposition tactics helped to blind many contemporaries to this.

Rather than there being any deep-seated fissure within the
political system, ministries were stable as long as they could
avoid serious problems, and in relative terms these were more
important an obstacle than in the twenty-first century because
ministries did not lose general elections. Lord North, Prime
Minister 1770–82, won the elections of 1774 and 1780, but
was brought down in March 1782 by his inability to secure a
satisfactory solution to the American Revolution. William Pitt
the Younger won the elections of 1784, 1790 and 1796, but
nearly fell in 1788–9 due to George III's apparent madness, and
fell in 1801 because he could not persuade the king to accept
Catholic emancipation.

More generally, government relied on cooperation between
the ministry and the social elite and lacked both a substantial
bureaucracy and a well-developed bureaucratic ethos. Policy
was contested: aside from the institutional framework of
contention – elections and Parliament – the Court and
ministerial context of elite politics was not one of uniform
opinions and an absence of debate. Nevertheless, differences
did not prevent effective government. Furthermore, there was
no permanent struggle between government and the world of
extra-parliamentary politics, and no consistent and coherent
challenge to the political system.

Yet it would be misleading to underrate the political problems
of the period. The loss of America led to a serious political crisis
in 1782–3, in which George III and his ministers sought to end

the war and wrestled with the problem of mutual mistrust in a system that required cooperation. Furthermore, the war had more than doubled the national debt. North was succeeded by Charles, 2nd Marquess of Rockingham, the leader of the Whigs, who formed a coherent political group in opposition to George III. His ministry, however, only lasted fourteen weeks because he suddenly and unexpectedly died before he could negotiate peace or push through the domestic reforms he believed necessary in order to lessen government power in Parliament. George III then chose as prime minister William, 2nd Earl of Shelburne, not the new leader of the Rockinghamites, William, 3rd Duke of Portland. This led to the resignation of prominent Rockinghamites, especially Charles James Fox, but the king's determination to defend his prerogative of choosing his own ministers was generally accepted.

Shelburne skilfully exploited the divisions between Britain's opponents in the War of American Independence, offering favourable terms to the Americans in order to persuade them to abandon France, Spain and the Dutch. In February 1783, however, he failed to persuade Parliament to accept the peace preliminaries which were genuinely unpopular, especially the lack of any guarantees for the Loyalists and for British debts. Aside from this issue and the isolated Shelburne's personal unpopularity, the two largest groups in the Commons, those led by Fox and North, were aiming to secure office. They were prepared to do so regardless of any claim by George III to choose his ministers.

Shelburne resigned in February 1783 to be replaced by the Fox–North coalition between former opponents, a ministry George III only very reluctantly accepted, but royal hostility helped to make this ministry unstable. In December 1783, George dismissed the coalition and called on William Pitt the Younger to form a government, despite the fact that it did not enjoy the support of the majority of MPs.

The second son of William Pitt the Elder, and only twenty-four in 1783, Pitt the Younger was classified as a Tory by his opponents, and regarded as unduly favourable to the king. He became the youngest prime minister ever. This provoked a

The 'Madness' of George III

'I have always had little or no hopes of the King. I have sent however by this day's courier a remede which they tell me est sure. It is tout simplement the blood of a jack-ass which after passing a clear napkin through it two or three times is given afterwards to the patient to drink.'

The owner of Knole, Kent, the womanising, cricket-playing John, 3rd Duke of Dorset writing back from his embassy in Paris in the winter of 1788/9 revealed the extent to which, in health, as in so much else, the notion of a division between a modernising, enlightened elite and a marginal populace sunk in superstition was, and is, misleading. Contemporaries had no idea how to cope with the 'madness' of the king, an episode highlighted in 1991 by a most successful play by Alan Bennett and the subsequent film.

George III was fifty in 1788, not old by the standards of the age, although his father, Frederick, Prince of Wales had died in 1751 at the age of forty-four, while four of George's six siblings died before the age of fifty. George had been seriously ill in 1765 but, thereafter, his health had been fairly good. He had survived an assassination attempt by the deranged Margaret Nicholson in August 1786. On 5 November 1788, however, George became delirious while at Windsor. He was incapacitated by an attack of porphyria, which to contemporaries appeared to betoken the onset of insanity.

This provoked a constitutional crisis. Ill health had none of the finality of death, but it became apparent that, while George was ill, it would be necessary to make provisions for a regency, and that this arrangement might have to last until the king's death, as his recovery seemed unlikely. George's eldest son, George, Prince of Wales, was no friend to his father or his ministers, and thus the question mark that the presence of an heir to the throne always posed to the politics and personnel of the current monarch's government was dramatically highlighted in Britain in 1788. It had been a serious problem for the governments of both George I and George II, most obviously in 1717–20 and 1747–51, when their respective heirs, the future George II and Frederick, Prince of Wales, had led opposition to them. The abrupt and sweeping differences that a new monarch could make had been demonstrated with the fall of the Tories after the accession of George I in 1714, and again when George III himself had succeeded to the throne in 1760 and destabilised the Pitt the Elder–Newcastle ministry.

Although George III's loyal wife, Queen Charlotte, was mentioned, it was clear that if there were to be a regency, the Prince of Wales would be regent, and the ministry would therefore change because the prince was close to Fox. The extent of his powers, however, was unclear, and that would have to be determined by Parliament.

It met on 20 November 1788, only to be adjourned for a fortnight while the politicians awaited developments in George's health. When on 3 December the king's five doctors were examined before the Privy Council they disagreed as to whether he was likely to recover, although two days later a new doctor, Francis Willis, under whose attention George was to improve, first saw his new patient.

Parliamentary debates on 10 and 16 December over the powers of the regent were very bitter and there was much opposition to Pitt's policy of restrictions. Ministerial cohesion slackened as some sought favour in the emerging political order round the prince. The situation was worrying for Pitt, for his position appeared to many to be one of delaying the inevitable and thus sustaining instability. Fortunately for him, from early February, George began to improve in time to prevent the creation of a regency and the formation of a Whig ministry. The Prince of Wales did not become regent until 1811 and, by then, he had broken with the Whigs and become a conservative figure.

The slaughtered jackass had been unnecessary and Dorset had not been recalled from his post as he had feared. Close to Marie Antoinette and to French courtiers opposed to reform, Dorset was no sympathiser with the early stages of the Revolution and he left Paris on 8 August 1789. Lord Steward of the Royal Household from that October until shortly before his death in 1799, Dorset's most lasting legacies are at Knole: the portraits he bought from his close friend Sir Joshua Reynolds that hang in the Reynolds Room, and the plaster statue of the nude Giovanna Zanerini that is at the foot of the Great Staircase. Known to the duke as Jannette, she was a dancer at the King's Theatre in the Haymarket, who became his long-standing mistress in 1779.

serious political crisis. George's actions, which were regarded by some as unconstitutional, were countered by the collective resignation of several office-holders. George saw himself as 'on the edge of a precipice', and in January 1784 stated his willingness to abdicate if the opposition gained office. However, public support turned toward the king and the free exercise of the royal prerogative in ministerial selection. Pitt's victory in the 1784 general election restored political stability and began a period of largely stable ministerial and parliamentary politics that lasted until his resignation in 1801. Pitt understood the need for sound finances. His prudent management and a growth in trade stabilised government finances.

This new-found order was challenged in late 1788 when an attack of porphyria, a blood disease producing symptoms akin to madness, led to the belief that George III was insane and near death. The resulting Regency Crisis nearly brought the fall of the government and its replacement by the Whig opposition under Fox, who was close to George, Prince of Wales. Fortunately for Pitt, the king recovered in early 1789.

The next crisis was caused by the advance of the forces of Revolutionary France across the Austrian Netherlands (modern Belgium) in November 1792 and the resulting threat to the Dutch, now British allies. This was an emergency played out in the public eye and one in which concern about popular views was a major factor.

In recent decades, the press had played a major role in the development of national political campaigns, such as support for the radical John Wilkes in the 1760s, the organisation of Lord George Gordon's anti-Catholic Protestant Association, the county petitioning movements of the early 1780s calling for economical and parliamentary reform, opposition to slavery, and the protests of 1787–90 against the Test and Corporation Acts. These campaigns arose from the increasing importance of national lobby and interest groups that reflected, although they were not limited by, urbanisation, professionalisation and the broadening strata of the middling orders in society. Care was taken to keep these groups informed of political developments and to win their support.

The French Revolution that began in 1789 excited widespread interest in Britain and it was crucially important for the government that hostility to the growing radicalism of the Revolution combined strongly with popular loyalism in late 1792 to provide a firm domestic basis for opposition to France. On 28 November 1792, John Hatsell, Clerk of the House of Commons, referred to the Association for Preserving Liberty and Property against Republicans and Levellers, which had been launched at a meeting at the Crown and Anchor tavern in London on the 20th.

I wish every county was like Devonshire – but I fear that in Ireland, Scotland, the manufacturing parts of Yorkshire and particularly in London, there is a very different spirit rising . . . the Society at the Crown and Anchor. This appears to me a better plan than trusting to the soldiery and brings the question to its true point – a contest between those who have property and those who have none – If this idea is followed up generally and with spirit, it may, for a time, secure us peace *internally*.

The 1790s and 1800s witnessed an upsurge in conservative propaganda, for example, in the *Star, Sun, True Briton, Observer, York Courant, Liverpool Phoenix, Caledonian Mercury and Edinburgh Herald*. Loyalist propaganda also flourished in such periodicals as the *British Critic, Anti-Jacobin, Anti-Jacobin Review and Magazine, Loyalist, Anti-Gallican* and *Annual Register*. In Leicester, Manchester and Newcastle, where there were both radical and conservative newspapers, the latter triumphed.

The war with France that started in February 1793 sorely tested not only the British military system but all aspects of state and society. In 1794, the British were driven from the Austrian Netherlands, in 1795 their alliance system collapsed, and from 1796 the country was threatened by invasion. The British and their allies were no more successful after Napoleon took power in France in 1799. In 1802, by the Peace of Amiens, the government had to accept terms that left Britain isolated and France dominant in Western Europe.

The situation would have been even more grave had the navy not won a series of victories that enabled it to counter the consequences of France's co-option of the other leading naval powers, Spain and the Dutch, in 1795–6. In 1794, the French Brest fleet was defeated on the Glorious First of June, but, when the French gained the support of Spain, the British were forced to evacuate the Mediterranean. The subsequent crisis was overcome in 1797 when the Spanish and Dutch fleets were defeated off Cape St Vincent and at Camperdown respectively. In 1798, Horatio Nelson's destruction of the French fleet at the Battle of the Nile in Aboukir Bay undercut the consequences of Napoleon's invasion of Egypt, ending the French threat to India. The victory was celebrated by the construction of the Naval Temple by a local dining club on the Kymin in South Wales, while, on their Thoresby estate in Nottinghamshire, the Manvers family celebrated the victory at the Nile by laying out a plantation in the order of Nelson's line of battle. The British navy had the advantage in technology and resources as well as effective commanders, good seamanship and well-drilled gun crews. Progress in metallurgy improved British gunnery so that enemy ships were reduced to wrecks in a comparatively short time.

Pitt quickly discovered the difficulties of wartime leadership. The cost and economic disruption of the war led to inflation, the collapse of the gold standard under which the bullion value of paper currency was met by the Bank of England (1797), the introduction of income tax (1799), the stagnation of average real wages, and widespread hardship, especially in the famine years of 1795–6 and 1799–1801. The situation resulted in serious food rioting. Lancashire cotton weavers were not alone in having their real wages plummet by more than half in 1792–9. The government was also faced by naval mutinies in 1797 that owed much to anger over pay and conditions.

Concern encouraged government action against radicals, who found their activities prohibited or limited. Habeas Corpus was suspended, radicals were tried for sedition, and their newspapers, like the rest of the press, suffered from a rise in duty. The Treasonable Practices Act and Seditious Meetings Act of 1795 sought to prevent denunciations of the constitution, and large unlicensed meetings. These measures hindered the radical societies. The membership of the London Corresponding Society, which had been founded in 1792 to press for radical reforms, declined. Most of the leadership of the relatively numerous Sheffield radicals had fled or been prosecuted by 1796. Nevertheless, clandestine activity continued, although there is controversy over its significance and over the threat of revolution at the end of the 1790s and in the early 1800s. In addition, trade unions were hindered, although not ended, by the Combination Acts of 1799 and 1800 which made combinations of employees for improved pay or conditions illegal. Although oppressive, the Acts in practice had only a limited impact.

Despite royal opposition, Pitt had supported parliamentary reform in 1785, but, once the war broke out, he and the bulk of the establishment lost interest. In May 1798, William, 1st Marquess of Lansdowne, formerly Earl of Shelburne and now a radical, pressed the Lords for parliamentary reform: 'while it could be done gradually, and not to delay its necessity till it would burst all bounds'. However, such policies were now unpopular; as public opinion had moved against change.

The greater popularity of George III after the Regency Crisis helped the government. George catered to middle-class assumptions through hard work, sobriety, and glorified domesticity. He cultivated the image of being a father to all, as his personality shaped the monarchy more than theories on his role and legitimacy. He was no Napoleon. A system of hereditary monarchy dealt with the basic question of legitimacy and was appropriate for a society structured around privilege and hereditary succession, and with a markedly inegalitarian distribution of wealth and opportunity; in 1802, the Hebdomonal Council of Oxford saluted George as 'the illustrious defender of the social order'. Such a society, however, confronted the problems of the continual need for energetic and talented leadership and administrators. Napoleon personified the strengths and weaknesses of meritocratic monarchy, but one of the major aspects of the success of the British state and of British monarchy was that there was no need for George III, or for his eldest son,

Prince Regent 1811–20 and then George IV (1820–30), to be a military leader: merit could be provided by others.

In May 1810, William, Lord Grenville, who had been Prime Minister in 1806–7, wrote from his seat at Dropmore to Henry Brougham, an energetic Whig MP with a commitment to reform:

> This fine weather is not favourable to speculations about Parliamentary Reform and must at all events be my excuse for not having earlier answered the rational and well considered suggestions which you had the goodness to communicate to me. My general view of the situation is this. I continue to object strongly to the vague and undefined notions of reforming merely for the sake of reform. That is determining to make some change without previously considering its extent, its principles or its objects. I hold on the contrary side in equal reprobation the opinions in the other extreme, that on this point alone all change is to be rejected without examination, merely because it is a change. The just sentiment seems to be that in this as in every other matter in which the public interests are concerned the constant and vigilant superintendence of Parliament is required, neither adopting nor rejecting change in the abstract, but weighing each particular position in detail by the scale of probable advantage or mischief to the community . . . all ideas should be disclaimed of extensive and as you justly call them wholesale plans of reform which are at once to strike out for us a new constitution of government and legislation.

Grenville was no Tory, but his letter makes clear that conservatism in this period was broadly based and not simply dependent on politicians termed, then or subsequently, Tory. Another aspect of conservatism was recorded by the architect Gilbert Scott:

> The inhabitants of Gawcott were a very quaint race. I recollect my father [Thomas Scott, 1780–1835] saying that when he first went there to reconnoitre he found the road to it

rendered impassable by a large hole dug across it in which the inhabitants were engaged in baiting a badger; a promising prelude to an Evangelical Ministry among them! However he succeeded in bringing the place in due time into a more seemly state as to externals though the old leaven remained and a certain amount of poaching and other forms of rural blackguardism, though there grew up amongst all this a good proportion of really excellent people.

Far from being remote from urban life, Gawcott was close to Buckingham.

Nevertheless, despite this widespread conservatism, the stability of the political system was not some God-given national right, but, rather, owed much to success in war, especially the avoidance of invasion, to political leadership, and to social and economic developments. Similarly, there was nothing inevitable in the earlier transition that occurred from conspiracy and battlefield to elections and parliamentary government, a transition that in 1762 led the 'bluestocking' Elizabeth Montagu to reflect that 'a virtuoso or a dilettanti may stand as secure in these times behind his Chinese rail as the knight on his battlements in former days'.

The nature, practices and purposes of parliamentary government were not accepted by all. This led to a series of crises, most obviously in the North American colonies in 1775, among British radicals in the 1790s and late 1810s, and in Ireland in 1798. However, the authority of the British state was only overthrown in North America. Elsewhere, the landed elite and their urban allies remained in control because of their shared interests and confidence in their role, the lack of a widely accepted alternative, and, in Ireland, coercion. Governments that might be termed Tory, such as those of Pitt in 1801 and 1806, could fall without any sense that the essential continuity and conservatism of social structures and political practices were being compromised.

Pitt's second ministry, which had been formed in 1804, did not survive his early death in 1806, but the succeeding 'Ministry of All the Talents' fell in 1807, in large part because of uneasy

Wellington and the British Army

Initially, the British were badly affected by the military dynamism of Revolutionary France within Western Europe. British forces were less successful in the Low Countries in 1793–5 than they had been there in 1689–97, 1702–12 and even 1744–8, and in Germany in 1704 and 1758–62. The French were in reasonably secure control of the Low Countries from 1795 until 1814, the longest period in British history when the region was controlled by a hostile power. British challenges, in Holland in 1799 and in the Scheldt estuary in 1809, were both short-lived and unsuccessful, humiliatingly so, and even in 1814 things went wrong. In peace negotiations in 1801–2 the British had to accept French control of the region which they had been unwilling to tolerate before the war in 1792–3.

British failure in the Low Countries has led to an underrating of the army prior to Wellington's successes in Portugal and Spain in 1808–13. Nevertheless, his achievements appear more striking against the background of numerous British failures elsewhere in 1805–15, especially in Argentina in 1806 and 1807, Egypt in 1807, and at New Orleans in 1815. These defeats indicate that there was no necessary superiority for British troops and tactics, nothing inevitable about British victory, although they were all failures on the offensive that occurred during short-term amphibious campaigns, in each case against local forces that were securely based and well led, for example by Andrew Jackson at New Orleans. On the defensive against the French in Iberia, the British situation was different.

Wellington was also helped by the decline in the quality of the French Army due to near-continual campaigning. This used up veterans and affected the tactical sophistication of the force, not to mention its morale. French success in battle had greatly relied on the exploitation of the cooperation between cavalry, close-order infantry, artillery and skirmishers. A combination of attacks by different arms reduced both the enemy's physical means to resist and his will. The French experienced great difficulty in Spain in trying to achieve this. Terrain factors frequently precluded the effective use of their frequently superior cavalry and artillery. Attacks were often executed sequentially, rather than simultaneously, and by one arm, usually the infantry. French failures to weaken the British lines, by the use of artillery or skirmishers before the column attack, left the columns exposed to heavy defensive fire. The lack of unity among the corps commanders also hit the French hard; mutual support was far below the standard they achieved in North-Central Europe.

Clearly the leading naval power, able to defeat not only the navy of France but also those of her allies, Britain enjoyed a quite atypical military capability. Her commanders were able to withdraw isolated, retreating or defeated forces, as from New Jersey in 1778, Germany in 1795, Egypt in 1807, Corunna in 1808, and Walcheren in 1809; and thus to thwart or limit attempts to achieve a decisive tactical or strategic victory at the expense of the British. If necessary, Wellington's army could have been withdrawn from Portugal. It was also possible, thanks to maritime strength, to overcome logistical constraints presented by limited local supplies. This ability enhanced the role of sea power in transporting forces. The navy was also crucial for communications.

Like Napoleon, much of Wellington's skill lay in adapting quickly to fresh intelligence and changing circumstances. He had an eclecticism that was a product of personality, experience, the need for an adaptive military system, and the variety of the tasks facing the British. A bayonet charge, preceded by a volley, had become a standard British tactic from the late 1750s, used with effect in the War of American Independence (1775–83), and, with his fine grasp of timing and eye for terrain, Wellington brought the system to a high pitch of effectiveness. He employed the thin red line of two ranks that the British army had utilised in North America, but, like Abercromby's force in Egypt, his men fought elbow to elbow.

In India, Wellington, like other British generals, benefited from the superior discipline of outnumbered British units under fire. This was a matter of controlled British evolutions on the battlefield. Conflict between European forces and the role of drill and discipline in European military culture had led to a situation in which the Europeans acquired a capability advantage over non-Europeans in keeping cohesion and control in battle. This permitted more sophisticated tactics in moving and withholding units on the battlefield, and more effective fire. This was true both of the Russians in their wars with the Turks and of the British in India.

There, the British benefited from their heavy reliance on firepower, especially from light field guns firing grape and case shot. Storming did play an important role in the capture of fortified positions, but it generally followed the use of firepower to create breaches and could involve particularly heavy casualties. Yet, battlefield advances were also important, as, for example, later at Ters-el-Kebir in Egypt in 1882. Wellington's report on the crucial victory over the Marathas at Assaye in 1803, printed in the London Gazette of 31 March 1804, noted: 'the troops advanced under a very hot fire from cannon, the execution of which was terrible . . . I cannot write in too strong terms of the conduct of the troops, they advanced in the best order, and with the greatest steadiness under a most destructive fire, against a body of infantry far superior in numbers, who appeared determined to contend with them to the last, and who were driven from their guns only by the bayonet'. That this was very different from the accepted image of the Wellingtonian battlefield reflects in part the dominance of the icon of a defensive position – line or square, assaulted by greater numbers – in the symbolisation of the British way of war in this period.

As with William III in 1689–97 and Marlborough in 1702–11, Wellington's battlefield skills had to be matched by the command and strategic demands of coalition warfare. Unlike them, he also faced the varied challenges and requirements that reflected the growing range of British military commitments. In his case, that was true of India, while his service in Iberia was a result of the British inability to sustain their position in the Low Countries. Varied challenges and requirements obliged the British military to have a multiple capability, and this was at least as important in their success as the crude resource level available. In contrast, Marlborough and Frederick the Great had not had to fight outside Europe, nor George Washington outside North America. Range of commitments is important in any judgement of the capability and skill of armies and generals, especially any comparative judgement.

Multiple capability was not restricted either to the Europeans or to the British, but Britain was the most successful of the European powers in developing and utilising it. In part, this reflected British skill and success in naval, amphibious and trans-oceanic operations, and, in part, the cultural, political and geographical factors that led Britain not to place as great a premium as its European opponents on warfare on the continent.

Britain's role in the defeat of Napoleon culminated at Waterloo in 1815. Having escaped from Elba and regained power in Paris from the restored Bourbons, Napoleon took the initiative and struck first at his nearest opponents: a British–Dutch–German army under Wellington at Brussels and the Prussians under Blücher at Liège.

The subsequent battle of Waterloo on 18 June found Wellington with 68,000 men, 31,000 of them British, holding his position against attacks by Napoleon's 72,000. This was not, however, the army with which Wellington had won the Peninsular War. Many of those units were involved in the war with America that broke out in 1812. Instead, many of the duke's British units were untried in battle. Nevertheless, although uncertain of Prussian moves, Wellington decided to stand and fight.

As in the Peninsular battles, the British line had not been weakened by prior engagement. Although the French attempted to do so with an artillery bombardment, its impact was weakened by Wellington's use of the reverse slope to shelter his men. Napoleon's tactical lack of imagination in launching successive poorly coordinated frontal attacks at Waterloo was in keeping with his earlier failure to obtain a decisive success while his opponents were divided. He was less brave and decisive on the battlefield than Wellington; more a distant commander who lost touch with the progress of the battle and failed to manoeuvre.

Furthermore, ruined by incessant warfare, the French Army was only a shadow of its former self. At best, Napoleon might have secured a Pyrrhic victory. Wellington had constructed a strong defence-in-depth which, even under better weather and other conditions, would have proved difficult to crack. Napoleon had only a slight numerical advantage, while Wellington had some 70,000–80,000 Prussians closing in on his left. Indeed, as the day wore on, Wellington was able to abandon his position on the left entirely to the Prussians, who also got round Napoleon's right flank and rear.

Yet, for all Napoleon's failings and the maladroit conduct of several of his generals, the French at Waterloo were still a formidable army and their defeat was a major achievement for Wellington and his force. This success has been called into question. Even if Napoleon had won at Waterloo, it is unclear whether his grand strategy was sustainable. He had triumphed before in battles without winning the war. Large allied forces, especially Austrians, were approaching France from the east. Yet Waterloo was not a strategic irrelevance. Napoleon was speedily crushed, and the war was ended beyond any hopes that events or allied divisions would provide him with opportunities.

After the battle, Wellington and the Prussians advanced into France. Napoleon surrendered on 15 July to an astonished Captain Frederick Maitland of HMS Bellerophon. The British naval blockade made it impossible for him to leave France by sea. The British were concerned to prevent Napoleon taking refuge in America. He was taken, instead, to the British island of St Helena in the South Atlantic, where he died, his imprisonment a consequence and sign of British power.

relations with George III over his determined opposition to Catholics gaining the vote. In 1807 the Pittite political system returned in the shape of a ministry led by the Duke of Portland and containing most of the leading Pittites. The Whigs, thereafter, spent many years in opposition. They were unable to take advantage of the unpopularity and divisions of the Portland ministry in 1809, and it was replaced by a government under Spencer Perceval that continued on a Pittite base. After Perceval was assassinated in 1812 by an embittered merchant, a firm and competent Pittite, Robert, 2nd Earl of Liverpool became Prime Minister. He held office until a major stroke hit him in February 1827. The Whigs were not to triumph until 1832.

The unpopular terms of the Peace of Amiens of 1802 reflected an acceptance of Napoleon's control over continental Europe. Peace brought a measure of economic revival in 1802–3, but distrust of Napoleon's aggressive expansionism then led to a resumption of the conflict. This was especially serious because Britain was initially isolated. Napoleon planned invasion, and, among the defensive preparations, the Royal Military Canal was dug along the inner edge of Romney Marsh. Volunteer units manoeuvred along the south coast, as the Home Guard was to do in the Second World War. However, the French attempt in 1805 to achieve a covering naval superiority in the Channel was thwarted by the mishandling of the scheme and the swift British response. Napoleon planned for his squadrons to escape from their blockaded ports, sail to the West Indies, join at Martinique, and then return as a united force able to defeat the British. He required superiority in the Channel for four days in order for his troops to cross, planned to land in or near Pegwell Bay in Kent, and intended to overrun London within a week before dictating peace.

Instead, there was no rendezvous. Cancelling his invasion plans, Napoleon turned east to attack Austria and ordered the Franco-Spanish fleet in Cadiz to sail for Italian waters. It was intercepted off Cape Trafalgar by Nelson on 21 October 1805 and heavily defeated in the greatest of all British naval triumphs. One French ship blew up and eighteen French and Spanish ships of the line were captured. Nelson died on the *Victory*.

This justly celebrated victory did not, however, prevent Napoleon from triumphing over first Austria (1805) and then Prussia (1806). The extension of his power threatened British interests. By implementing the Continental System, which was inaugurated in November 1806, he sought to bring Britain to her knees by economic means. The Berlin Decrees declared Britain blockaded and banned trade with her. In turn, Britain blockaded France.

The Imperial Power

The attempt to exclude Britain from the continent exacerbated Napoleon's urge to control Europe, and this led his system to unravel. An attempt to impose control on Spain and Portugal in 1808 misfired and gave the British an opportunity to resist Napoleon in an alliance that did not collapse before French strength. British troops were sent to Iberia from 1808. The struggle was a long one, but by late 1813 the Duke of Wellington was leading the British army into South-West France. Napoleon's invasion of Russia had failed the previous year, he had been defeated at Leipzig in 1813, and his system was rapidly collapsing. With Austrian and Prussian forces invading eastern France in early 1814, Napoleon was forced to abdicate.

Napoleon was not only defeated in Europe; France had also lost the struggle for oceanic mastery and colonial predominance. Thanks to repeated naval victories from the Glorious First of June in 1794 on, the British had been left free to execute amphibious attacks on the isolated colonial centres of non-European powers, and also to make gains at the expense of non-European peoples. The route to India was secured: Cape Town was captured from the Dutch in 1795 and, after it had been restored in 1802, again in 1806. The Seychelles were taken in 1794, Réunion and Mauritius in 1810. The British were able to consolidate their position in India. Seringapatam, the capital of the Sultanate of Mysore, which had been a serious foe since the 1760s, was stormed in 1799. India became the basis of British power and influence around the Indian Ocean, and it proved possible to expand the colony that had been founded at

Botany Bay in Australia in 1788. The Pacific became a sphere for British, rather than Spanish, expansion. The Congress of Vienna that sought in 1814–15 to settle the problems of the European world, left Britain with a dramatically stronger position. Her control of Cape Colony, the Seychelles, Mauritius, Trinidad, Tobago, St Lucia, Malta, Surinam, and Ceylon (Sri Lanka) was recognised, and France's position within Europe was weakened.

The growth of British trade registered her oceanic success. It was accompanied by a major expansion in shipping and docks. The London Dock was excavated in 1801, followed by the West India Docks in 1802, the East India Docks in 1805, and the start of work on the Surrey Commercial Docks in 1807. In 1815, most of the trans-oceanic European world in the eastern hemisphere was British. The collapse of the Spanish American empire was to ensure that by 1830 this was true of the entire world. Britannia ruled far more than just the waves.

TWO

FROM WATERLOO TO THE GREAT
EXHIBITION, 1815-51

The Great Exhibition opened at the specially built Crystal Palace in Hyde Park in 1851. Planned in 1849 by Queen Victoria's husband, Prince Albert, a keen moderniser, the event was intended as a demonstration of British achievement and a reflection of the country's mission, duty and interest to put itself at the head of the diffusion of civilisation. The Exhibition, with its 24-ton block of coal by the entrance, was indeed a tribute to British manufacturing skill and prowess. Joseph Paxton's iron and glass conservatory – the central space of the Exhibition – was 1,850 feet long, 460 feet wide and 108 feet high. The event was also a product of self-confidence, and a sense of superiority that led the British to feel that they were able to define civilisation and liberty, and to appropriate the resources of the world to their own ends. There were 6.2 million visitors, some coming to London by means of the recent and expanding rail system.

The Millennium Dome at Greenwich in 2000 was fancifully compared by some to the Great Exhibition, but by then the world and attitudes of 1851 seemed very distant. Confidence in Western values had been assailed over the previous forty years, and a modern world of multiculturalism finds nineteenth-century attitudes abhorrent. Secondly, even within the context of the Western world, there is far less interest in Britain as a model, while British self-confidence has fallen dramatically. A sense of the country, its constitution, institutions and society, as failed has been propagated actively by influential groups seeking to remould Britain as part of a 'modernising' Europe. The confidence and international respect of 1851 thus seem almost as distant as the world of Magna Carta (1215) or the Civil Wars (1642–8).

Moreover, there is a strong sense that even the achievements of 1851 should be qualified by a much fuller understanding of the iniquities of that society. Although late twentieth- and early twenty-first-century attitudes have been ambiguous or contradictory, 'Victorian values' are generally deplored, and the period is presented as cruelly inegalitarian, with a public ethos that was sanctimonious, smug and repressive. In short, if modern Britain is held to have failed, this is part of a larger critique that British history itself is a record of cruelty and oppression, an unsatisfactory tale that offers no cause for celebration.

It would be easy to ignore such charges in this book, and to present an apparently unproblematic narrative of the age. Yet such an approach would be unhelpful, because it slights the wider question of our response to the past. The Victorian age epitomises this question for modern Britons, for it is apparently close and vivid. The Victorians and their age were captured in photographs. This closeness ensures that the period can be used as a contrast with the contemporary world; and this can serve to condemn either or both. These contrasts can be personalised. William John Bankes (1786–1855), the beautifier of Kingston Lacy, Dorset, was prosecuted in 1841 for a homosexual act with a soldier and fled to spend the rest of his life in Italy. Modern attitudes to homosexuality are different.

The Victorian age is also seen as the seedbed of much in the modern world, ranging from extensive male suffrage and trade unionism to the modern Christmas, electricity and the motor car. The 'origin myths' of such developments, as well as views on their current role, condition our scrutiny of the past.

The context that is generally forgotten is that of the world outside Britain at that time. To criticise social conditions, the treatment of women, or attitudes to empire, as if Britain could have been abstracted from the situation elsewhere, is unhelpful and, in a profound sense, like much criticism of the Victorian period, ahistorical. Clearly the benefits of the British state, society and economy were distributed unequally, but it is, also, worth noting how far, within the constraints of the technologies and attitudes of the age, the British were more liberal than other major European powers. The Chinese who were attacked in the Opium War of 1839–42 and the Sikhs who were defeated in 1847–8 would not have appreciated the point, but Britain offered a powerful support to the struggle for independence in Latin America, and it was the British who were instrumental in ending the slave trade, despite the fact that this hit the economy of their colonies in the West Indies. In addition, self-government was rapidly granted to colonies settled by European immigrants. Quebec and Ontario achieved self-government in 1846, New Zealand in 1852, Newfoundland, New South Wales, Victoria, Tasmania and South Australia in 1855, Queenslandin 1859.

In Europe, where her prestige owed much to her economic sophistication and quality of government, Britain was seen as a force for liberalism in politics, economics, religion and culture. Catholics were granted the vote in Britain in 1829 and by the 1830s there were at least forty Catholic MPs, all bar one sitting for Irish constituencies. Although a devout Anglican, Queen Victoria was prepared to attend Presbyterian services in Scotland and Lutheran services in Germany.

This context is worth grasping before turning to consider developments within Britain itself. There it was the pace of technological innovation and economic development that was most powerful. These phenomena deserve attention ahead of domestic politics and imperial expansion. Britain set the pace in mechanisation, and the ideology and thrill of modernisation, not least with the dramatic development of the railways. Technological change brought the outer world closer, enabling the more rapid and predictable movement of messages, people and goods. In 1821, the Dover–Calais packet service was converted to steam, leading to a more predictable service. Thirty years later, the first messages were sent through the new submarine cable between Dover and Calais. The telegram was the Victorian equivalent of the internet in speeding up communications. More generally, the harnessing of technological change contributed to an economic transformation of the country, as did the benefits of readily available capital, an increasingly productive agricultural sector, and the burgeoning markets of a growing home and colonial population.

The British economy became dramatically different to those in the rest of Europe, encouraging a sense that Britain was exceptional. A crucial ingredient of industrialisation, the annual average production of coal and lignite, in million metric tons, amounted to 18 for Britain in 1820–4, and 2 for France, Germany, Belgium and Russia combined; and the comparable figures for 1855–9 were 68 and 32. The annual production of pig-iron in million metric tons in 1820 was 0.4 for Britain and the same for the whole of the rest of Europe; in 1850, 2.3 and 0.9, an even larger gap. Behind these figures, there was a vivid reality. The radical journalist William Cobbett wrote from Sheffield in January 1830:

All the way along, from Leeds to Sheffield, it is coal and iron, and iron and coal. It was dark before we reached Sheffield; so that we saw the iron furnaces in all the horrible splendour of their everlasting blaze. Nothing can be conceived more grand or more terrific than the yellow waves of fire that incessantly issue from the top of these furnaces. . . . Nature has placed the beds of iron and beds of coal alongside of each other, and art has taught man to make one to operate upon the other, as to turn the iron-stone into liquid matter, which is drained off from the bottom of the furnace, and afterwards moulded into blocks and bars, and all sorts of things. The combustibles are put into the top of the furnace, which stands thirty, forty, or fifty feet up in the air, and the ever-blazing mouth of which is kept supplied with coal and coke and iron-stone, from little iron wagons forced up by steam, and brought down again to be re-filled. It is a surprising thing to behold; and it is impossible to behold it without being convinced that . . . other nations . . . will never equal England with regard to things made of iron and steel. . . . They call it black Sheffield, and black enough it is; but from this one town and its environs go nine-tenths of the knives that are used in the whole world.

Other sectors of the economy also boomed. Raw cotton consumption in thousand metric tons totalled 267 for Britain in 1850 and 162 for the rest of Europe. The British economy benefited from the rising demand of a growing population (excluding Ireland: 1801, 10.5 million; 1831, 16.3; 1851, 20.8), and from its ability to export to less dynamic economies, but more than this was at stake in British growth. The application of technology was fundamental.

The plentiful availability of capital for investment was also crucial. The development of Penshaw Colliery in County Durham, for example, cost £60,000 in 1816. The financial system improved in 1826 when the Bank Charter Act permitted the formation of joint stock banks more than 65 miles from London, thus spreading risk. Later Acts in 1833 and 1844 brought considerable improvement by giving the Bank of England a central role in the issue of bank notes, bringing a degree of much-needed regulation. Changes in banking were an important aspect of the institutional dynamics of economic development.

Communications improved both with the coming of the railways and with improvements to roads and to river crossings, so that Britain became more effective as a manufacturing and marketing system. The Union Chain Bridge, opened over the Tweed near Berwick in 1820 for the Berwick and North Durham Turnpike Trust, was the first British suspension bridge able to carry loaded carriages. Turnpike roads focused on new crossing places, such as the suspension bridge across the Tees at Whorlton opened in 1831. The Conwy Suspension Bridge, built by Thomas Telford and completed in 1826, replaced the ferry that had previously been the sole means to cross the river. It was part of an improvement to road transport that helped open up North Wales, ensuring that Holyhead became a more important port for Dublin. The opening of the Menai Suspension Bridge between mainland Wales and Anglesea in 1826 contributed to bringing about the end of ferries at Porthaethwy (1826), Beaumaris (1830), and Abermenai (1840s). There were also transport improvements to open up the slate mining district, especially in the 1820s, and in the early 1840s, a regular coach service was established from Caernarfon to Harlech.

The cause of suspension bridges was put back in 1830, however, when the newly completed one over the South Esk at Montrose partially collapsed, when 700 spectators rushed from one side to another during a boat race. As a result, the proposal to build a similar structure across the Tamar was abandoned. Nevertheless, suspension bridges continued to be built. The design submitted in 1831 by Isambard Kingdom Brunel (1806–59) for a suspension bridge over the Avon at Clifton near Bristol was accepted as the most mathematically exact of those tendered. Brunel was appointed engineer and work began in 1836, but remained unfinished in his lifetime due to a lack of funds. The bridge was eventually completed in 1864 according to Brunel's plans, and using chains taken from the Hungerford suspension bridge which he had constructed over the Thames in 1841–5.

There were important improvements in many regions of the country even before the steam railway reached them. Non-suspension bridges had been opened over the estuaries of the Teign and the Plym in 1827, making much of South Devon accessible to road traffic; the former was then the longest in Britain. Steam and chain floating bridges followed at Dartmouth, Saltash, and Torpoint. The widening of Devon roads in the 1820s also helped in the replacement of packhorses by wheeled traffic. Such improvements served to integrate regions into the national economy, and to create demand for further such development. Journey times and, thus, costs fell. R.W. Newman, an Exeter MP of the 1820s, told a House of Commons Select Committee that 'since the roads have been improved . . . a very large amount of the economy of the county is daily sent from Devon to the Metropolis'. By 1828, coaches were running four times a day between Exeter and both Exmouth and Teignmouth, while journey times to London and other centres had been greatly cut. That decade, the turnpike through the Snake Pass from Glossop to Sheffield helped open up the northern Peak District. By then, London mail coaches could reach Manchester in one day. More generally, many roads were improved by resurfacing. In Cheshire, the Wirral did not get most of its turnpike roads until after 1820, although other parts of the county were better served early on. Coastal shipping also improved in frequency and speed. Steamships were introduced to carry passengers in the Thames estuary in 1815.

The Coming of Railways

The British led the way in the coming of the railways. Wagonways had existed for many years, with horses drawing wagons along rails, especially from the collieries to the coal-loading staithes on the Tyne and Wear, but also elsewhere. Other products, such as stone, were also transported this way. The Surrey Iron Railway Company, the world's first railway company and public railway, operated between Wandsworth and Croydon from 1803. The company had proposed to improve links between London and Portsmouth. It advertised the idea of the railway in Parliament, for the company could only go ahead after permission was granted by an Act passed in 1801.

Self-propelled steam locomotives changed the situation, not least by making long-distance movement possible. In 1804, Roger Hopkins built a tramroad between Pen-y-darren and Abercynon in South Wales upon which Richard Trevithick tried the first steam railway locomotive engine, essentially a mobile beam engine.

The development of the locomotive from the stationary steam-engine provided the technology for the rail revolution, and industrialisation supplied the necessary demand, capital and skills. George Stephenson opened the Hetton Railway in 1822. The more famous Stockton & Darlington Railway followed in 1825, opened with a ceremonial journey from Witton Park colliery to Stockton; the Manchester & Liverpool Railway followed in 1830. Economic considerations were foremost. Thomas Meyneel, a wealthy merchant who was a leading promoter of the Stockton & Darlington Railway, had argued that a railway was preferable to a proposed canal, as it was likely to yield a better return. The 40-mile-long line was designed to transport coal from the mines near Bishop Auckland to the port of Stockton. The Stockton & Darlington was extended to Middlesbrough in 1830 and a suspension bridge took the line across the Tees.

Locomotives improved. When Goldsworthy Gurney's steam-jet (or blast) was applied to Stephenson's *Rocket* locomotive in 1829 speeds rose from 16 to 29 miles per hour. *Rocket* won the Liverpool & Manchester Railway's locomotive trials at Rainhill. Direct drive from the cylinders and pistons to the wheels increased efficiency, as did an engine design that boiled water more rapidly. Railways quickly proved superior to steam coaches which had been tried on Scottish roads in the 1820s and 1830s.

Railways offered new links and cut journey times for both freight and passengers. Initially, they were mostly small-scale, independent concerns providing local links and the movement of coal was crucial to their business. The first public railway in the Midlands, the Leicester & Swannington Railway of 1830, was designed to move coal to the expanding Leicester market and to undercut canal-borne supplies from Nottingham and Derby. The company paid an 8 per cent dividend in 1839.

The impact of the railway was local as well as national. Sunderland was reached by the Durham & Sunderland Railway in 1836, the Newcastle & Darlington Junction Railway in 1852, and the Londonderry Railway in 1854. On the northern bank of the Wear, branches of the Brandling Junction Railway reached Wearmouth and North Dock in 1839. The same railway reached Gateshead in 1839, a year after the Newcastle & Carlisle.

Companies competed. The Clarence Railway offered a shorter route for West Durham coal to the coast than the Stockton & Darlington, and was, in turn, likewise challenged by the Great North of England, Clarence & Hartlepool Junction Railway. The West Durham Railway was laid from Crook to Byers Green to compete with the Clarence line. The speculative schemes of George Hudson, the 'Railway King', whose frauds caused the financial crisis that hit the railways in 1849, were important in the development of rail routes in the region. The large number of companies led not only to competition, but also to different services supplementing each other, as at Carlisle where seven railway companies operated. This availability furthered the general use of the rail system.

With time, bolder trunk schemes were advanced and financed, and, in addition, already existing lines were linked to create long-distance networks so that they became important to more than their localities. This was true of the 1838 Carlisle–Newcastle line. Glasgow and Edinburgh were linked by rail in 1841. Services from London reached Birmingham in 1838, Southampton in 1840, Bristol and Brighton in 1841, Oxford in 1844, Norwich in 1845, Portsmouth and Plymouth in 1847, and Holyhead in 1850. A formidable amount was invested in building the rail system. The London to Brighton line, including the spur to Shoreham, alone cost £2,569,359.

Rivers were bridged, and the Menai Strait was crossed in 1849. Tunnels were blasted through hills: the Kilsby tunnel (1834–8) between London and Birmingham, and the Woodhead tunnel (1839–52) between Manchester and Sheffield.

Canals and coastal shipping now faced significant competition, especially as the rail companies developed processes and policies to handle through-freight movements. The Railway Clearing House created in 1842 established standard rates for freight and apportioned through revenues. Three years earlier, Thomas Edmondson had developed what was to become the standardised type of ticket for passengers. Rail was quicker than its competitors and canal building stopped in the 1830s. To meet the new competition, canal companies drastically cut tolls in 1840.

The use of steam tugs, instead of horses, speeded up canal transport but rail remained more flexible, and, in some cases, railways directly replaced canals. In Plym Bridge Woods the railway was built on the canal towpath, to bring stone and peat from Dartmoor to Plymouth. The canal from Carlisle to Port Carlisle closed in 1853 and was converted into the Port Carlisle Railway. The railway also hit river traffic. The opening of the railway to Barmouth in 1867 wrecked the lighterage carriage up-river to Dolgellau: 167 ships entered and left the port in 1866, but only eleven in 1876.

New links were created. Much development continued to focus on coal, a crucial source of investment income. The Taff Vale line between Cardiff and Merthyr Tydfil was opened in 1841 and, in conjunction with the development of the port of Cardiff, this permitted a major increase in the export of coal from South Wales. Other products and industries were also greatly affected. Use of the railway from the 1840s enabled the brewers of Burton-upon-Trent to develop a major beer empire, and also helped speed North Wales slates towards urban markets. The Ffestiniog Railway of 1836 linked the slate mines with Porthmadog harbour, and the rail network in the area improved from 1867. The press also took major advantage of the rail system: London newspapers could be transported rapidly round the country. In the 1870s the railway companies opened up urban markets for liquid milk, encouraging dairy farmers to produce 'railway milk', rather than farmhouse cheese. Horse race meetings, such as those at York and Stockton, benefited from 'specials' and came to enjoy a national or regional following. Thanks to the railway, large numbers travelled at an unprecedented speed and with increased frequency.

William Gladstone used the railways to campaign nationally in the 1870s and 1880s, and Queen Victoria and the royal family to visit Balmoral and to see more of Britain than their predecessors. Thousands of visitors used the railways to 'view' great houses and their parks, a hobby that attained great popularity, before ebbing in the 1880s as criticism of the aristocracy rose.

The impact of rail was also psychological. 'Space' had been conquered. New sounds and sights contributed to a powerful sense of change, and this was overwhelmingly seen as progress. This sense of progress helped to encourage the venture capital that was so important to the expansion of the rail system. A speculative risk element was important.

Railway stations, such as Sir Gilbert Scott and W.H. Barlow's St Pancras (1873), Thomas Prosser's York, Queen Street (1877), and Isambard Kingdom Brunel's Paddington, were designed as masterpieces of iron and glass, and many, such as John Dobson's Newcastle Central, were planned with bold, often classical, facades. Trains swiftly came to play a role in fiction. In Dickens' *Dombey and Son* (1846–8), one runs over the villain Carker 'and licked his stream of life up with its fiery heat'. They were also celebrated in art, with paintings such as William Frith's *The Railway Station* (1862).

The railway was seen as better than the canal, not just another form of transport. It helped bring uniformity. Time within Britain was standardised. The railways needed standard time for their timetables in order to make connections possible, and, in place of the variations from east to west in Britain, adopted the standard set by the Greenwich Observatory as 'railway time'. Clocks were kept accurate by the electric telegraph that was erected along lines.

News and fashions sped round the country. A travelling post office ran between Birmingham and Warrington from 1838 and a system to pick up and drop off the mail at stations without breaking was speedily introduced. In 1840, the Penny Black, the world's first postage stamp, was released as part of a system that set a uniform postal rate based on weight in place of a postal tariff system based on distance. In 1848, the first of what was to be the network of W.H. Smith railway bookstalls was opened at Euston Station. William Henry (W.H.) Smith made a fortune and embarked on a political career that was satirised in Gilbert and Sullivan's HMS *Pinafore* with its account of a 1st Lord of the Admiralty who did not like to go to sea. In fact he was competent and popular and when he died in 1891, both First Lord of the Treasury and the Leader of the Commons. He had opened 150 station shops.

Commuting developed, and London and other major cities spread: the railway helped to create suburbs and suburban environments. Rail services from London Bridge reached Deptford in 1836 and Greenwich in 1838. The London to Croydon line opened in 1839, to Margate in 1846, and to Southend in 1856. The spread of suburbia inspired the Commons Preservation Society, founded in 1865, and a campaigning base of figures who were instrumental in the foundation of the National Trust in 1893–5, especially Octavia Hill and Robert Hunter. In 1875 Hill had failed in a campaign to save Swiss Cottage Fields from development.

The shape of towns was changed as lines both joined and bisected. There was much demolition to make way for track, for example in Birmingham. Urban street patterns focused on railway stations, and commercial patterns changed. Pubs were built near stations, for example the Crown Liquor Saloon in Belfast, originally the Railway Tavern, across the street from the terminus of the Great Northern Railway.

Both locally and nationally, railways also contributed to industrialisation. Demand for ironwork encouraged the industrialisation of Gateshead, with the major growth of Hawks' ironworks, so that it employed over 1,000 workers by 1841, and also the opening of locomotive works in 1839 and 1852. On the Newcastle side of the Tyne, locomotives were made at Forth Banks. Train works and employment for the railway were very important in a number of other towns, such as Brighton, Carlisle, Crewe, Darlington, Derby, Horwich, Shildon, Stratford (London), and Wolverton. The coming of the railway could transform villages such as Swindon into major centres of employment when a company like the Great Western selected it for its locomotive works. Existing ironworks also began to produce for the railway. The Gaunless Bridge in York was the first example of an iron railway bridge. The Britannia Foundry at Derby came to make bridges and turntables, carriage wheels, locomotive tenders and steam-engine castings. The foundry was linked by sidings to the Great Northern Railway, and the company built another site linked to the Midland Railway.

For reasons of topography and economics, some areas had less rapid development. This was especially true of agricultural and upland areas. The former initially seemed to offer only limited traffic, while the latter also posed the problem of gradients. Predominantly rural Suffolk was slow to acquire rail links. The railway only reached Ipswich and Bury St Edmunds in 1846, and Newmarket in 1848. In 1852 there was still no link between London and Cornwall, and none between London and Aberystwyth until 1864.

A national network was not really in place until mid-century. By 1845, however, it was possible to travel via the Newcastle & Carlisle and Maryport & Carlisle Railways from the North to the Irish Sea. There were about 4,600 miles of track by 1848, but the main-line system was not completed until the early 1870s, and many local and branch lines were built thereafter. Across the Pennines the original cross-country Carlisle–Newcastle link of 1838 was not supplemented until the line from Durham to Barrow was constructed in 1861 and the Carlisle–Settle route opened in 1876. The first took Furness iron east and Durham coke west, helping the iron and steel industries on both sides of the Pennines.

In addition to the construction of new routes, existing ones were improved, and the railway system as a whole became more durable and effective in meeting both freight and passenger needs. Wooden bridges were replaced by iron, as on the North Midland Railway at Belper. New stations were built. The first in the Wolverhampton area, opened in 1837, was at Wednesfield Heath; because the line did not come into the town centre, passengers had to take a cab. This changed in 1852, when the London & North Western Railway opened the High Level Station, followed in 1854 by the Great Western Railway's Low Level Station.

There were important improvements in the quality of rail transport. Early rails were not strong enough for heavy steam locomotives, but by 1820 wrought-iron rails, that were less brittle than cast iron, were being successfully produced. The far more resilient steel rails were introduced from 1857, creating a permanent way that could bear heavy weights. The industry became a major employer and by 1873 there were 274,000 railworkers.

In areas with limited rail penetration, such as Cumbria, scheduled country carriers remained very important. In many respects, their business supplemented the rail system, providing cartage focused on railheads. Even in Cumbria, however, rail links spread. The Eden Valley Railway (1862), the Cockermouth, Keswick & Penrith Railway (1864–5), and the Cleator & Workington Junction Railway (1880), all aided the development of the West Cumberland iron industry. Routes were also planned into the Lake District, to further quarrying in Borrowdale and into Ennerdale and Ullswater. William Morris complained, 'You will soon have a Cook's tourist railway up Scawfell – and another up Helvellyn – and another up Skiddaw. And then a connecting line, all round.' This was overly pessimistic. A public campaign, launched by Hardwicke

Rawnsley, one of the founders of the National Trust, and backed by the Commons Preservation Society, blocked the Borrowdale, Ennerdale and Ullswater plans.

Elsewhere, the arrival of the train led to the decay of existing routes and of related facilities. Food for horses had been a major overhead for wagon and carriage services, but coal for trains was less expensive. Transport networks changed. Crawley had been an important town on the London to Brighton coaching route, but the train went via Three Bridges instead. The coaching town of Honiton was hit by the opening of a new rail route to Exeter, only, in turn, to benefit when a new line via Honiton began operating in 1860. Some turnpikes were bankrupted; for example, in Dorset, the Wimborne to Puddletown was hit by the introduction of the Southampton & Dorchester Railway.

At sea, steamships put pressure on less expensive, but less reliable and slower sailing ships, and harbours were built or improved to benefit from steamships, Porthmadog harbour being opened in 1824 to export slates from North Wales. But for the railway, more freight within Britain would have gone by steamships. Instead, frequent shipments were linked to railways at ports and the two developed together.

Rail travel reflected a social system stratified by wealth. There were three classes, with different conditions and fares. On the London to Brighton line, the third-class carriages lacked roofs until 1852, and were thus exposed to the weather and the hot ash from the engine. Return fares on the line in 1845 were 21 shillings (£1.10p) first class, 9 shillings (45p) second, and 5 shillings (25p) third. Brighton developed as a popular resort thanks to the train, as did other coastal towns. The timing of development was often linked directly to the introduction of services, as at Littlehampton in 1863. This was true of commuting as well as holiday resorts. The building of a direct route from London to Southend via Upminster avoiding the Tilbury detour, opened in 1888, cut the express journey time from 95 to 50 minutes, and was followed by an alternative route via Shenfield opened in 1889. Commuting from Southend rose rapidly. Some resorts, however, sought to preserve 'tone' by keeping the railway out. This was true, for example, of

Sidmouth. When such resorts finally had to accept the train, they ensured that the station was some way inland in order to deter day-trippers.

The rail system continued to spread in the following century. The last main line to London – the Great Central – only ran through to London in 1899. The line that killed river traffic on the Tamar on the Cornwall–Devon border was not opened until 1908. Light railways in Essex to Tollesbury and Thaxted were opened in 1907 and 1913. However, most of these later lines were never very profitable, the Great Central being a case in point. By 1914 the system was very largely complete. Subsequent expansion was to be minor, and was greatly outweighed by contraction. The system, meanwhile, had served society in ways that had not been imagined when the *Rocket* won its trials.

Economic Development

Aggregate figures for economic change were the product of the development of regional economies, and their interaction through better communications. The detailed geography of economic growth was broadly similar to that in the late eighteenth century. Coalfields were crucial, although the spread of the rail system introduced new transport routes and reduced costs on others. Areas without coal, such as East Anglia and the South-West of England, suffered de-industrialisation, although other factors were also important. Bruton in Somerset had been a major centre of silk production, with the largest manufacturer employing 700 to 900 hands on about 15,700 spindles in 1823; but, due to foreign competition, by 1831 it was down to 230 hands, 7,000 spindles and a four-day week.

As factories became more important, so the investment required for the most efficient implementation of particular processes rose, and this further encouraged a concentration and specialisation of activity. Across the entire economy, factory production did not predominate until the second half of the century, and much industrialisation was less a matter of technological change than of organisational improvement, most obviously in the specialisation of labour. Nevertheless, the foci of economic change underwent dramatic change. In Bradford, which became the global centre of worsted wool production and exchange, factory horsepower rose 718 per cent in 1810–30, and the population climbed from 16,012 in 1810 to 103,778 in 1850. Mechanisation brought profit, larger factories and a wave of migration, and the pace of innovation was continual. The mechanisation of yarn spinning in Bradford was followed in 1826 by that of worsted weaving. By 1850, the work formerly done by thousands of rural handloom weavers was now performed by 17,642 automatic looms, mass-producing women's dress fabrics in Bradford's factories. By 1821, Manchester had over 5,000 power looms. As another sign of economic expansion, by 1850 Sunderland was the greatest shipbuilding town in the world.

The same process was repeated on a smaller scale in smaller towns. The population of Carlisle, a centre of cotton manufacture, rose from near 10,000 in 1801 to over 35,000 by 1841. Carlisle also saw the development of biscuit manufacturing. Jonathan Dodgson Carr adapted a printing machine to cut biscuits, replacing cutting by hand, and then, helped by Carlisle's position as a major transport junction, sold his product throughout the country, transporting it by rail. Companies and towns that wished to stay at the leading edge of economic development had to become and remain transport foci. Mills that had been located earlier to benefit from fast-flowing streams in upland areas, such as the western Pennines, faded because they lacked the access enjoyed by large-scale steam-driven urban mills.

The importance of new technology was demonstrated at Tiverton where John Heathcoat founded a machine-made net and lace factory. The threat to jobs posed by his patented bobbin net machines had led to the riotous destruction of his Loughborough factory in 1816, and Heathcoat moved his machines to a disused Tiverton cotton mill. This became the largest lace factory in the world and hit lace-making in East Devon. A former partner of Heathcoat, John Boden, opened the Derby Lace Works at Barnstaple in 1825. By 1830, he was employing 1,000 people and, largely as a result, the population of the town rose from 5,079 in 1821 to 7,902 in 1841. The lifestyle and densely-inhabited working-class neighbourhood that developed there and in Tiverton were relatively uncommon in Devon.

New technology also affected other activities, such as the press. In 1814, the largest-selling newspaper, *The Times*, switched to a steam press, leading to a larger circulation, and other papers followed from the 1820s. In 1838 Jeremiah Garnett devised new methods of feeding the presses of the *Manchester Guardian*, so that 1,500 impressions an hour could be produced. There were no significant developments in typesetting, however, until the 1880s. Steam power was also used in book publishing. When in 1832 Oxford University Press opened its new site in Walton Street, it introduced a steam engine to power the works. Industries such as brewing were also influenced by new technology.

Social and Political Tension

Economic change generated tension, as did social pressures. Postwar depression and demobilisation exacerbated the situation from 1815. Population growth led to under-employment and unemployment, and, combined with low wages and limited social welfare, to poverty for those in and without work. Difficulties were accentuated by poor harvests. Moreover, dominated by the landed interest, Parliament passed the Corn Law Act of 1815, which prohibited the import of grain unless the price of British grain reached 80 shillings a quarter. This kept the price of supplies artificially high, leading to food riots among hungry agricultural labourers, with attacks on farmers and corn mills, and demands for higher wages. 'Bread or blood' was their call. In 1828, the Corn Law system was adapted to include a sliding scale by which duties fell as prices rose.

In addition, new machines threatened jobs, both on the land and in industry. The replacement of hand flailing by threshing machines led to machine-breaking, as in South Norfolk in 1812. In Carlisle, the handloom weavers rioted in 1819.

Tensions lessened during the relatively prosperous years of the early 1820s, but in the late 1820s an industrial slump and high bread prices helped cause a revival in popular unrest. The invention of friction matches in 1826 by the Stockton chemist John Walker, and their subsequent manufacture as 'strike anywhere lucifers', made arson easier. In 1830 'Swing' riots affected large parts of southern and eastern England. Machine-breaking, arson and other attacks often followed letters signed by 'Swing', threatening trouble if job-destroying machines were not removed. Over ninety threshing machines were broken in Wiltshire alone. The identity of 'Captain Swing' is unclear, and the riots probably spread spontaneously, rather than reflecting central control.

The diversity of protest, both social and economic, was a striking feature of the Swing Riots. Large farms were targeted for action, as small-scale farmers, who also opposed new machinery, attacked agrarian capitalists. 'Swing' brought unease to the owners of agricultural estates, a disquiet far from obvious to subsequent viewers of the splendid houses of the period. The building of such houses was helped by the higher prices and rents that flowed to landlords from the Corn Laws and by the repeal in 1816 of income tax, seen as a temporary wartime measure.

Political awareness was heightened by the growth of the press. The number of provincial papers rose from 50 in 1782 to over 100 in 1808, 150 by 1830, and over 230 by 1851. Publication began in new centres, and new titles were launched in existing ones. Cornwall's first paper, *The Cornwall Gazette and Falmouth Packet*, was launched in 1801; the first in North Devon was established at Barnstaple in 1824. After two or possibly three failures in the eighteenth century, the continuous publication of papers in Plymouth began in 1808. The first newspapers in Wales were founded: Swansea's *The Cambrian* in 1804 and Bangor's *North Wales Chronicle* in 1808. In 1797, there was only one paper in Cumbria, the *Cumberland Pacquet*, but it was joined by the *Carlisle Journal* (1798), the *Westmorland Advertiser* (1811), the *Patriot* (1815), and the *Westmorland Gazette* (1818), all of which lasted into the present century, only the *Carlisle Chronicle* (1807–11) meeting with a speedy demise. In Herefordshire, the *British Chronicle*, or *Pugh's Hereford Journal*, launched in 1770 and lasting into the twentieth century, was joined by the *Hereford Independent* (1824–8) and the *Hereford Times* (1832 until twentieth century). The number of Liverpool papers rose markedly between 1812 and the late 1820s.

Radical papers both attacked the government and focused on local issues, usually abuses, criticism of which could develop and elicit popular support. In 1812, the *Montrose, Arbroath, and Brechin Review*, a Scottish paper launched in 1811, began to publish attacks on local abuses, which revived the campaign for burgh reform and against self-elected corporations. In 1818, Montrose burgesses won the right to elect the magistracy. The paper also supported a wider franchise (right to vote), education for the working class, liberal economics, and combinations (trade unions), and criticised Church patronage.

Conservatives responded with alarm. The *Nottingham Gazette* was launched in 1813 in order to stem 'the torrent by which the minds of the lower classes were being overwhelmed'. Charles Dibdin, junior, the proprietor of Sadler's Wells, claimed that year that: 'there really is an impudence in the press of this age that does the country more disservice in disorganising the people than all the democratic leaders can do, I think; and I'm afraid it is sowing the seeds of a commotion that our children or grandchildren will feel the dire effects of'.

By 1817, sales of William Cobbett's *Political Register*, a radical weekly, were estimated at 60,000–70,000. It was joined by Thomas Wooler's weekly, the *Black Dwarf* (1817–24), which pressed in clear and ringing tones for political and social justice, and by other papers that called into question the pretensions and prerogatives of the entire landed order, including the *Cap of Liberty* (1819–20).

Public interest in reform rose. On 16 August 1819, about 60,000 people turned out in St Peter's Field, Manchester, to hear 'Orator' Henry Hunt demand parliamentary reform. The excited Manchester magistrates read the Riot Act and ordered the Manchester and Salford Yeoman Cavalry to seize the speakers, but the untrained, amateur cavalry also attacked the crowd, leading to eleven deaths and many injuries. There was public outrage at what was termed, by analogy with Waterloo, the Peterloo Massacre. *The Times* deplored 'the dreadful fact that nearly a hundred of the King's unarmed subjects have been sabred by a body of cavalry in the streets of a town of which most of them were inhabitants, and in the presence of those Magistrates whose sworn duty it is to protect and preserve the life of the meanest Englishman'.

Government and elite attitudes in the 1810s, however, were hostile to the development of popular activism. Discontent and violence led to repressive legislation, most prominently the Six Acts of 1819, passed after Peterloo. These included the Blasphemous and Seditious Libels Act and Publications Act, which were intended to limit press criticism. Cobbett fled to America in 1817, when Habeas Corpus was suspended.

There were calls for revolution in Britain, but the radicals were divided and most, including Hunt, rejected the use of force as dangerous, counter-productive and undesirable. In the Cato Street Conspiracy of 1820, a small group of London revolutionaries, many cobblers, under Arthur Thistlewood, planned to surprise the Cabinet at dinner, kill them, and establish a republican government, but they were arrested; while a rising in Huddersfield that year was also unsuccessful. Tension in Scotland culminated in major strike action in 1820, while in Wales the Merthyr Rising of 1831 was defeated by military action and its own divisions, with at least twenty rioters killed. There were also attacks on local privileges. Opposition to the tolls on the bridge over the Tees at Stockton led to a riot in which the gates were pulled down and thrown into the river. The tolls were abolished in 1821. The American envoy, Richard Rush, a bitter critic of the British political system, claimed in 1820:

this is essentially a military government. The regular army is too strong for the unarmed millions, who would otherwise not allow the government to stand for six months; and while the government has the direction of the army, the latter will continue to be paid, and the former supported by the bayonet in its authority. That this state of things will be very permanent, I do not think forever!

Popular discontent did not set the agenda for national politics, but it helped increase the volatility of politics in the early 1830s. In the late 1810s and early 1820s, George IV and the Tory government of Robert, 2nd Earl of Liverpool (1812–27) had essentially contained the situation, firmly resisting both agitation and reform, but in the late 1820s religious issues focused and contributed to a sense of change. The Test and Corporation Acts that maintained the Anglican ascendancy were repealed in 1828 and Catholics gained the vote the following year. Arthur, Duke of Wellington, the victor at Waterloo in 1815 and Prime Minister from 1828 to 1830, had had to press the obdurate George IV very hard to obtain his consent to the Roman Catholic Relief Act. The issue split the Tories, with the ultra-Tories seeing it as a betrayal. In Ireland, the Catholics had had the vote already, subject to property qualifications, under Hobart's Act of 1793.

George IV had a sustained and general unpopularity greater than that of his Hanoverian predecessors. He was not a man able effectively to resist the trend towards a lesser political role for the monarch, however much he might spasmodically insist on his views of his own importance. He lacked his father's strong sense of duty, as well, quite clearly, as his moral concern, and the absence of both was reflected in his failure to follow George III's pattern of royal diligence. Fifty-seven at his accession in 1820, his stamina weakened by laziness, self-indulgence and poor health, George IV's agenda was dominated by more immediate concerns. It was difficult for a monarch to speak convincingly about the constitution when he was perceived as more interested in the Civil List (payments voted by Parliament for the Crown).

At the outset of his reign, George sought to divorce his long-estranged wife, the allegedly disreputable Queen Caroline, whom he had married in 1795 and separated from in 1796 after she had borne a daughter, Princess Charlotte, who died in 1817. He also sought to remove Caroline's royal status. The ministry

The Workhouse

The National Trust has recently acquired the Thurgarton Hundred Incorporated Workhouse in Southwell, Nottinghamshire, the best preserved workhouse in England and the only one with grade II* listed building status. Built in 1824, it retains most of its original fabric and its rural setting, and was regarded by the Poor Law Commission as a model for the Union Workhouses created under the 1834 Poor Law Amendment Act. The workhouse was built by one of the leading writers on poor relief, the Reverend J.T. Becher (1770–1848). He believed that a workhouse would offer care for the deserving poor and deter those who were 'idle and profligate'. Instead of 'outdoor relief' – paying, but not housing, the poor – which was seen as expensive and unable to provide an improving environment, the poor were to be scrutinised and controlled, at a lower cost, in a purpose-built workhouse. Becher described his system in his pamphlet The Antipauper System (1828). His workhouse, built at the cost of £6,596 to house 158 paupers, became in 1836 the Southwell Union Workhouse, serving sixty parishes. Most of the inmates were younger women or older men. Initially there was a punishment regime for reprobates of breaking stones and being locked in solitude, but this was dropped. The original function of managing the unemployed was replaced by that of care of the old and infirm, and new infirmaries were built on the site in 1871 and 1926.

Transferred to local authority control in 1929, the buildings still fulfilled the same function: county and county borough councils had taken over responsibility for poor relief from the poor law unions. After the Welfare State was introduced in 1948, the former workhouse provided temporary accommodation for the homeless and became a centre for social services activity, while the infirmaries became a home for 'elderly and confused ladies'.

The main block of the workhouse provided an architecture of control. Aside from the central hub for the master's accommodation, there were wings for the three segregated groups, men, women and children, a design that derived from prisons, while the stairs were intended to extend the segregation to divide the idle and profligate poor from the blameless and infirm, a segregation that extended to the exercise and work yards.

introduced a retrospective Bill of Pains and Penalties in the House of Lords to dissolve the marriage and deprive Caroline of her royal title. The press lapped up the sexual details of Caroline's alleged affairs and engaged in a vicious and personal debate about whether Caroline was a wronged woman or a disgrace to her sex. Her cause was taken up by the public, the debate lent focus and interest to political controversy, and the government felt obliged to abandon George's campaign against her, although she was successfully denied a coronation.

The contrast with the domestic life of the uxorious George III was readily apparent. George IV could scarcely have issued a proclamation against vice and immorality, as his pious father had done in 1787. In addition, George IV scarcely displayed the ability to manage scandal. Instead, there was much that was ridiculous as well as degrading about the Divorce Bill and the coronation of 1821. Fortunately for George, Caroline died that year.

The coronation, a ceremony of great pomp and expense, was followed in 1821–2 by popular visits to Ireland, Hanover and Scotland, none of which had been visited by George III; Ireland and Scotland indeed had not been visited by any monarch during the eighteenth century. George IV's wearing of Highland dress was particularly successful in courting popularity in Scotland. Thereafter, he retreated from the public face of monarchy, and after 1823, bar the ceremonial opening and proroguing of Parliament, he made no public appearances in London, in large part because he was very unpopular there. He also felt ridiculous as a result of his girth and was affected by poor health. Instead, he spent most of his time in Brighton and Windsor, much of it in the company of his mistress Lady Conyngham. This was no longer the exuberant prince who had built so grandly and strove in his own fashion to compete with Napoleon. It was the restoration French court, not that of George, that set the tone and fashion for court life throughout Europe.

Politically George benefited from the stability of the ministry of Lord Liverpool, as his father had benefited when Pitt the Younger was in power. However, after Liverpool had a stroke and retired in 1827, George IV found politics troubling. The crisis of Liverpool's succession was eventually resolved by making George Canning head of the government, against the initial wishes of the king, but Canning's death in August 1827 reopened the political situation. George helped to put in a weak government under Lord Goderich (1827–8), and, after that collapsed, a stronger ministry under Wellington. However, ministerial stability was challenged by the pressure for Catholic emancipation. George was adamantly opposed, but was forced, under ministerial pressure, to accept the Act passed in 1829.

George IV might have been termed the 'first gentleman in Europe', and there is little doubt that his colourful flamboyance was as one with elevated taste in architecture and fashion, but, as monarch, he lacked charisma, and was widely believed to have no sense of integrity. The *Monthly Repository*'s obituary declared: 'He was too regardless of the decorum which his father so steadily maintained for it to be decent in religionists to become his apologists.' His reign was a lost opportunity for assertive monarchy. In some respects, the history of the British Crown has been often such. James VI and I failed to unify England and Scotland, and his Stuart successors found it impossible to create a domestic consensus or to win glory abroad. The Glorious Revolution of 1688–9 did not produce an uncontested succession, or lead to the accession of vigorous monarchs with healthy children. George I, II and III were not without success, but under George IV, British monarchy lacked political flair, skill and dedication.

The First Reform Act

In the early 1830s, pressure for political change increased. This focused on demands for a reform of Parliament in order to make it more representative of the wealth and weight of the community, a view that reflected the notion of social groups as interests. These demands were not confined to the world of high politics. An easing in political tension had reduced interest in political publishing for a popular market in the 1820s, but the situation altered in the early 1830s as parliamentary reform came to the fore as an issue. The protracted nature of the crisis, at once national and local, high political and electoral, led to sustained excitement as well as violence. During the riots in 1832 Nottingham Castle was burned down.

The Whig government of Lord Grey that took power in November 1830 from Wellington's Conservative administration, after the general election that followed the death of George IV, supported reform. Grey believed the situation 'too like what took place in France before the Revolution'. Rejected by the Commons in April 1831, the Reform Bill, which outlined changes in the franchise and in the distribution of seats, passed in June after another general election, only to be thrown out by the Tory-dominated House of Lords in October 1831. One staunch Tory, John, 1st Earl Brownlow, established and trained a militia to protect his seat at Belton, Lincolnshire, from rioters; the feared attack did not come. In Exeter, the opposition of Henry Philpotts, the Bishop, to the Reform Bill led to violence with his son using coastguards to garrison the episcopal palace against an attack by local radicals. This, however, was a crisis that was rapidly overcome.

The Lords gave way in June 1832, when William IV (1830–7), who was more willing to accept reform than his predecessor, reluctantly agreed that he would make sufficient new peers to create a majority for change. He was influenced both by the widespread support for reform, by the view that the choice was between reform and widespread disorder, and by Grey's opposition to further changes, and thus the sense that the Reform Bill would not be followed by a total transformation of British politics.

In the cartoon *The Reformers' Attack on the Old Rotten Tree,* which advocated electoral changes, William was portrayed on 'Constitution Hill', applauding the process of reform. He was seen as seeking to be a 'constitutional' monarch, which is indeed what he wanted to be. He had to, and could, adapt to political reform.

It is only in hindsight that patterns appear clear. There was nothing predictable about political developments in 1827–32 and a different attitude on the part of the monarch, and indeed a different position for the monarchy, might well have been crucial. That cannot, however, imply that the 'wrong' course was followed, but simply that British political culture in the early nineteenth century had been changed by the decline of the monarchy in the person of one of its most flamboyant and, in many respects, pathetic figures, the self-centred George IV.

Born in 1765, William was somewhat eccentric and his conversations often went off at a tangent, which led to his nickname – 'Silly Billy'. But he was popular and was seen as having integrity. His personal life caused less offence than George's had. Between 1790 and 1811 William lived publicly but quietly with the actress Dorothy Jordan, and they had ten children. He separated from her in order to get married to a socially acceptable wife, Adelaide, whose father was the Duke of Saxe-Meiningen, but their two daughters both died in infancy. William was succeeded by his niece, Victoria, daughter of his brother Edward, Duke of Kent, who had already died.

William's reign began the process of monarchical revival that was to culminate in the development of imperial splendour under his niece, Victoria (1837–1901), and her son, Edward VII (1901–10). His was not the cause of the ultras (reactionaries). Indeed, from William's reign, the British monarchy was not associated with the forces of political conservatism, as it would have been had his brother Ernest, Duke of Cumberland, been king. Ernest became King of Hanover on William's death, for Victoria, as a woman, was not eligible to succeed there. Thereafter, the two thrones remained divided.

The First Reform Act of 1832 was the first major change to the franchise (right to vote) and political geography of England and Wales since the short-lived Interregnum constitutions of the 1650s. Separate acts were also passed for Ireland and Scotland. The Reform Act for England and Wales extended the franchise to sections of the middle class. A uniform borough franchise, based on households rated at £10 annually, was established. The English electorate increased by 50 per cent, so that about one-fifth of all adult males could vote after 1832. The number of those who voted rose dramatically from the 1826 to the 1832 elections. The distribution of seats was radically altered in order to reward growing towns that had not, hitherto, had their own MPs, such as Birmingham, Bradford and Manchester, and also under-represented counties. 'Rotten boroughs', seats with a small population, that were especially open to influence, lost representation. Minehead, which had been a pocket borough under the control of the Luttrells of nearby Dunster Castle, was one such. Between 1734 and 1831, indeed half of all English and Welsh constituencies were contested three times or fewer, in large part because it was not thought worth challenging established interests.

The distribution of seats had been very unequal. Prior to the Reform Act, County Durham had had only four MPs, but the most heavily represented county, Cornwall, had returned forty-four, many from pocket boroughs. The Act gave Durham an additional six, including two for Sunderland and one each for Gateshead and South Shields. Stockton, however, where the Tory Marquess of Londonderry was influential, remained without its own MPs. This led to accusations of bias against the Whig Earl of Durham, Grey's nephew, who had been influential in drafting the bill and was powerful in the north of the county where the towns gained representation. The Whigs won the subsequent general election easily.

Although the changes in the Act were important, they neither amounted to a constitutional revolution, nor led to a social one. The political system remained under the control of the socially powerful. John, Viscount Althorp, who became 3rd Earl Spencer in 1834, was Chairman of the Northamptonshire Quarter sessions from 1806 until his death in 1845. From 1803 until 1906 every heir to the marquessate of Bristol sat at one time or another as MP for West Suffolk or for the borough of Bury St Edmunds, adjacent to the family seat of Ickworth.

The Reform Act was not, however, the end of pressure for reform. The electoral changes excluded the working class, and the distribution of seats was still seen as unfair. London remained under-represented. A series of unstamped radical papers, including the *Prompter* (1830–1), *Republican* (1831), *Poor Man's Guardian* (1831–5), *Working Men's Friend* (1832–3), *Reformer* (1832), *Cosmopolite* (1832–3), and *Man* (1833), produced by

The Novelists' Britain

Much of our image of Victorian Britain comes from the famous novels of the period, especially those of Charles Dickens (1812–70). Whereas Jane Austen (1775–1817), now the best-known novelist of Regency England, is noted foremost for her acute observation of provincial propertied society, and Sir Walter Scott (1771–1832), the leading Scottish novelist of the period, for his historical works, Dickens deliberately addressed social conditions and urban society. In his childhood, Dickens had experience of hardship. His father went to the Marshalsea Debtors' Prison and, at the age of twelve, Dickens began menial work in London in Warren's blacking factory, a shocking experience for him. Later, after being employed as an office boy, a court reporter and a journalist, Dickens became a writer, the successful serialisation of his *Pickwick Papers* starting in 1836. He was a committed reformer, especially over capital punishment, housing and prostitution.

Dickens' novels presented the inadequacies of existing institutions. In *Nicholas Nickleby*, published in monthly parts in 1838–9, Nicholas, sent to teach at Dotheboys Hall in Yorkshire, is horrified by the headmaster, Wackford Squeers, who, knowing their uncaring parents will not intervene, mistreats and starves the pupils and doses them with brimstone and treacle. Nicholas rebels and thrashes Squeers unconscious. The story also featured Ralph Nickleby as a dishonest and callous financier, and Sir Mulberry Hawk as a selfish and sinister member of society. *Bleak House* (1852–3) is an indictment of the coldness of law and Church, the delays of the former and the smugness of the latter in the person of the righteous Reverend Chadband. Society, in the persons of Sir Leicester Dedlock – 'his family is as old as the hills and infinitely more respectable' – and his wife, is revealed as haughty and as concealing a guilty secret. As with the orphan Smike in *Nicholas Nickleby*, society also fails the poor, in this case Jo, a young crossing-sweeper. Both die.

In *Hard Times* (1854), Dickens attacked utilitarianism in the person of the fact-obsessed, unloving hardware merchant Thomas Gradgrind. In *Little Dorrit* (1855–7), society worships Merdle, a great but fraudulent financier, 'a new power in the country', while government, in the shape of the Circumlocution Office, is callously inefficient. At dinner at Merdle's, 'Treasury hoped he might venture to congratulate one of England's world-famed capitalists and merchant-princess. . . . To extend the triumphs of such men, was to extend the triumphs and resources of the nation'.

Not only a novelist, Dickens also launched the weekly magazine *Household Words* in 1850 and held public readings of his works. He won great success. *The Old Curiosity Shop* (1840–1) sold 100,000 copies, his weekly magazine from 1859, *All the Year Round*, as many as 300,000. A fine observer of people, Dickens was also a recorder of a changing society. This was captured in his short story 'Dullborough Town', published in *All the Year Round* on 30 June 1860. The story was about a return to childhood haunts:

> . . . Most of us come from Dullborough who come from a country town . . . the Station had swallowed up the playing-field. It was gone. The two beautiful hawthorn-trees, the hedge, the turf, and all those buttercups and daisies had given place to the stoniest of jolting roads. . . . The coach that had carried me away, was melodiously called Timpson's Blue-Eyed Maid, and belonged to Timpson, at the coach-office up-street; the locomotive engine that had brought me back, was called severely No. 97, and belonged to SER [South Eastern Railway], and was spitting ashes and hot-water over the blighted ground.

Dickens was not alone in his concerns. His one-time collaborator Wilkie Collins (1824–89) dealt with issues such as divorce, vivisection, and the impact of heredity and environment. In *The Woman in White* (1859–60), Anne Catherick is incarcerated in a mental asylum in order to conceal a secret. Evangelical busybodies are attacked in the person of Miss Clack in *The Moonstone* (1868). *Man and Wife* (1870) condemns the cult of athleticism and criticises the marriage laws. In *The New Magdalen* (1873), Collins condemns sexual hypocrisy. Wracked by gout, Collins took large quantities of laudanum and the drug had a major impact on his work.

Elizabeth Gaskell (1810–65) wrote about industrial strife, working-class living standards, and the role of entrepreneurs in *Mary Barton* (1848); and again about industrial strife in *North and South* (1855). George Eliot, the pseudonym of Mary Anne Evans (1819–80), depicted a seducing squire in *Adam Bede* (1859), social ostracism in *The Mill on the Floss* (1860), the cruel selfishness of the two sons of the squire in *Silas Marner* (1861), corrupt electioneering in *Felix Holt* (1866), a hypocritical banker in *Middlemarch* (1871–2), and the decadent mores of society in *Daniel Deronda* (1878). Her work also recorded the pressures of social organisation and mores. Social rank is seen as divisive in *Middlemarch*. Both writers exemplified the importance of women in the writing of novels; they were also very important in readership.

Hardy's Cottage, the birthplace of Thomas Hardy (1840–1928), was the home he returned to in 1867 to write. His novels, including *Far From the Madding Crowd* (1874) and *The Mayor of Casterbridge* (1886), recorded the bleaker side of country life and the corrosive pressure of urban mores on rural ways. Rural society was presented as steeped in folklore and customs, and suspicious of new men of business. Hardy's *Jude the Obscure* (1895) dealt with exclusion from scholarship as a result of class. Earlier, the agricultural labourer John Clare had depicted the plight of the rural poor in *Poems Descriptive of Rural Life* (1820). George Gissing (1857–1903) presented urban poverty and the harsh binds of heredity in *Workers in the Dawn* (1880).

Other novelists were less noted for social criticism, although in *The Way We Live Now* (1874–5), Anthony Trollope (1815–82) condemned the corruption of what he saw as 'the commercial profligacy of the age'. Yet there was little social criticism in the works of Edward Bulwer Lytton (1803–73), now little known, but, in his prime, frequently seen as the country's foremost man of letters for works such as *The Last Days of Pompeii* (1834). Scottish fiction tended to abandon confrontational attitudes towards contemporary industrialisation in favour of historical, ruralist and fantasy writing often intended to reinforce a separate identity for Scotland. This was true of James Hogg (1770–1835), the self-styled 'king of the mountain and fairy school', George MacDonald (1824–1905), an accomplished fantasy writer, and R.L. Stevenson (1850–94).

The writers of the age sought a wide readership, not only for personal profit but also because they thought it important to write for a mass audience, in order to broaden horizons and change minds. This was not seen as incompatible with literary excellence, and these attitudes reflected the distance between the literary world of the nineteenth century and that of two centuries later.

bold and energetic publishers, such as Richard Carlile and Henry Hetherington, launched sweeping attacks on the Establishment, its pretensions, prerogatives, privilege and personnel. The government responded with prosecutions, not least of the vulnerable news-vendors, but the expression of working-class radicalism was not staunched.

Politics, 1833–51

Reform was not at the pace demanded by the radicals. In 1831, indeed Henry Hunt, the Peterloo orator, had told a Manchester meeting that he opposed the Reform Bill, as it would join the middle to the upper classes 'in order to raise yeomanry corps and keep up standing armies'. The Whigs, in fact, sought a stable civic society, serving progress and prosperity, not an uncertain situation vulnerable to disorder and demagogues. Such notions reflected a social stratification that treated the bulk of the population as prone to self-indulgence and a lack of wisdom.

The middling orders, in contrast, were seen as a vital prop to society. Hobhouse's Vestry Act of 1831 was an important extension of their participation in the localities. The Municipal Corporations Act of 1835, passed by the Whig government of William, 2nd Viscount Melbourne, Prime Minister in 1834 and 1835–41, standardised the situation in England and Wales, replacing self-selecting oligarchic corporations, mostly run by Tories, and giving elected borough councils – based on a franchise of rated occupiers – control over the local police, markets and street lighting. This change was to be the basis of an upsurge in urban politics and a wave of urban reformism. A sense of public accountability was captured in the *Sherborne Mercury* of 6 February 1837 under the heading 'Reform Meeting at Lyme Regis':

A public meeting was held on Thursday the 26th instant [January], at the Guildhall in this borough, the Mayor in the chair, for the purpose of enabling their respected representative, William Pinney, Esq., to state his opinions upon the leading political questions of the day, and to take the sense of his constituents on his parliamentary conduct during the past session.

The article continued by providing details of the meeting.

Other parliamentary acts of the period indicated the spreading role of reform agitation, the greater scope of legislation, and, also, the extent of accommodation with existing interests. In 1833, there was both a Factory Act, regulating hours of employment for those under eighteen and establishing a factory inspectorate, and a Bank Charter Act. The latter gave the Bank of England new powers, renewed its charter for twenty-one years, and established its notes for sums of £5 or more as legal tender throughout England and Wales – a measure of national standardisation. The legislation also added the accountability that was a steadily increasing theme of public office: the Bank was required to publish its accounts on a quarterly basis.

The Poor Law Amendment Act, or 'New Poor Law', followed in 1834. It created a centrally controlled bureaucracy, rather than the earlier, varied system of local provision. Parishes now had to join together into 'unions' to support workhouses. The Tithe Commutation Act of 1836 was another work of standardisation, while the introduction of civil registration of births, marriages and deaths in 1837 lessened the role of the established Church. In 1839, state responsibility for elementary education was introduced. Moreover, the number of offences carrying the death penalty was greatly cut.

Melbourne's Whig ministry rested on Tory support and was acceptable to the Tories, because Melbourne was largely concerned to consolidate Grey's legacy, rather than to press on with radical reforms. William's removal of the Melbourne ministry in 1834 was the last time a British ruler dismissed the government and called on other ministers. Contemporaries saw parallels with George III's removal of the Fox–North ministry in December 1783 and his appointment of Pitt the Younger, but the sequel was crucially different. Pitt won the 1784 election, while the Tory leader Sir Robert Peel lost the one in 1835.

Although Melbourne regained office in 1835, he was no radical, and indeed, held off radical rebels. Melbourne's position, however, was challenged by new issues and by their impact on divisions within the government. In addition, there was a Tory revival and, in 1841, the Tories under Peel won a comfortable majority in the general election, thanks to the support of the counties and the numerous small boroughs. It is all too easy to forget the latter when concentrating on the industrial towns that dominate our image of the period.

Meanwhile, Chartism, a variegated popular protest movement, had developed. The Chartists pressed, in the Six Points of the People's Charter, for universal adult male suffrage, a secret ballot, annual elections, equal electoral districts, abolition of property qualifications for MPs and payment for MPs. Parliament, however, resisted Chartist mass-petitions in 1839, 1842 and 1848, and the movement's uneasiness about any resort to violence ensured that there was no parallel to the Year of Revolutions on the continent in 1848. Nevertheless, the scale of government preparation to counter any insurgency was impressive. It benefited from modern technology, as trains and the telegraph greatly increased the speed and effectiveness of the response.

There had been considerable anxiety about the possibility of insurrection. A bill to create a national police had failed in 1832, but under the County Police Act of 1839 Parliament enabled counties to raise uniformed police forces. These were designed to supersede parish policing which was no longer regarded as adequate to the tasks of maintaining law and order in what was seen as a disorderly society. The move from the parish to the county level represented a major shift not only in policing but also in the surveillance, control and governance of the countryside. It contributed to a bureaucratisation, or at least systematisation, that replaced earlier more personal and diverse relationships. Attempts were also made to maintain and improve parochial policing, but these proved unsuccessful, and this led to the County and Borough Police Act of 1856, which consolidated the 1839 legislation.

The forces raised under the latter were a powerful new arm of government. That in County Durham consisted of seventy officers under Major James Wemyss, a Waterloo veteran. This force was used to police the miners' strike of 1844, while troops were used against miners in St Helens and Wigan in Lancashire. Labour relations were volatile, not least because of the difficulties of creating and negotiating industrial relations and work practices in a rapidly changing situation. In addition to the police, there were also new county gaols.

Meanwhile, Peel, who had become Prime Minister in 1841, had pressed for the repeal of the Corn Laws because he saw their continuation as likely to increase popular radicalism, as well as hitting the free trade that exporting industries required. The Anti-Corn Law League was pressing hard on the issue and in 1845–6 Peel divided his party by deciding in favour of phasing out the laws over three years: much of the party saw repeal as a threat to farming. Repeal was only carried in 1846 thanks to the support of Whig MPs, and, having lost control of his party, Peel resigned. This Tory baronet was seen as the man who had given the people cheap bread, and, when he died in 1850, Peel was commemorated in statues, engravings, street names and celebration mugs and plates.

Chartism collapsed as a result of its failure to achieve its goals in 1848 and of a measure of growing prosperity, but many of its ideas, including democratic accountability, influenced popular Liberalism from the 1850s.

Social Conditions

Social conditions for much of the population remained grim. This was especially true for those who lacked employment. In 1834, Henry Stuart found three main groups of inmates in the East Anglian parish workhouses, which he described as often 'abodes of misery, depravity and filth': they were the old and infirm, orphaned and illegitimate children, and unmarried pregnant women. The Poor Law Amendment Act of 1834 introduced national guidelines for the treatment of the destitute, but the workhouse system was deliberately designed to discourage all bar the very destitute from being a charge on the community. Conditions and discipline were harsh, and workhouses were unpopular. Men and women were kept apart.

In Charles Dickens' novel *Our Mutual Friend* (1864–5), Betty Higden was terrified by the workhouse, and in Thomas Hardy's novel *Far From the Madding Crowd* (1874), the unmarried Fanny Robin died in childbirth in the harsh Casterbridge workhouse.

Life outside was also bleak. A review of rural conditions around Street in Somerset in 1845 depicted labourers' families subsisting largely on potatoes and able to spend very little on clothes. Ambrose Batson, a trenching labourer with five children, could not afford meat or butter and used burnt crust as a substitute for tea or coffee. More generally near Street, '5, 6, 7 and sometimes 8 children live together in one room and sleeping in the same room with their father and mother with scarcely a rag to cover them when laid down. And the whole of them to subsist on 5s to 7s weekly and often not that.' The housing of much of the British population was crowded and insanitary. Most houses were cold and damp, because of an absence of damp-proof courses, inadequate heating, insulation and ventilation, and construction on poorly drained land. Rural poverty was a major problem, although less frequently reported than the situation in towns. But the Industrial Revolution would not have taken the form it did if working-class living standards as a whole were this low; domestic demand for goods was important to industrialisation.

Whether indigent or not, everyone was threatened by the ecological situation. Fast-expanding polluted towns proved breeding grounds for disease, and the spread of cholera from Asia was especially fatal. Cholera, a bacterial infection largely transmitted by water infected by the excreta of victims, struck first in 1831, and by 1866 about 140,000 people had died of it. In the industrial centre of Bilston in Staffordshire 692 of the 14,500 population died of cholera in 1832: Bilston Brook provided both water and a sewage outflow. Exeter was hit in 1832 and 1833. Another water-borne infection, typhoid, killed Prince Albert in 1861. Glasgow, which was hit by a serious outbreak of cholera in 1832, and of typhus in 1817–18 and 1837, had annual average death rates of 33 per 1,000 in 1835–9.

More generally, dysentery, diarrhoea, diphtheria, whooping cough, scarlet fever, measles and enteric fever were major problems. Smallpox declined, thanks in part to vaccination, but, due to crowding, poor diet, hard working conditions and pollution, the life of many was grim. As far as mortality figures were concerned, the situation was worse in cities than in poor rural areas. Mortality under five was about 50 per cent in Manchester from 1789 to 1869. In 'Peter Bell the Third' (1819), Shelley wrote 'Hell is a city much like London – A populous and a smoky city.'

Imperial Power

London was also the capital of a growing empire. Turning away from Europe's conflicts gave Britain the opportunity to expand elsewhere. Equilibrium in Europe provided opportunity abroad, and a sense of Britain as a major military power naturally followed the Napoleonic Wars. Wellington was Prime Minister in 1828–30, while Trafalgar Square, begun in the 1820s, soared with Nelson's column, which was topped by Edward Bailey's 18-foot-high statue. The bronze lions followed in 1867. Nelson monuments were also erected in Dublin and Edinburgh, while his victorious death at Trafalgar was commemorated in paintings, engravings, songs and dinners.

Between 1815 and 1851, while other European states made only modest colonial gains, the British Empire expanded across several continents. India was the most important area of expansion, and the British showed that they were capable of conceiving and sustaining strategies and logistics that spanned all of the subcontinent. Although the British lost an entire Anglo-Indian division in a poorly conducted winter-time evacuation of Afghanistan in 1842, they acquired the Maratha dominions in Western India in 1818, Arakan and Tenasserim from Burma in 1826, Mysore in Southern India in 1831, Sind in 1843, and the Punjab in 1849. Kashmir became a vassal state in 1848.

The British also expanded in Malaya, gaining Malacca and Singapore; and annexed Aden in 1839, the first time it had been captured by a European power. British warships moved into the Persian Gulf, while Argentinian and American interest in the Falkland Islands was countered by their occupation by the British in 1832–3. Success against China in the Opium War led to the acquisition of Hong Kong in 1842. The British presence in Australia and New Zealand spread. In South Africa, the British expanded from Cape Colony. Natal was annexed in 1845.

British success owed something to the new-found potential of steampower at sea. Warships were now able to manoeuvre in calms and make headway against contrary winds. In the First Burmese War of 1824–5 the 60 horsepower engine of the British East India Company's steamer *Diana* allowed her to operate on the swiftly flowing Irrawady, and was crucial to the British advance 400 miles upriver.

Territorial expansion provided raw materials, markets and employment, and, combined with evangelism, encouraged a sense of Britain as at the cutting edge of civilisation. The country's destiny increasingly seemed imperial and oceanic. The varied consequences included the ability to send plant-hunters all over the world, enriching British gardens with plants never seen before in Britain, and encouraging the creation of arboreta, such as that at Westonbirt, to display trees from far-flung places. At Killerton, Devon, these included the Californian giant redwood, named Wellingtonia after the duke because it stood so high above its fellows.

Another legacy of British prestige can be seen on the Embankment in London. In 1820, Mehmet Ali, ruler of Egypt, presented an obelisk known as Cleopatra's Needle to George IV. The collecting instinct filled museums. Augustus Pitt-Rivers (1827–1900) served abroad as a soldier, became a noted collector of ethnographic material, and donated his collection to serve as the basis of the Pitt-Rivers Museum in Oxford. Other legacies of empire in Britain included badminton, polo, snooker and curry.

British capital and expertise played a major role in many parts of the world. Banking houses such as Barings provided the credit for the development of railways abroad, as with America's first railroad, the Baltimore & Ohio. The British also exported to the world. Coal from ports such as Cardiff, Seaham, Hartlepool and Sunderland powered locomotives and forges overseas.

At the time of the Great Exhibition, James Wyld built a large model of the globe. 'Wyld's Great Globe' was displayed in a large circular building in Leicester Square in 1851–62. Gas-lit, it was 60 feet high, about 40 feet in diameter, and the largest hitherto constructed. No eccentric, Wyld was an active parliamentarian, Master of the Clothworkers' Company, and a leading promoter of technical education. He reflected a widespread British confidence in their superiority and rule. In the Notes to Accompany his globe, dedicated to Prince Albert, Wyld wrote:

> What comparisons suggest themselves between the condition of the Pacific region in the time of [Captain] Cook and now? What was then held by illiterate savages now constitutes the rising communities of New South Wales . . . the civilizing sway of the English crown . . . an empire more extended than is governed by any other sceptre.

THREE

VICTORIAN HIGHPOINT, 1851–86

Many of the events that are identified with the lengthy reign of Victoria (1837–1901) occurred in the years 1851–86. It was the age of the Crimean War (1854–6), the Indian Mutiny (1857–9), the purchase of control over the Suez Canal (1875), the creation of the title of Empress of India (1876), war with the Zulus (1879), and the loss of General Gordon at Khartoum (1885). The Whig Lord Palmerston was Prime Minister in 1855–8 and 1859–65, the Conservative Benjamin Disraeli in 1868 and in 1874–80, and the Liberal William Gladstone in 1868–74, 1880–5, 1886 and 1892–4.

The Whigs were transformed, largely thanks to Gladstone, into the more reformist Liberals. Building on Peel's work, under Disraeli, Conservatism was effectively redefined as different from and opposed to Liberalism, but not as a creed of reaction. Instead, Disraeli sought to fuse social legislation with a sense of national continuity.

The economy expanded, there was a measure of social progress, and only limited popular discontent. Extensions to the franchise in the Second (1867) and Third (1884) Reform Acts were accomplished without the tension that had surrounded what was now called the First Reform Act of 1832. Although there were doubts and panics, there was also a reasonable degree of confidence in Britain's international position. Certainly, in contrast to the 1890s and 1900s, let alone later decades, these seemed to be golden years.

As earlier in the century, this was a period of economic expansion, and Britain remained the workshop of the world. In 1880–4, the annual average production of coal and lignite in million metric tons was 159 for Britain, and 108 for France, Germany, Belgium and Russia combined; that of pig-iron in

1880, 7.9 for Britain and 5.4 for the rest of Europe; and of steel 1.3 and 1.5 respectively; while raw cotton consumption, in thousand metric tons, in 1880 was 617 for Britain and 503 for the rest of Europe. Middlesbrough, Gladstone's 'infant Hercules', was a symbol of Britain's achievement in iron and steel production. Increased industrial production interacted with expanding trade. This led to an increase in shipping and shipbuilding. On the Tyne, the Palmer brothers opened a shipyard at Jarrow that became crucial to the development of the town. Trade also led to the building of new docks. In London, the St Katharine Docks, opened in 1828, were followed by the Poplar Docks (1852), Royal Victoria Dock (1855), Millwall Dock (1868), Royal Albert Dock (1880) and Tilbury Docks (1886). Factories located near the quaysides.

Aggregate figures for economic growth concealed a regional geography of great variations. As industrialisation gathered pace, so did the contrast between industrialised regions and the rest of the country, between, for example, Clydeside and South-West Scotland. The world of work changed. By the mid-nineteenth century, for example, fewer than 10 per cent of those employed in the Scottish central-belt counties of Lanark, Midlothian and Renfrew worked in agriculture, forestry and fishing. The population of regions experiencing industrial growth rose rapidly. The number of people in County Durham rose from 390,997 in 1851 to 1,016,562 in 1891, with a growth of 34.7 per cent alone in the decade 1861–71. Four major iron and steelworks were established at Workington on the Cumberland coast in 1862–74, and the population there rose from 6,467 in 1861 to 23,749 in 1891. In Newcastle the increase was from 28,294 in 1801 to 215,328 in 1901. In such areas, the landscape changed. Paintings such as Myles Foster's *Newcastle upon Tyne from Windmill Hill, Gateshead* (*c.* 1871–2) showed formerly prominent buildings – the castle keep and the cathedral, now joined by factory chimneys and the railway bridge. The city centre had been transformed in the 1830s. At a smaller scale, the Derbyshire town of Staveley had grown at an average rate of 1.3 per cent per year between 1741 and 1841. When it industrialised rapidly between 1841 and 1861 the rate rose to nearly 5 per cent.

Major increases in population were only achieved by migration. The dislocation caused by extensive movement of people was part of the pattern of economic growth, essential to provide labour and yet disruptive for individuals and communities. Areas with limited economic growth, such as Cornwall and Ireland, produced large numbers of migrants, who were soaked up by growing cities and by emigration. Thanks to growth on and near the South Wales coalfield, Glamorgan and Monmouthshire had about 20 per cent of the Welsh population in 1801, but 57.5 per cent by 1901. Eleven per cent of Swansea's population in 1861 had been born in South-West England. London, Britain's largest industrial city as well as much else, drew heavily on East Anglia and the West Country. Of the 225 iron workers at the Britannia Foundry at Derby in 1871, over half were born outside the town, although most came from the county.

Industrial regions that failed to maintain earlier growth rates, for example the Staffordshire coal and iron area, also provided migrants. Staffordshire and Shropshire ironworkers were partly responsible for the expansion of the population of Tudhoe in County Durham from 400 in 1851 to 1,359 in 1861: an ironworks had been opened there in 1853. By 1871, the population was 5,007: pits were sunk in 1866–9. Most of the new inhabitants of Tudhoe came from exhausted mining areas in the west of the county and from the Midlands.

Industrial growth in Britain in the second half of the century increasingly focused on engineering, shipbuilding and chemicals, rather than the textiles and metal smelting of earlier in the century, and this led to changes in the location of industrial expansion. Such economic changes helped to foster the further expansion of the rail system, as indeed did the growing practice of commuting by workers, especially those of a senior grade.

The socio-economic impact of a developing national economy affected all regions. The most remote – the Scottish Highlands and Islands – was changed by new pressures of commercialism and agrarian change, as, more generally, was the whole of rural society. There were also important changes throughout industry, not just in the major concerns. These focused on the mechanisation of production. Thus, a Tewkesbury industrialist invented and patented the reinforcing of the underfoot and heels of stockings, and, by 1860, Owen and Uglow's factory at Tewkesbury employed 600 men and 150 women, all servicing a large number of machines.

The new society of urbanisation and industrialisation created new needs. The development of urban working-class leisure, away from traditional customs and towards new mass, commercialised interests, was one of the responses to the new society. Music-halls and football clubs were founded in large numbers. This was commercial and institutionalised leisure, a form more open to regulation, so that it would not challenge the requirements of the established order. At the 1852 Annual Meeting of the Darlington Horticultural Society, the Reverend H. Harries pontificated: 'this society . . . was calculated to improve and elevate the taste of all classes, especially the poorer classes, by withdrawing them in their leisure hours from grosser indulgences to a pleasurable and improving pursuit'. Such bodies provided opportunities for the dissemination of established views. The Marquess of Londonderry said at one of the society's exhibitions in 1848 that 'by rallying round the throne and the constitution he entertained not the least doubt that the glories of England would continue to the end of the world'. So much for Chartism.

Alternative entertainments were scrutinised. Under the Vagrancy Act of 1824, and later laws, the police were able to arrest street entertainers, and, by the end of the century, these were figures of the past. Instead, popular activities were regulated, for example, with the growing standardisation of the organisation of brass bands in the 1860s and 1870s. Public spaces were controlled. The new policing of the period was much concerned about the moral threat of the urban environment and sought to bring order and decorum to the streets. For instance, the popularity of the Clent Hills with trippers from the West Midlands led to problems, not least due to drunkenness and disorder. In 1881, conservators were appointed and they were given powers by Parliament to make by-laws. This involved regulation, the licensing of the erection of booths, the sale of goods and the hiring of horses and donkeys. More generally, in 1854 pubs were forced to close at midnight on Saturday and, except for Sunday lunch and evening, not reopen until 4 a.m. on Monday. Complete Sunday closing was enforced in Scotland from 1853 and in Wales from 1881.

Aside from disquiet about urban crowds and conduct, there was also a cultural reaction to industrialisation. By the 1840s, the horrors of industrialisation were encouraging, in some quarters, a nostalgic return to medievalism. The most obvious manifestation of this was architectural – a very historicist Gothic revival. But, indirectly, in art it led to the Pre-Raphaelite movement, launched in 1848.

In stark contrast, the living conditions of the bulk of the population were poor, and increasingly seen as such. Population density rose as the urban population grew. The number of people in Sunderland nearly trebled between 1825 and 1865, but the built-up area little more than doubled. Overcrowding could be acute, and was accompanied by a lack of facilities. In 1843, Pipewellgate in Gateshead had 2,040 people crammed into a street 300 yards long and mostly only 8 feet in breadth; there were only three privies in the street. That year, only 110 homes in Gateshead had water laid on, while, in Newcastle, fewer than 10 per cent of homes had water directly supplied. Instead, part of the Newcastle supply came from the Tyne, especially during summer droughts, and this was linked to major cholera outbreaks in 1832, 1850 and 1853. In the last, 1,500 out of the city's 90,000 people died in five weeks. The overcrowded east end of Sunderland was the centre of the 1831 cholera epidemic in the town. The crowded, insanitary part of Carlisle was badly hit by cholera: the city had an unsatisfactory water supply. There were major epidemics of cholera in Britain in 1848–9, 1854 and 1866. An orphanage was founded in Wolverhampton after the 1849 epidemic in order to provide for cholera orphans. Southampton, like many cities, had an area known as 'the rookeries' from the network of courts, alleys and paths that were inhabited by thieves and the destitute. In one cholera outbreak there, a doctor found a family in a room over a stable overcome by ammonia from the sewage below.

Lord Armstrong and Cragside

The Northumbrian house Cragside was a product of Victorian enterprise and technology in two senses, first in terms of the house itself and, secondly, as a product of the fortune of its self-made creator, William Armstrong (1810–1900), one of the leading industrialists of the age. With the installation of arc lighting in 1878, Cragside was the earliest house in the world to be lit by electricity derived from water power. Joseph Swan's carbon-filament incandescent light bulbs followed two years later. Armstrong also used the latest hydraulic technology to ensure a plentiful supply of water.

Cragside was built in the Debdon valley, much of it bare hillside. Armstrong initially constructed a small stone lodge, but the projected extension of the railway to nearby Rothbury led him to make it his main home, and, to that end, in 1869 he hired the architect Richard Norman Shaw. The house was not finished until the late 1890s. A dramatic work of man was stamped on the wild Northumbrian countryside.

Son of a Newcastle corn-merchant, Armstrong was initially a solicitor, but his interest in hydraulics led him in 1845 to mastermind a new water company to supply Newcastle. This provided a basis for his fortune, and in 1846 he employed the pressure of this new water supply to develop the world's first effective hydraulic crane for the Newcastle docks. Founding an engineering firm at Elswick west of Newcastle in 1847, he swiftly expanded the manufacture of cranes to include bridges and locomotives also. Armaments followed from the late 1850s, and eventually ironclad warships. The 110-ton, nearly 44-foot long, Armstrong breech-loaders manufactured for HMS *Victoria*, which was launched in 1887, were the largest and most powerful guns in the world.

Armstrong's armaments were also sold abroad. The Afghan force that defeated the British at Maiwand in 1880 had three rifled 14-pounder Armstrong guns, while his shipyard built for a host of foreign powers, including Argentina, Chile, Italy and Japan. Monarchs seeking arms deals, including the Shah of Persia in 1889 and the King of Siam,were entertained at Cragside. Aside from arms, engineering continued to be important to Armstrong. He supplied the hydraulic equipment to raise Tower Bridge, a potent symbol of empire opened in 1894, and also the hydraulic lifts that enabled the London Underground system to expand with deep stations.

Armstrong was defeated when he stood for Parliament in 1886, but in 1887 he went to the Lords. A great local benefactor, who supported local education and health, Armstrong was President of the Arts Association and a purchaser of the works of contemporary British painters, such as Dante Gabriel Rosetti, a member of the Pre-Raphaelite school. The changed nature of society was underlined in 1894 when this greatest of modern British warlords spent £60,000 buying Bamburgh Castle, the ruined centre of Northumbrian power for much of the Anglo-Saxon period and a great medieval fortress, restoring it and making it habitable again.

This was one example of a widespread attempt to preserve castles and an interest in the Middle Ages. The Somerset Archaeological Society purchased Taunton Castle in 1874 and then restored it. John, 3rd Marquess of Bute, acquired Falkland Palace in 1887 and began its restoration. George, Marquess Curzon bought and helped restore Bodiam and Tattershall castles in East Sussex and Lincolnshire respectively, giving them to the National Trust in 1925. Stuart Rendel, who was Armstrong's managing partner in London, bought the eighteenth-century Hatchlands Park, Surrey, made alterations, and took his peerage title from the property.

None of Armstrong's successors possessed his dedication or business acumen. The heavy debts of the 1st Lord Armstrong of the second creation led to the sale of many of Cragside's valued appurtenances in 1908, and in 1977 death duties led to Cragside passing to the Treasury.

Public knowledge and awareness of disease increased during this period. In 1849, Dr John Snow argued, in his *On the Mode and Communication of Cholera*, that the disease was transmitted through drinking water contaminated by sewage. In the *Punch* cartoon 'Father Thames Introducing His Offspring To The Fair City of London' of 3 July 1858, a facetious design for a fresco for the new Houses of Parliament, a filthy Thames, polluted by factories, sewage and steamships, presented diphtheria, scrofula and cholera.

There was also action, an impressive effort, and investment in public works. In 1848, the Public Health Act created a General Board of Health and an administrative structure to improve sanitation, especially water supply. The new act provided for the creation of local boards of health, and they took action. The board established in Leicester in 1849 was instrumental in the creation of a sewerage system and in tackling slaughterhouses and smoke pollution. The report on the Sussex town of Battle, drawn up in 1850 by Edward Cresy, a superintending inspector under the General Board of Health, noted: 'There is no provision for the removal of any offensive or noxious refuse from the houses and gardens of the poorer classes; all the decomposing and putrescent animal and vegetable matter which is brought out of the house is thrown into a pool, around which is engendered an atmosphere favourable to the production of febrile epidemics.' Cresy's critical report on Derby led the Liberal councillors to embark on a programme of works, including public baths and washhouses.

With its population rising from just over 1 million in 1801 to over 7 million by 1911, London presented the most serious problem, but, from 1859, under the direction of Joseph Bazalgette, Chief Engineer to the Metropolitan Board of Works, a drainage system was constructed. Fully completed in 1875, this contained 82 miles of intercepting sewers that took sewage from earlier pipes that had drained into the Thames, and transported it to new downstream works. Pumping stations provided the power. Storm-relief sewers followed in the 1880s. Other aspects of Bazalgette's work showed how man-made constraints were being stamped on the environment. He was responsible for the Victoria, Albert and Chelsea embankments, each of which limited the river bank and lessened the risk of flooding. Bazalgette also created new routes in London – new bridges at Putney and Battersea, the Woolwich steam ferry, and Northumberland Avenue.

Disposing of sewage was not the sole problem. Clean drinking water for all was crucial. On Tyneside, reservoir storage capacity rose to 215 million gallons in 1848, 530 million in 1854, over 1,200 million in 1871 and over 3,000 million by the end of the 1880s. Filter beds were installed in 1863, and stricter filtering controls imposed in 1870. Distant upland areas were tapped by reservoirs, including from 1905 the Catcleugh Reservoir in Redesdale, and these were linked to the cities by pipelines. The Tyne itself was dredged from 1863 by the combination of a reforming body – the Tyne Improvement Commissioners, an able engineer – J.F. Ure, and new technology – the world's most powerful bucket dredgers. The Souter Lighthouse, opened nearby in 1871, was the first to be powered by alternating electric current.

The process of improvement was widespread. Manchester began to get water from Longdendale in the early 1850s. Brighton obtained adequate water in the 1860s and an intercepting sewer in 1874, Carlisle a reservoir at Castle Carrock in 1909. The average death rate per 1,000 from typhoid in Ffestiniog fell from 12.9 in 1865–74 to 1.3 in 1880–90, thanks to piped water and a better sewerage system. In addition, electric lighting systems were installed in towns, the first in Godalming in 1881.

It is important not to exaggerate the degree and pace of improvement. Industrial expansion led to new sources of pollution. Gasworks produced coal-gas tar which drained into rivers. In 1866, 43 per cent of Newcastle's population was still living in dwellings of only one or two rooms; in 1885, 30.6 per cent. Gastro-intestinal disorders linked to inadequate water and sewerage systems were responsible for Bradford's very high infant mortality rate, and for comparable problems in crowded parts of Newcastle and elsewhere. Death rates, especially due to the infectious diseases of early childhood, such as measles and scarlet fever, were higher in urban areas, so that the redistribution of the population towards the cities through migration delayed the decline in national mortality.

Furthermore, the decision to tackle public health essentially through engineering directed by administrators ensured that alternative responses, such as measures to alleviate poverty, were sidetracked. The focus was on sewerage systems and clean water, not on securing the supply of food and work or income at levels sufficient to lessen the impact of disease. This priority accorded with that of the reforming middle classes, but to underline the existence of an alternative is not to engage in anachronism: there were suggestions from informed contemporaries. William Alison, Professor of Physiology at Edinburgh, linked cholera and poverty and argued in his *Observations on the Management of the Poor in Scotland, and its Effects on the Health of the Great Towns* (1840) and his *Observations on the Epidemic Fever in Scotland, and its Connection with the Destitute Condition of the Poor* (1846) that the latter had to be addressed. This helped lead to a reform of the Scottish poor law system in 1845, but the 1848 Public Health Act represented a triumph for the focus on drains.

Working conditions were frequently grim. The death rate from fatal accidents per 1,000 workers underground in 1875–93 was 2.09 for coalminers and 2.34 for Cleveland ironworkers. Rates among Ffestiniog slate miners were higher – 3.23, despite the inclusion of slate mining in the Metaliferous Mines Acts of 1872 and 1875 which sought better working conditions by, for example, improving ventilation. A total of 189 men and boys were killed due to an underground gas explosion at Wood Pit in Haydock, Lancashire, in 1878.

Public health problems also existed in small towns and rural areas; rural poverty, opposition to the interference of central government, and the preference for traditional practices (including inaction), could be a potent mix. Reports on the situation in Bruton in Somerset in the 1870s and 1880s described insufficient and defective toilet arrangements, inadequate sewage disposal, and a lack of clean water. A reluctance to spend money ensured that plans to alleviate the situation were delayed: although the sewerage system was finally improved, Bruton did not construct a water supply system in the Victorian period. The lead-working settlement of Leadhills in South-West Scotland did not receive an improved water supply until the 1920s.

Nevertheless, there were steadily greater attempts to create a legislative framework for reform. In place of a reliance on self-help and the efforts of local communities, there was a stress on institutional provision and national standards. This was seen in many aspects of administrative, social and economic activity. The Factory Acts of 1833, 1844, 1847, 1850, 1860 and 1874 regulated conditions of employment. The shocking conditions of child labour in the calico printing industry revealed by the Print Works Commission of 1843 led to the prohibition of employment of children under eight in the Calico Print Works Act of 1845. Conditions, however, remained hard throughout industry.

Attempts were made to improve and regulate society, especially the urban environment. The County and Borough Police Act of 1856 made the formation of paid police forces obligatory. The Recreation Grounds Act of 1859 and the Public Health Act of 1875 encouraged the laying out of public parks, while the Commons Act of 1876 sought to protect from development land outside towns that was beneficial to the community. Municipal parks and buildings testified to the strength of local identity and the desire to improve the local environment. Wolverhampton gained a town hall in 1871 and a people's park in 1881. The East End Public Park in Wolverhampton followed in 1895.

The governments of both Gladstone (1868–74, 1880–5, 1886, 1892–4) and Disraeli (1868, 1874–80) pushed for social improvement. Under Gladstone, the 1870 Education Act divided the country into school districts under education boards, and stipulated a certain level of educational provision. The Endowed Schools Commission established that year redistributed endowments and reformed governing bodies. Open competition was introduced in the Civil Service in 1870, an important step in the move from patronage to merit; and voting made less open to coercion with the secret ballot (1872).

The institutionalisation of Easter, Whitsun and bank holidays in 1871 provided more opportunities for organised leisure. Southend grew rapidly as a resort for London East Enders after the Bank Holiday Acts of 1871 and 1875.

Under Disraeli in 1874–80, there was much social reform, although his commitment was limited, certainly far less than that of Gladstone. Some of the legislation was inherited from the Gladstone government, and most of it did not receive Disraeli's full attention. Nevertheless, whatever the practical impact, legislation on factories (1874), public health, artisans' dwellings, and pure food and drugs (1875), systematised and extended the regulation of important aspects of public health and social welfare. The Artisans Dwellings Act of 1875 made urban renewal possible. The Prison Act of 1877 established state control. The Definition of Time Act of 1880 made the use of Greenwich Mean Time compulsory throughout Britain.

That year, Gladstone returned to power. The 'People's William' had fought a vigorous campaign, reaching the electorate by train and through the 'penny' press, and firing them up as his opponents could not do. The beneficiary of working-class support, the new Liberal government moved to the left, alienating the Whig landed aristocracy who distrusted further extensions of the franchise and opposed land reform. The party was to split for good over Irish Home Rule in 1886.

A Royal Commission on the Housing of the Working Class was held in 1884–5, and, under the 1890 Housing Act, the London County Council established in 1889 by the 1888 Local Government Act, was given the right to rebuild cleared slums and to build on greenfield sites. The Crofters Act of 1886 sought to deal with economic problems and social tension in the Scottish Highlands and Islands, and was followed in 1897 by the establishment of the Congested Districts Board.

As government became more activist and regulatory, so the goal of the political groupings that controlled it increasingly became seizing the opportunity to push through policy, as much as office-holding for personal profit and prestige. The nature of power within society was now discussed to a greater extent than a century earlier. The expanding middle class expected power and status, and was dubious of established institutions and practices that did not seem reformist or useful. Deference was eroded. Middle-class views and wealth stimulated a demand for, and process of, improvement, civic and moral, that was central to the movement for reform. It was directed as much against the habits of the poor as those of the Establishment.

Inherited privilege that lacked purpose was criticised. To take one example, London's development challenged conventional beliefs that certain areas were inhabited only by certain types of people, as it became necessary to define new and redefine established neighbourhoods. Adolphus Longestaffe, the snobbish squire seeking both a loan and a railway directorship in Anthony Trollope's novel *The Way We Live Now* (1874–5), had a town-house in Bruton Street:

> It was not by any means a charming house, having but few of those luxuries and elegancies which have been added of late years to newly built London residences. It was gloomy and inconvenient, with large drawing-rooms, bad bedrooms, and very little accommodation for servants. But it was the old family town-house, having been inhabited by three or four generations of Longestaffes, and did not savour of that radical newness which prevails, and which was peculiarly distasteful to Mr. Longestaffe. Queen's Gate and the quarters around were, according to Mr. Longestaffe, devoted to opulent tradesmen. Even Belgrave Square, though its aristocratic properties must be admitted, still smelt of the mortar. Many of those living there and thereabouts had never possessed in their families real family town-houses. The old streets lying between Piccadilly and Oxford Street, with one or two well-known localities to the south and north of these boundaries, were the proper sites for these habitations.

Such a hierarchy based on past values could not be sustained, and Trollope had no sympathy for Longestaffe. In contrast, Lady Bracknell, the snobbish, but acute, social observer in Oscar Wilde's satirical play about English social distinctions, *The Importance of Being Earnest* (1895), was keen to respond to the matrimonial prospects of money, and noted that it was possible to change the fashionable side of London squares.

The middle class also had a strong sense of place, of where it was acceptable to live, and of the conduct deemed appropriate in those areas. Immorality was criticised as debasing and unproductive. Combined with concern about the impact of venereal diseases on the armed forces, this led to the Contagious Diseases Acts of 1866, 1867 and 1869, under which a harsh system of control was established over prostitutes in garrison and port towns. The prostitutes, rather than their clients, were blamed for venereal disease.

'Morality' was not only a middle-class cause. Self-improving artisans were also involved, especially in expanding towns such as Sunderland, where there was a high percentage of owner-occupiers of property. Similarly, reform agitation was not limited to the propertied. In the 1870s, textile workers campaigned hard for an eight-hour day. Many of the ideas that were to influence the Labour movement were being developed in this period. For example, John Ruskin's attack on capitalist society, *Unto This Last*, was published in magazine articles in 1860 and in a book in 1862.

Reform Acts

In the 1850s the decline in anxiety about radicalism, after the collapse of Chartism, made it easier to consider fresh reforms. The abolition of the tax on advertisements in 1853 and of the stamp tax on newspapers in 1855 permitted a cheaper, and thus more active, press. The first provincial dailies in Birmingham, Liverpool, Manchester and Sheffield appeared in 1855, in Newcastle in 1857, in Bristol in 1858, Plymouth in 1860, Nottingham in 1861 and Bradford in 1868.

Existing voting arrangements in this expanding society appeared redundant to many mainstream politicians. The Second Reform Act of 1867 nearly doubled the existing electorate and, by offering household suffrage, gave the right to vote to about 60 per cent of adult males in boroughs. In addition to all ratepaying householders, £12 occupiers in the counties and £10 lodgers in the boroughs were given the vote. The opponents of reform had stirred up popular anger by claiming that the workers were 'unfit' to have the franchise; Gladstone and Lord John Russell, Whig Prime Minister 1865–6, believed, in contrast, that the more affluent workers should be trusted with the vote. Unable, in the face of a Whig split, to convince the Commons, they resigned and the Conservatives (as the Tories were now increasingly called), under the sickly Edward, 14th Earl of Derby, took office and pushed through their own Reform Bill. Disraeli was responsible for much of the parliamentary work and roused the suspicions of the Conservative right, including a future Prime Minister, Lord Salisbury. Disraeli needed Liberal votes in order to get the Bill through the Commons, and Liberal amendments were responsible for all borough ratepayers gaining the vote, a measure that enfranchised many manual workers.

There was also a redistribution of seats. Less populous boroughs, such as Honiton, lost their seats. New parliamentary boroughs in County Durham – Darlington, Stockton and the Hartlepools – and elsewhere, reflected population growth. However, the continued deficiencies of the system encouraged pressure for more reform.

In 1884, the Third Reform Act extended to the counties the household franchise granted to the boroughs in 1867, so that over two-thirds of adult males in the shires, and about 63 per cent of the entire adult male population, received the vote, although the eighteen-month residence qualification limited numbers. This was the first time that the whole of the United Kingdom had been brought under the same electoral system. Initially rejected by the Conservatives in the Lords, the Bill was passed in return for the Redistribution of Seats Act of 1885, which led to a move to single-member seats and a major reorganisation that included the division of many county seats. In County Durham, the number of MPs went up to sixteen, and the electorate expanded greatly as a result of the miners gaining the vote. As in 1868, the Conservatives were defeated in November 1885 in the first election held under the new franchise; they had also been defeated in the last election under the old franchise.

In November 1885, many rural electors voted against their landlords: democracy challenged the existing social politics, and, in particular, the rural strongholds of Conservatism. But the defeats were not only in the countryside. In 1868, the Marquess of Londonderry's son lost at Stockton to a Liberal. In the 1885 general election, the Tories were routed in County Durham, only winning the City of Durham, a more conservative constituency. Working-men Liberal–Labour candidates were more successful, two of the Durham Miners' Association agents winning seats, although Labour sympathy was mostly contained within Liberalism.

The democratisation of local government followed, thanks to Local Government Acts in 1888 and 1894, with elected county and town councils taking over functions formerly performed by the magistrates and the Poor Law Unions. The first Act alienated Conservative landowners, but was pushed through by a Conservative government under Robert, 3rd Marquess of Salisbury in an attempt to pre-empt something more radical from a future Liberal government.

Electoral geography was also changing; Salisbury had supported redistribution because he felt it would increase the representation of middle-class areas, such as suburbs and seaside resorts, taking them out of county seats. He thought this would benefit the Conservatives, not least because he sensed middle-class disaffection with growing Liberal radicalism. Salisbury was correct to discern the possibilities of 'Villa Torydom'. From the mid-1880s, politics began to conform to a pattern that would seem more familiar to twentieth-century observers.

Maps and Mapping, 1791–1914

War brought Britain into a new cartographic age. A degree of modernisation resulted from the challenge of the French Revolutionary and Napoleonic Wars (1793–1815). This modernisation included the introduction of income tax and a national census, and parliamentary union with Ireland. In addition, a government department, the Board of Ordnance, was given responsibility for mapping the British Isles in order to help cope with an apparently likely French invasion. The Trigonometrical, later called Ordnance, Survey, the basis of the detailed maps of Britain to this day, began in 1791, although it continued triangulation work first begun in 1784. A 1 inch to the mile map of Kent was published in 1801. Thereafter, the surveyors moved to the South-West of England, another potential invasion area.

The triangulation was virtually completed by 1824, when the survey began work on a 6-inch map of Ireland, finished, in 1,875 sheets, in 1846. The first ninety sheets of England and Wales, covering up to a line from Preston to Hull, at 1 inch to the mile were published between 1805 and 1844, and sheets for all of England and Wales had been published by the end of 1869. There was also mapping at 6 inches and 25 inches to the mile, and at 5 feet and 10 feet to the mile.

Mapping also played a major role in the extension of British power. Imperialism was territorial. This territoriality required knowledge – the ability to locate, and the construction and acquisition of that knowledge was part of a more general process by which the British sought to understand the world in their own terms. Physical geography was measured: seas charted, heights gauged, depths plumbed, rainfall and temperature graphed. All was integrated, so that the world was increasingly understood in terms of a British matrix of knowledge.

In a process that had been actively pushed forward since the third quarter of the eighteenth century, hitherto uncharted waters were sounded. Commander Edward Belcher and HMS Sulphur surveyed the sea around Hong Kong in 1841, part of the process by which the British took control. Reliable maps became easier to provide and to publish. From 1823, the extensive range of charts produced by the Admiralty was offered publicly for sale.

The methods of mapping reflected imperialist assumptions. In surveying India, especially by means of the Great Trigonometrical Survey undertaken by the East India Company, the British discarded information from Indian sources. Underlying the unreasonably low British opinion of the Indians' worth as surveyors were some basic assumptions about their alleged inability to conceive of space and distance in European terms. The British carried out most of the surveying, with the Indians largely employed as labourers, guards, and bearers; not until the 1820s did some Indians begin to assume positions hitherto reserved for Europeans.

As with other aspects of the British economy and British culture, technological changes were of great consequence. Mechanised papermaking became commercially viable in the 1800s, leading to the steam-powered production of plentiful, inexpensive supplies, and the steam-powered printing press developed in the same period. Aside from the changes resulting from the mass production of printed material, there were also specific developments in map production that led to a greater process of specialisation. This reflected and encouraged the foundation of new specialised map publishers, such as W. and A.K. Johnston in 1826 and John Bartholomew & Son in the 1820s, both in Edinburgh, and George Philip & Son in London in 1834.

Map-colouring ceased to be a manual process and was transformed by the onset of common colour printing. Colour came to play a more prominent role in mapping, and was seen as both a commercial opportunity and challenge. Colour conventions developed. The use of pink or red to denote the British Empire began. Henry Teesdale's *New British Atlas* (1831) was one of the first recorded examples of the use of red to show British possessions. This did not become a general convention until after 1850, with the development of colour printing, and was popularised by school wall maps and atlases.

Within Britain, there was steadily more mapping. Much was functional. The reorganisation of farmland and common land through enclosure continued to require the production of maps. Aside from specific acts, General Enclosure Acts were passed in 1801, 1836 and 1845. Population growth and wartime pressures on food supplies combined to ensure much enclosure in 1793–1815, including nearly one-third of Bedfordshire, Cambridgeshire and Huntingdonshire. Furthermore, the 1836 Tithe Commutation Act led to the mapping and valuation of titheable land. The development of the railways also resulted in much mapping to plan new routes and then individual journeys. Timetables often contained maps – George Bradshaw's first *Railway Timetable* appeared in 1839. More generally, improvement maps registered planned changes.

The establishment of mass schooling increased the demand for maps. With growing literacy and wealth, the general book-reading public swelled and readers became more used to seeing maps, for example in bibles, newspapers and magazines, and on stamps and consumer products, especially tins. They were avid for information. There was also a great interest in statistics, and increased mapping was a part of this process. Maps played an increasing role in scientific investigation and exposition, whether with the science of mankind, such as Charles Booth's maps of London poverty and Henry Mayhew's of London crime, or with biological and physical sciences. Mapping was central to geology.

More generally, a conviction of the influence of environment encouraged an interest in mapping. Atlases devoted more attention to physical details. In his *New Student's Atlas of English History* (1903), Emil Reich claimed: 'The paramount importance of geography as the basis of a study of history has been brought home to Englishmen by the late war in South Africa [Boer War].' Reich also chose to map 'British Genius'. Analysing the *Dictionary of National Biography* (1885–1900), a scholarly statement of British importance, Reich mapped the 21,000 people whose birthplaces had been traced in order to correlate locality and types of genius. He saw this approach as a means to indicate 'the influence of the locality, which is both spiritual, through its historical traditions, and physiological, through its climatic and other physical factors'.

Environmentalism could be combined with a 'Whiggish approach' to history that regarded it as teleological, optimistic and progressive – a triumphal march towards a pre-ordained liberal present. Thus Charles Pearson presented geography as playing a major role in his *Historical Maps of England* (1869). He suggested that although 'man triumphs over the elements', this triumph was essentially a matter only of the previous half-century. Pearson also saw geography at work in the great political divisions of the country's history. He saw the mountains as 'the conservative element . . . in our history', where the Roman presence was limited and the Angles and Saxons were resisted. Similarly, for the civil war of the reign of King Stephen in 1135–54, the 'oppressive' Matilda was presented as drawing her support from the upland west, and Stephen from London 'and the commercial towns of the east'. In the 1260s 'London and the south and east were with the great constitutional leader De Montfort; the north and west sided with the king'. Similar remarks were made about the Wars of the Roses, the Civil War and the Jacobite rising in 1745. To Pearson, the nineteenth century was a record of geography overcome: 'the hills are losing their old influence'.

British atlases expressed confidence in the national destiny. The text accompanying the last map, of the British Isles from 1485 onwards, in Edward Gover's *The Historical Geographical Atlas of the Middle and Modern Ages* (1853), was triumphalist:

> This map serves to connect the history of the British Isles with the period of their greatest progress in the arts of civilization, and which is best evidenced by a reference to any modern map upon which the greatest network of their railways, canals, and turnpike-roads is accurately laid down. The map of the British Isles of the reign of her most gracious Majesty Queen Victoria, is the best and truest record of the indomitable perseverance and skill of the Anglo-Saxon race.

The Victorian Press

One of the many ways in which Victorian London was at the centre of life in Britain and its empire was provision of the news. Much of the news was, of course, made in London, but much was not; whichever was the case, it was London newspapers that spread information and orchestrated opinion through its press. London newspapers created the image and idiom of empire, shaped its opinions and lay claim to the title of the 'fourth estate' of the realm. Aside from its political function, the press also played a central economic, social and cultural role, setting and spreading fashions, whether of company statements or through

Empire and War

In the second half of the nineteenth century, the British fought across the globe as never before. It is easy to underrate these conflicts, as none was a war for survival and none transformed British society, but their cumulative impact for Britain was important and their individual impact on other societies formative. Britain's role was part of the wider story of European imperialism, but greater than that of any other state, because of her limited role in European power politics, her unprecedented naval and commercial strength, and the already extensive character of the empire in 1851.

Empire helped to change Britain's identity, including notions of masculinity. Soldier heroes, such as Field Marshal Garnet Wolseley, General Charles Gordon, Field Marshal Frederick Roberts and Field Marshal Herbert Kitchener, fed a tradition of exemplary imperial masculinity, a combination of Anglo-Saxon authority, superiority and martial prowess, with Protestant religious zeal and moral righteousness. This was given form in adventure novels such as those of G.A. Henty, including *With Kitchener in the Soudan* (1903). Empire also changed the details of British life in many respects. Gin was mixed with quinine-rich tonic water, a drink developed to provide resistance to malaria in India. Indian words also entered the language, and games such as badminton and polo were introduced.

There were two difficult conflicts in the 1850s. In the Crimean War of 1854–6, a Franco-British force eventually achieved its target – the Russian naval base of Sevastapol, attacked in order to reduce Russian pressure on the Turks – but only after heavy casualties and some flawed generalship, most famously the unsuccessful Charge of the Light Brigade at Balaclava in 1854. The Indian Mutiny of 1857–9 was triggered by the British demand that their Indian soldiers use a cartridge greased in animal tallow for their new Enfield rifles, a measure that was widely unacceptable for religious reasons. The rising was violently suppressed by British and loyal Indian troops, especially Gurkhas and Sikhs, in the largest deployment of British forces between the Napoleonic Wars and the Boer War of 1899–1902. At the end of the 1850s, the British attacked China. After initial checks, an Anglo-French force advanced to and occupied Beijing in 1860.

After the Crimean War, Britain did not fight another European power until the First World War broke out in 1914. There was concern about the danger of conflict with France and Russia, and invasion fears directed at France led to the construction of defensive positions, such as the Needles Old Battery on the Isle of Wight. In the event, competition with other European powers stopped short of war, and only encouraged the drive to empire.

In the 1860s and 1870s, the pace of British expansion increased. Native resistance was overcome in New Zealand, although the Maoris used well-sited trench and pa (fort) systems that were difficult to bombard or storm, and inflicted serious defeats on the British. In Africa, Lagos was annexed in 1861, and, although an expedition against one of the more powerful African people, the Asante, was wrecked by disease in 1864, in 1873–4 a fresh expedition under Garnet Wolseley was more successful. Wolseley benefited from the assistance of other African peoples, especially the Fante, but his superior fire-power – Gatling machine guns, breech-loading rifles and 7-pounder artillery – was crucial. Ethiopia had been successfully invaded in 1868, although no attempt was made to annex it. By 1900, the British had an empire covering a fifth of the world's land surface and including 400 million people.

There were defeats on the way. At Isandlwana in southern Africa in 1879, a 20,000-strong Zulu army defeated a British force of 1,800, by enveloping the British flanks and benefiting from the British running out of ammunition. In 1880, at Maiwand, an Afghan army armed with British cannon, defeated an outgunned and smaller British force. Elsewhere the British were more successful in battle. At Gingindlovu, Khambula and Ulundi in southern Africa in 1879, heavy defensive infantry fire from prepared positions, supported by artillery, stopped Zulu attacks before the Zulus could reach the British lines. Wolseley stormed the Egyptian earthworks at Tel el-Kebir in 1882. Egypt and the Sudan became protectorates that year. In 1885, Mandalay was captured, and in 1895–6 the Asante, Matabele and Mashona were defeated in Africa. The fate of the Sudan was settled at Omdurman in 1898 when British artillery, machine guns and rifles devastated the attacking Mahdists, with 31,000 casualties for the latter and only 430 for the Anglo-Egyptian force. Technology and resources were not only at stake on the battlefield. In 1896, the British invading force built a railway straight across the desert from Wadi Halfa to Abu Hamed.

Extended to Atbara in 1898, it played a major role in the supply of the British forces. By 1900, the British had also constructed 20,000 miles of railways in India.

Britain's most difficult transoceanic conflict was, as it had been in the eighteenth century with the War of American Independence, with people of European descent, the Afrikaner republics of the Orange Free State and the Transvaal in Southern Africa. In the First Boer War, the British were defeated at Majuba Hill in 1881 and forced to accept Boer independence. A lengthier struggle in 1899–1902 initially found the British outnumbered and poorly led, while the Boers' superior marksmanship with smokeless, long-range Mauser magazine rifles, and their effective combination of the strategic offensive and a successful use of defensive positions, inflicted heavy casualties in the winter of 1899/1900.

More effective generalship by Roberts and Kitchener changed the situation in 1900, and the ability of Britain to allocate about £200 million and deploy 400,000 troops was a testimony to the strength of both her economic and imperial systems, although the dispatch of so much of the regular army left it far below normal strength in the British Isles. Other colonies, such as Australia and New Zealand, also sent troops. Once the Boer republics had been overrun in 1900, their mounted infantry challenged British control, leading to a blockhouse system with barbed-wire fences, scorched earth policies and reprisals. This resulted in the 1902 Treaty of Vereeniging, a bitter but conditional Boer surrender. Income tax had had to be doubled in Britain to pay for the war, and it also greatly pushed up government borrowing. The Conservative policy of low taxation, especially low income tax, and financial retrenchment had to be abandoned under the pressure of imperial expansion.

Near-continual conflict ensured that the British Empire was created and sustained by force as well as trade. It also encouraged notions of superiority and manliness that were to be challenged by the First World War.

theatrical criticism. In what was increasingly a commercial society, the press played a pivotal role, inspiring emulation, setting the tone, and fulfilling crucial needs for an anonymous mass readership in a society in which alternative means of spreading opinion, such as the Church, appeared increasingly weak or redundant.

The press was itself affected by change, by the energising and disturbing forces of commercialisation and new technology. It was to be legal reform and technological development that freed the Victorian press for major development. Newspapers had become expensive in the eighteenth century, in large part due to successive rises in Stamp Duty. In the mid-nineteenth century, these so-called 'taxes on knowledge' were abolished: the Advertisement Duties in 1853, the Newspaper Stamp Duty in 1855 and the Paper Duties in 1861. This opened up the possibility of a cheap press and that opportunity was exploited by means of a technology centred on new printing presses and the continuous rolls or 'webs' of paper that fed them. Web rotary presses were introduced in Britain from the late 1860s: the Walter press was first used by *The Times* in 1868 and by the *Daily News* in 1873, while the *Daily Telegraph* purchased the American Bullock presses in 1870. Mechanical typesetting was introduced towards the end of the century, linotype machines appearing in newspaper offices in the 1890s.

New technology was expensive, but the mass readership opened up by the lower prices that could be charged after the repeal of the newspaper taxes justified the cost. The consequence was more titles and lower prices. The number of daily morning papers published in London rose from eight in 1856 to twenty-one in 1900, and of evenings from seven to eleven, while there was a tremendous expansion in the suburban press. The repeal permitted the appearance of penny dailies. The *Daily Telegraph*, launched in 1855, led the way and by 1888 had a circulation of 300,000, while that of the *Daily News* rose from 50,000 in 1868 to 150,000 in 1871. The penny press was in turn squeezed by the halfpenny press, the first halfpenny evening paper, the *Echo*, appearing in 1868, while halfpenny morning papers became important in the 1890s with the *Morning Leader* (1892) and the

Daily Mail (1896), which was to become extremely successful with its bold and simple style. The *Echo* peaked at a circulation of 200,000 in 1870.

In comparison an eighteenth-century London newspaper was considered a great success if it sold 10,000 copies a week (most influential papers then were weeklies) and 2,000 weekly was a reasonable sale. Thus an enormous expansion had taken place, one that matched the vitality of an imperial capital, swollen by immigration and increasingly influential as an opinion-setter within the country, not least because of the communications revolution produced by the railway and better roads. The development of the railways allowed London newspapers to increase their dominance of the national newspaper scene. Thanks to the trains, these papers could arrive on provincial doorsteps within hours of publication.

The public, among whom literacy rates were rising, sought cheap, entertaining reading matter. As in the previous century, this was only partly provided by the expanding press. A literature of chapbooks and almanacs had been more popular in the 1700s than the newspapers, and in the Victorian age much of the daily press did not provide the lurid tales that were sought by many.

The papers that best served popular tastes were the Sundays, *Lloyd's Weekly News*, the *News of the World* and *Reynolds's News*. *Lloyd's*, the first British paper with a circulation of over 100,000, was selling over 600,000 by 1879, over 900,000 by 1893 and in 1896 rose to over a million sales per issue.

The Sunday papers relied on shock and titillation, drawing extensively on police court reporting, a cheap source of exciting copy and one that linked the popular press to the world of works produced specifically to deal with particular crimes. This overlap was exemplified in special editions or larger print runs produced to capitalise on public interest in individual crimes, trials and executions. The *Illustrated Police News*, a penny weekly, owed its popularity to such accounts. But such interests could also be found in the 'quality press'. In 1888, *The Times* devoted six editorials and thousands of words to the activities of Jack the Ripper, providing charts and plans, and on 10 November a report of 5,000 words on yet another of the murderer's 'revolting and fiendish acts'. The same issue revealed that interest in crime had no national boundaries when it carried three paragraphs on a Parisian murder trial.

This lurid world was far removed from the weighty political comment and lengthy parliamentary reports that were carried in much of the press, but it should not be forgotten. The circulation of *The Times*, the most influential serious newspaper, was between 60,000 and 68,000 in the 1860s and 1870s, when the paper cost 3d. For the average Londoner, the favoured read was more likely to have been *Lloyd's Weekly News*, and the circulation figures of the Sundays suggest that in the 1850s and 1860s artisans bought them rather than dailies, which they could not afford. A penny was not an inconsiderable sum.

Reporting reflected the growing importance of organised sport, in part a response to the clearer definition of leisure time in an industrial and urban society. By 1895, the *Daily News* covered racing, yachting, rowing, lacrosse, football, hockey, angling, billiards, athletics, cycling and chess. There was also an expansion in the coverage devoted to financial news, a relatively easy subject to report given the proximity of the City to Fleet Street. The balance between the different sections of news varied considerably in response to developments, and the press was essentially reactive. There was relatively little attempt to organise the news in pursuit of an editorial objective and much of the copy printed was material sent in by interested individuals and bodies or by penny-a-liners, rather than items obtained by journalists. Indeed, investigative journalism was rare, which helps to account for the particular impact of specific revelations, such as William Russell's attacks on the mismanagement of the Crimean War in *The Times* in the winter of 1854–5, the *Daily News*'s reports on Turkish massacres in 1876, and the revelations in the *Pall Mall Gazette* about prostitution in London.

If the bulk of the newspaper-reading public appear to have preferred revelations about the last words of a condemned man or the putative identity of Jack the Ripper to speculations about the plans of foreign governments, there was, nevertheless, a growing interest in foreign news, one that inspired newspapers to obtain foreign exclusives, which were generally far more expensive than their domestic counterparts. Britain was a great imperial power, London the seat of empire, and in the Victorian age the empire expanded considerably. The use of the telegraph helped to satisfy a growing popular demand for information. Telegraphic links were established to the Black Sea in 1856 and to India in 1869, and during the Franco-Prussian War in 1870–1, which was followed closely in Britain, the *Daily News* established the habit of using telegraphs routinely.

The period witnessed major conflicts involving Britain in India, Egypt and South Africa, and a series of spectacular wars, such as the American Civil War and the Wars of German Unification. The French Revolution had largely been reported from French newspapers and only one British correspondent, James Perry of the *Morning Chronicle*, had gone to Paris. In contrast, the reporting of the Franco-Prussian War relied more heavily on British correspondents. Napoleon III had banned correspondents at the front during his Italian war with Austria in 1859 and maintained his ban during this new conflict. British correspondents in Metz were imprisoned and news from the French side consisted essentially of communiqués from the French correspondents. The Prussians, in contrast, allowed correspondents to visit their positions, though not the actual front line. William Russell, who had outraged Union supporters by his sympathy with the Confederates and his criticism of the Union army at the battle of Bull Run in 1861, was sent by *The Times* to the more congenial headquarters of the Crown Prince of Prussia, where there were other correspondents, including those from the *Daily Telegraph* and the *Daily News*. However, the Prussians refused to give the unsympathetic G.A. Henty of the *Standard* a pass – he subsequently wrote a pro-French novel about the war – and Alfred Austin, his replacement, was only given one as a result of his pro-Prussian views. Bismarck gave Austin interviews which were at variance with the *Standard*'s pro-French editorial line. News from besieged Paris for *The Times* was carried out by hot-air balloons. The paper was sent into the city by carrier pigeon in a reduced microscopic size.

Partisanship was not restricted to events in France. Reporting of the struggle in the Balkans was divided between pro- and anti-

Russian views, as in the *Pall Mall Gazette* and the *Morning Post* respectively. Again, this division was far from new. The fate of the Balkans, as much as the flight to Varennes, had been a major topic in the London press in 1791, the year when Britain nearly went to war with Russia in the Oczakov Crisis. Readers who were interested in international politics were amply served by a press that expended considerable sums on telegraphy. *The Times* by the 1870s was spending about £40,000 a year.

As Britain was actually or potentially closely involved in most international developments, this concern with foreign news cannot be presented as remote from the interests of the average reader, though the press can be criticised for providing relatively little background analysis and for presenting a view of foreign countries that was resolutely metropolitan. Similarly, it was London politics that dominated the reporting of British news. There was relatively little political control of this reporting, but this owed much to a culture in which government and newspapers were not generally adversarial and in which, by European standards, the precept of freedom of the press was largely observed.

Newspapers did not conduct market research and the impact that they made is impossible to gauge. However, the very expansion of their circulation helped to make them a crucial medium for the spread of information and opinion. Their profitability ensured that their spread would be essentially due to market influences and indeed the capitalist nature of their publications was to be an essential feature of the Anglo-American newspaper tradition. The other characteristic was the pluralistic nature of the Victorian London press. There was no uniformity in content, style or political allegiance. This variety reflected the dynamic nature of British society. The press profited from it and in turn fostered and propagated the dynamism and variety.

FOUR

MASS POLITICS AND WAR, 1887–1918

In 1887, Britain was still adjusting to an expanding rail system, while the bicycle craze had recently begun in 1885. By 1918, the internal combustion engine had brought lorries and tanks, as well as buses and the motor car; there were also electric trams, submarines, aircraft and airships. There were 132,000 private car registrations by 1914. What had merely been on the drawing board in 1887 had now become commonplace. Distance had changed. The first successful powered flight, by the American Wright brothers, occurred in 1903. Six years later, Louis Blériot flew across the Channel. 'Britain is no longer an island' reflected the press baron Lord Northcliffe. In January 1904, Leo Amery, a journalist who was to become a Conservative politician, emphasised the onward rush of technology when he told the Royal Geographical Society that sea and rail links and power would be supplemented by air, and then: 'a great deal of this geographical distribution must lose its importance, and the successful powers will be those who have the greatest industrial basis. It will not matter whether they are in the centre of a continent or on an island; those people who have the industrial power and the power of invention and of science will be able to defeat all others.'

The geopolitical threat was in the future; but the economic challenge was all too present. Britain's industrial power was affected by the rising economic strength of other countries, in particular of Germany and the USA. This hit manufacturing hard from the 1880s. Coal mining had been affected from the 1870s, slate mining from 1903. By the 1880s, the Durham coalfield had passed its peak and miners were leaving the county.

In the Sunderland shipyards there were empty order books and wage cuts in the 1880s. The West Cumberland Iron & Steel Company closed in 1891; the Britannia Foundry at Derby in 1910, in part due to poor management. In Gateshead, the major ironworks ceased trading – Hawks, Crawshay in 1889 and Abbot's in 1909 – the chemical industry declined from the 1880s and the Railway Works was much cut in 1910.

Nevertheless, manufacturing decline was relative, rather than absolute, and Britain was still a leading economy. Her share of world trade had fallen, but that trade was now far larger. Britain was the largest overseas investor and the greatest merchant shipper in the world, as well as the centre of the world's financial system: commodity prices, shipping routes and insurance premiums were all set in London. The expansion of the service sector, focused on the City of London, was fundamental to Britain's continued (and still continuing) economic strength and influence. Thanks to her prominence in submarine telegraphy, Britain was also at the centre of the world's communications. The landing point for sub-oceanic cables was Porthcurno Beach in Cornwall.

Aside from her major, sometimes leading, role in the production of traditional goods, such as coal, textiles, steel, iron and ships, Britain was also playing a major part in the development of new sectors, in the growth of production in chemicals, and in new consumer products, such as motor cars and telephones. The British Empire also dominated the production of many important goods. Gold and diamonds came from South Africa, copper from Canada, tin from Malaya, cocoa from Ghana, palm oil from Nigeria.

Empire was linked in the public mind not only to the army but also to maritime dominance. In 1906, HMS *Dreadnought* was launched, the first in a new class of big gun battleships designed to fulfil its name, and the first capital ship in the world to be powered by the marine turbine engine, invented by Sir Charles Parsons in 1884. Completed in one year, her construction reflected the industrial and organisational efficiency of British shipbuilding. The creation and spread of electric tram systems had more of an impact on ordinary people.

Alongside new possibilities generated by new inventions, there was also change in the sheer scale of activity. The cotton industry was well-established, but in 1900–9 15 million spindles (35 per cent) were added to the capacity of the industry.

It was no longer a case of change affecting society, politics, the economy and culture. Instead, change became integral to their structures and, in part, ethos. This challenged all institutions and was unsettling to much of the population. The varied manifestations of this unease included hostility to immigrants in the East End of London, some of it bitterly anti-Semitic, and a wider disquiet about the state of the nation. This encouraged social analysis, calls for public action, and private missions. Toynbee Hall was founded in Bethnal Green in 1884 in order to provide help to the poor from Oxford students. The social surveys of Charles Booth in East London in the late 1880s and of Seebohm Rowntree in York in 1899 revealed that over a quarter of their population were living below the perceived poverty level. Booth attributed poverty to the role of seasonal and casual labour, the problems of child-rearing and old age without social welfare. He called for old-age pensions. Booth also presented poverty as a threat to civil society. In his *Life and Labour of the People in London . . . Poverty I* (1889), he depicted: 'The lowest class, which consists of some occasional labourers, street sellers, loafers, criminals and semi-criminals. . . . Their life is the life of savages, with vicissitudes of extreme hardship and occasional excesses . . . their only luxury is drink. . . . From these come the battered figures who slouch through the streets, and play the beggar or the bully.' This unsympathetic view highlighted a sense of menace.

Poor urban housing, sanitation and nutrition were widely blamed for the physical weakness of much of the population. The army found this a serious problem at the time of the Boer War, the Metropolitan Police thought their London recruits physically weak, and defeats at the hands of the visiting New Zealand All Blacks rugby team in 1905 led to discussion about a supposed physical and moral decline arising from the country's urban and industrial nature. A preoccupation with national degeneration dated back to the 1880s, however, and the Welsh team beat the All Blacks in 1905.

Victorian social reform had not ended all abuses. In 1907, for example, there were still about 5,000 half-timers under thirteen working in Bradford. The state of the populace encouraged Liberals, Labour, and Conservative paternalists to support measures for social welfare.

Problems were not restricted to what strikes the modern observer as poverty-riddled urban slums. There was also much rural poverty. This resulted from a combination of traditional social inequalities and the consequences of a protracted agricultural depression caused by competition from foreign supplies, particularly North American grain, Argentinian beef, Australasian wool, mutton and lamb, and Danish bacon. Britain's food market was flooded with cheap American imports. Thus, the technological advances of steamships, refrigerated holds, railways and barbed wire that helped the development of export agriculture in distant areas and were frequently financed by British capital, badly affected British farming in what became the Great Agricultural Depression. Arable farmers bore the brunt of an agricultural decline that was absolute, not relative. Dairying and some livestock husbandry expanded, however. Meanwhile, the impact of food imports in lowering prices greatly benefited the urban working classes and, thus, encouraged electoral support for free trade. As Disraeli appreciated in 1879, it was not practical to revive agrarian protection by relaunching the Corn Laws.

Agricultural problems hit rural workers hardest, but landlords were also affected, and the economics of rural estates were far worse than is suggested by visiting many of the houses of the period. Rent rebates were common: 10 per cent on the Blanchland estate in County Durham of Lord Crewe's Charity from 1887 until 1893, and on most of the estate's holdings the 1895 rent was equal to or less than the 1870 figure. Rents there did not improve until the decade after 1900. Derelict farms could now be found in once prosperous areas, such as South Essex.

Frequently, the show of landed wealth was no longer based on agricultural income but resulted in large part from mineral rights or from marriage with heiresses, increasingly, towards the close of the century, Americans. The decline in the wealth and power of the aristocracy was a major theme in the history of this period.

There was also considerable tension in some rural areas. In 1888, the 3rd Earl of Sheffield, a Sussex landowner, with his seat at Sheffield Park, received a letter including the passages: 'my duty to let you know, as I do not think you do, or you would not have the heart to turn an old tenant like poor Mrs Grover out of her home after such a hard struggle to maintain and bring up her family . . . you and your faithful steward want it all. . . . My knife is nice and sharp.' The letter was signed Jack the Ripper, then at his murderous work in Whitechapel. Nothing happened to the earl. Mrs Grover, in fact, was staying with her children after a fall, and Edward Grover, a failed butcher, admitted writing the letter. This was not an isolated episode. In 1889, the earl wrote an open letter to the Secretary of Sussex County Cricket Club, explaining his resignation as President, in which he referred to 2½ years of pestering by anonymous threats.

There were also problems for workers who managed to avoid poverty. Thus in Sunderland, where shipbuilding brought good jobs and a large percentage of workers owned their houses, life took place under a thick layer of coal dust, which was definitely detrimental to health. The sky was smoke-blackened. Such pollution ensured that industries that required clear air located to the west of cities so the prevailing wind took noxious gases away from them: film-making at Ealing, Kodak at Harrow. Both film-making and Kodak were aspects of a changing industrial world that focused on electricity and the internal combustion engine. By 1907, the Britannia Foundry at Derby included a motor cylinder line making 400 to 500 parts a week for car manufacturers, such as Jowett Motors of Bradford. The sense of the new possibilities presented by electricity was captured in the name of the cinema opened in Harwich in 1911, the Electric Palace.

Alongside new products, there were also changes in industrial and commercial organisation. Ownership and production became more concentrated, as in the Northumberland and Durham brewing industry. More generally, control by national chains became more pronounced, and public limited companies developed. Big retail chains became important. John Sainsbury opened his first dairy in London in 1869, Thomas Lipton his first grocery in Glasgow in 1871. By 1900, Sainsbury had 47 provisions stores. By 1914, Lipton had 500. In 1883, Julius Drewe and his partner opened a shop in the Edgware Road in London called the Home and Colonial Stores. By 1890, there were 107 shops in Drewe's company, and by 1906 over 500. Drewe did the buying, and encouraged the drinking of Indian not Chinese tea to gain commercial advantage. He also entered the Establishment, becoming a justice of the peace in 1900, deciding he had Norman antecedents, accumulating a Devon estate, and commissioning a country house, Castle Drogo, in Devon. In 1894 Marks & Spencer was founded.

Major chains of banks also developed. In 1896, twenty private firms merged to form Barclays. Strongest in East and South-East England, Barclays spread by amalgamating with the Consolidated Bank of Cornwall in 1905, the United Counties Bank (an important Midlands institution) in 1916, the London, Provincial & South Western Bank in 1918, and the Union Bank of Manchester in 1919. This was part of the process by which the local and regional levels of activity and organisation were increasingly subordinated to the national.

Concern over the state of the nation now led to growing activism in social welfare, and this was increasingly politicised. Relevant agencies became more responsive to the needs of the population. The Local Government Act of 1888 created directly elected county councils and county boroughs, and the London County Council.

Thanks to the divisive effect of Irish Home Rule on the Liberals from 1886, the Conservatives, under Robert, 3rd Marquess of Salisbury and, from 1902 his nephew, Arthur Balfour, with the support of Liberal Unionists, were in office in 1886–92 and from 1895 to 1905. The Conservatives also benefited from their growing urban strength following the 1885 constituency redistribution, from the long-term expansion of the middle classes, and from the popularity of their imperialist policies. The Conservative Party gained an effective popular organisation with the foundation of the Primrose League, which stood for Church, crown, empire, property and order. Although headed by the Establishment, the Conservatives were keen to reach out and win the active backing of what they saw as the inherent conservatism of the populace.

The Conservatives followed a cautious policy on domestic reform, ceding workmen's compensation for injury but not old-age pensions. However, growing pressure for more radical policies increasingly led political opinion to coalesce and polarise along social and class lines. In 1891, Gladstone called for a reduction in factory work-hours, free education, electoral reform, and the reform or abolition of the House of Lords. Radical Liberalism of this kind encouraged a coalescence of opinion in defence of property and order in the shape of the Conservatives, but in 1905 the Liberals, under Sir Henry Campbell-Bannerman, came into office, going on to win a landslide election victory in early 1906. In 1903, they had secretly allied with Labour, the two parties agreeing not to fight each other in certain seats lest they help the Conservatives. Campbell-Bannerman did not see Labour as a threat, was happy to cooperate with it, and appointed John Burns, President of the Local Government Board, the first member of the working class to join the Cabinet.

Liberal Reform

Some Liberals, especially the dynamic David Lloyd George, Chancellor of the Exchequer 1908–15, were determined to undermine the power and possessions of the old landed elite, and keen to woo Labour and the trade unions. As President of the Board of Trade in 1905–8, Lloyd George had greatly increased state regulation of the economy. In 1906, the Liberals passed a Trade Disputes Act that gave unions immunity from actions for damages as a result of strike action, and thus rejected the attempts of the courts, through the Taff Vale case of 1901, to bring the unions within the law, and therefore make strike action potentially prohibitively expensive. The Mines Regulations Act of 1908, limited the number of hours that miners could spend underground.

In 1909, Lloyd George announced a 'People's Budget', introducing new taxes for the wealthy: land taxes, supertax and increased death duties. The opposition of the Conservative-dominated House of Lords, only overcome in 1910, led to the Parliament Act of 1911 which replaced the Lords' ability to veto Commons' legislation with the right simply to delay it. The entire dispute was accompanied by strident social criticism of the aristocracy. The Parliament Act was only passed as a result of the threat of creating many more peers to pack the Lords with Liberal supporters.

Other ministers also pressed forward state-directed reform. As the President of the Board of Trade (1908–10), Winston Churchill, then a Liberal and a keen supporter of Lloyd George's budget, tried to improve wages in the 'sweated' trades where they were very low, and to develop unemployment insurance. As Home Secretary (1910 11), Churchill attempted to reduce sentences for petty offences, although he dealt forcibly with both the militant suffragettes (supporters of votes for women) and labour unrest. Legislation extended government responsibility to all children, while child imprisonment was ended. In 1911, Lloyd George's National Insurance Act provided for unemployment assistance and for all males eligible for insurance to be registered with a doctor who was to receive a fee per patient, irrespective of the amount of medical attention provided. Payment for MPs, a measure which looked back to Chartism and was pressed by the Labour Party, was introduced in order to help win Labour support for the Liberal government.

Widespread urbanisation and industrialisation had brought massive social change. Deference and traditional social patterns, never as fixed as some thought, had ebbed, and the new and newly expanded cities and towns created living environments in which the role and rule of the old world was far less. Only 10.4 per cent of the United Kingdom's workforce was employed in agriculture in the 1890s, compared to 40.3 per cent in France, and this had implications for the nature of rural society and its gentry leadership.

The changes in society not only challenged traditional social assumptions. There were also important shifts in the nature of public religion, as well as objections to customary gender practices. In the case of the first, the political, religious, intellectual and educational authority of the Anglican Church, the established Church in England, Wales and Ireland, was challenged. The assault came from social and economic developments, especially the expansion of industrial cities, from other faiths and from government. Sir Thomas Acland MP had a chapel built at his stately home of Killerton in 1838–41 and would note absentees from Sunday service among his servants, estate workmen and tenants. Such social control was far less possible in the expanding cities. The rise of Dissent was a problem for the Church of England, especially in Wales and the North of England. The religious census of 1851 revealed that in County Durham on 30 March out of a county population of 411,679 there were 176,282 attendances at worship. Of these 55,987 were Church of England, 98,066 Nonconformist, 10,741 Catholic; and there were 169 Church of England places of worship, 351 Methodist, 72 Dissenter and 20 Catholic. The re-emergence of 'public' Catholicism, with the re-establishment of the Catholic hierarchy in England in 1850–1 and in Scotland in 1874, and massive Irish immigration between 1845 and 1848, the years of the potato famine, caused more tension. Between 1850 and 1910, 1,173 Catholic churches were opened in England and Wales, the largest number in London and Lancashire.

The changing role of government also challenged the established Church, although many within government were responsive to Church reform which became particularly active from the 1830s. Nevertheless, the role of the Church altered. The position of the parish in local government, education and social welfare declined in favour of new governmental agencies. Municipal and county government was better able than the Church to channel and implement the aspirations of society for reform and control. For example, the only means of separation from a spouse, other than expensive parliamentary divorce hearings, had been an action through ecclesiastical courts. This did not permit remarriage. In 1857, marital legislation transformed the situation. The Marriage Act of 1837 had ended the situation whereby unions between Catholics and Nonconformists were illegal in England and Wales unless conducted by the Church of England.

Oxford and Cambridge were reshaped by reformers, and religious 'tests' for undergraduates and academics that had kept the universities Anglican strongholds were repealed. In addition, the traditional curricula were changed. In 1850, modern history and natural sciences were introduced as courses at Oxford, and in 1879 the first female students arrived.

The very notion of an established Church was criticised, leading to a stress on the voluntary principle for religion. Although many Liberals, such as Gladstone, were churchmen, some pressed for disestablishment, and there were attempts to abolish church-rates, taxes for the maintenance of church buildings, in the early 1860s. The Church of Ireland (the Anglican established Church in Ireland where the population was overwhelmingly Catholic) was disestablished by Gladstone in 1869. Moreover, in Wales, there were bitter political disputes over disestablishment. Welsh Liberals were strongly opposed to Church schools, especially to measures to provide public assistance to them. The 1902 Act providing for school finance from the rates, passed by a Conservative government, led to the 'Welsh Revolt' as county councils refused to implement it. A Liberal government voted through Welsh disestablishment in 1914, although, due to the First World War, it was not implemented until 1920. There was also pressure for Scottish disestablishment.

Demand for disestablishment, and its eventual passage in Ireland and Wales, provided a new form of difference between the parts of the British Isles that was important as a constituent of distinct identities. This was part of the process by which relations between areas of the British Isles began to change, although, thanks to the impact of nationwide legislation and the financial power of the City of London, at the same time, national organised institutions lessened regional autonomy. In Ireland there was widespread demand for Home Rule, and a minority terrorist movement emerged, initially conducted by the Fenians, a secret organisation founded in 1858.

In Wales, after the failure to stamp out the Welsh language in schools, there was a growing interest in Welsh cultural history and identity. This led to the 'revival' of the eisteddfod in 1858, and to a range of new institutions that provided a focus and platform for those seeking to assert Welsh identities. Both the National Library and the National Museum were authorised by royal charter in 1907; £11,000 towards the cost of the former was raised in penny contributions from South Wales miners. The Sunday Closing Act for public houses in Wales, passed in 1881, was the first since the 1650s to introduce regulations in Wales that differed from those in England, and was a testimony to the self-righteous determination of Welsh Nonconformity.

The Cymru Fydd home-rule movement launched in 1886 was less successful, in part because of the antagonism between South and North Wales, and, in part, because at that time the demands of Welsh nationalism centred upon the eradication of Anglican privilege in a largely Nonconformist country, not on home rule. The big expansion of the South Wales coalfield in the late nineteenth century also brought in many English workers and thus changed South Wales significantly. Furthermore, the rise of Welsh cultural and political nationalism was tempered by the extent to which the key Welsh issues of the period – land reform, hostility to tithes, disestablishment and public education – could be presented in radical Liberal terms and thus incorporated in British politics.

In Scotland, a sense of national identity developed, centring on a re-emergent cultural identity that did not involve any widespread demand for independence. Kilts and an interest in Burns and Scott, Wallace and Bruce did not lead to a home-rule party, and may have even delayed the establishment of one. The past was used to celebrate Scotland and to present it as equal to England, not to encourage demands for separatism. There was no equivalent to the religious dimension of Irish politics nor the religious and linguistic aspects of Welsh politics. In 1843, the Church of Scotland divided on the matter of lay patronage, a dispute that had a nationalist dimension because of the issue at stake, but there was no equivalent to the role of Nonconformity in energising Welsh discontent with a landed,

Labour Relation: Penrhyn and the Slate Strike of 1900–3

Penrhyn Castle, Gwynedd, is a masterpiece of Norman revival, built in the 1820s on the profits from the Penrhyn slate quarry, the largest 'hand-made' hole in the Earth's surface, and the leading producer of slate in the world throughout the nineteenth century. Production rose from 40,000 tons in 1820 to 120,000 tons in 1859, as demand rose following the repeal of the slate duty in 1831, and the workforce rose from 1,000 in 1820 and 2,500 in 1859 to 3,000 in 1893, despite the greater use of machinery from the 1850s. The profits were vast and the quarry's net annual income in 1859 was £100,000. Much was spent on roads, schools, houses and churches on the Caernarfonshire estate of Lord Penrhyn, which by 1893 comprised 72,000 acres, as well as on the house and its major collection of paintings.

The family were paternalistic employers, not that that eased the workers' respiratory problems produced by slate dust and the effects of silicosis. They were strongly opposed to trade unionism. In 1865, the 1st Lord Penrhyn had a recently formed union of quarrymen dissolved. In 1874, however, a strike led to the recognition in the quarry of the newly formed North Wales Quarrymen's Union. Union recognition was withdrawn by the Tory 2nd Lord Penrhyn in 1889, but paternalism failed to hold industrial tension at bay. At Penrhyn, as elsewhere, a new, more adversarial and combative working-class consciousness developed. There were major strikes in the London gasworks and docks in 1888–9, in the South Wales coalfield in 1893 and 1898, and in the engineering industry in 1897–8, and these helped to radicalise sections of the workforce. Two striking miners were killed by troops at Featherstone in 1893. That year the Independent Labour Party was founded, and in 1897 the first Welsh-language Socialist newspaper.

A major strike at Penrhyn in 1896–7 led to an angry debate in the House of Commons, but ended without major concessions from Lord Penrhyn. Similarly, a strike in the slate mines at Llechwedd in 1893 failed. At Penrhyn, in 1900 a riot against the employment of individual contractors led to the conviction and dismissal of six workers, and a strike by the entire workforce. Union recognition became the crucial issue, and the strike attracted national press and political attention; Lloyd George, the most prominent Welsh Liberal, was a bitter critic of Lord Penrhyn. In June 1901, the quarry reopened, but the majority of strikers refused to return to work. Violence by strikers exacerbated the dispute. Eventually the press and the Trades Union Congress ceased their support and the strike ended in November 1903. This coincided with a slump in the building industry and a fall in production at the quarry.

Penrhyn quarry was a focus of a growing wave of industrial militancy which led to a questioning of the ability of the system to solve disputes. Important political consequences followed. In 1899, the Trades Union Congress advocated an independent working-class political organisation, leading in 1900 to the formation of the Labour Representation Committee, the basis of the Labour Party. In 1900, too, Keir Hardie was elected for Merthyr Tydfil. By 1906, there were twenty-nine Labour MPs, and by 1910 there were five Welsh Labour MPs.

Labour relations nationwide deteriorated from 1909, when there were major strikes in the shipyards. Difficult economic circumstances led in 1910 to downward pressures on pay, industrial disputes, sabotage and riots. Disputes in the coal industry arose from pressure on the profitability of pits and on miners' living standards, due, in part, to geological factors which reduced pit productivity. Employers tried to restrict customary rights and payments. Sabotage by striking miners in 1910 against collieries, strike-breakers and the trains attempting to bring them in, as well as extensive looting, was resisted and led to much violence. At Tonypandy a miner was killed by police, and troops were sent in by the Liberal Home Secretary, Winston Churchill, although he held them back and was criticised for allowing the rioters to destroy property. The following year, the first general rail strike led to sabotage at Llanelli, and also to the deployment of troops who killed two strikers in Liverpool. Nearly 41 million working days were lost through industrial action in 1912. As with other such disputes, those involved were a potent mixture of workers dissatisfied with specific conditions and others seeking political transformation.

Yet in Britain as a whole in 1914, the Liberal Party, with its desire for the cooperation of capital and labour and its stress on class harmony for all bar the aristocracy, still displayed few signs of decline at the hands of Labour, and showed much confidence in its future. Another election was due by 1915 and, although the Conservatives were in a better shape than they had been after the 1905 election, there seemed many reasons to assume that they would face a fourth election defeat, not least because they had fewer political allies than the Liberals. On the other political flank, the Liberals were in a strong position. Lib-Labour, not Syndicalism (a working-class radical movement), held sway in the valleys of the Rhondda. Over 75 per cent of the working population were not members of trade unions and many voted Liberal or Conservative. This was to change significantly within a decade.

Anglican ascendancy. Within the framework of a generally non-interventionist British state, Scottish communities were essentially self-governing. Moreover, social tensions within Scotland did not focus on an ascendancy that could be presented as English. Instead, the problems of industrial society encouraged political alignments comparable to those in England.

In the Highlands, 'clearances' led to a displacement of much of the population, which possessed no secure and long-term legal rights to land. Indeed, nearly 2 million Scots emigrated to Australasia and North America, and from the 1820s there was widespread opposition to clearances in Highland and Island Scotland. Yet, the peasantry were being evicted by their clan chiefs, not English absentees.

More generally, Scottish identification with the idea of Britain and the benefits of the British Empire lessened any tendency towards separation. Gladstone was elected for Midlothian in 1880 in a campaign that indicated the national concerns of the newly democratic Scottish electorate. In 1885, the Scottish Office and Secretary were created, in response to some pressure, and in 1894 a Scottish Grand Committee in the House of Commons. Five of the ten prime ministers who held office between 1880 and 1935 were Scottish and another two had important Scottish links. The fact that Scotland retained considerable independence within the United Kingdom also militated against the development of political nationalism. Scotland possessed its own established Church and educational system. Its legal system was also different and Scotland could issue its own bank notes.

Women

Women across Britain were affected by the processes of change, but modern standards of equality were still a long way off. The general notion of equality then was one of respect for separate functions and development. Women's special role was defined as that of running the home and family, and was used to justify their exclusion from other spheres. The ideology of separate spheres, in part stemming from a substantial body of medical and philosophical literature on the supposedly natural differences between men and women, was well established from the late eighteenth century. Gender relations were now affected by the declining influence of religion and the rise of scientists who became the new authorities. Older ideas of the intellectual superiority of men over women were given new vigour by men such as George Romanes, who claimed that the greater brain size of men proved the point. In other ways, science, more specifically medicine, 'legitimised' the inferiority of women by stressing their hormonally unstable natural state. The medicalising of 'crimes' such as kleptomania and nymphomania drew attention to supposedly natural differences between men and women which apparently rendered the latter unsuitable to hold public positions. If all women were seen as potentially hysterical, could they be trusted with the vote?

At a more day-to-day level, women ate less well, and this was publicly endorsed. For the celebration of Queen Victoria's Golden Jubilee in 1887 the women and children of Ashby-de-la-Zouch sat down to a tea of sandwiches, bread and butter, and cake in the marketplace, while the men had earlier had a meal of roast beef, mutton, potatoes, plum pudding and beer, which had been prepared by women.

The world of work was also biased against women. Industrialisation ensured that, alongside the continued demands of domestic service, more, predominantly single, women worked in factories, although rural opportunities, such as spinning, were reduced. Women mostly moved into the low-skill, low-pay 'sweated' sector, and were generally worse treated than men, a practice in which the trade unions cooperated with the management. The absence of an effective social welfare system and the low wages paid to most women ensured that prostitution was the fate of many. Part-time prostitution was related to economic conditions. Sexual harassment of women in the workplace and on the streets was a problem, as was the sexual abuse of children. Women, both single and married, suffered from the generally limited and primitive nature of contraceptive practices. Many single women resorted to abortion, which was both treated as a crime and hazardous to health. There was an emphasis on maternity, but very much within marriage. Frequent childbirth was exhausting and many women died giving birth, ensuring that many children were brought up by stepmothers. It was not until the introduction of anti-bacterial sulphonamides after 1936 that mortality figures fell substantially.

It is important, nevertheless, to notice nuances and shifts, for many of our current views about Victorian society are misleadingly two-dimensional. Recent work, for example, has re-evaluated notions of Victorian sexuality and suggests that the image of universal repression is misleading. Sexual pleasure was generally given discreet approval within marriage, but, in the case of women, was harshly treated outside it.

The complexity of the position of women is indicated by the extent to which it is possible to look at the rise of the 'new woman' in the late nineteenth century in two ways. The fact that there was an articulate and public challenge to both established and new gender roles cannot be dismissed. The degree to which the journalist and novelist Eliza Linton (1822–98) could write, in works for women, so extensively against the 'new woman', as in *The Girl of the Period and Other Essays* (1883), is an indication of the fears that were aroused. On the other hand, the practical impact of the idea of the 'new woman' is easily overstated, even for middle-class (let alone working-class) women. The 'separate spheres' ideology displayed both resilience and adaptability, and was to continue to do so during the twentieth century.

The extensions of the franchise in the nineteenth century had brought no benefit to women, and in the 1900s a vociferous suffragette movement demanded the vote in national elections – some women did have the vote in local elections. The militant tactics of the Women's Social and Political Union founded by Emmeline and Christabel Pankhurst in 1903 were designed to force public attention. The Labour Party officially endorsed women's suffrage in 1912 but a limited vote for women was not to be introduced until 1918. Less dramatically, but also indicative of pressure from women for a different society, the Co-operative Women's Guild, founded in 1884, had 100 branches and 6,000 members by 1889. Campaigning for rights for women workers, the guild also pressed for a different society, arguing in the early twentieth century for divorce reform, pensions and better schools.

In this, as in many other respects, British society in 1914 was very different from a century earlier. Although the strains and consequences of the First World War dissolved much of the old order, it was already fast eroding before the pressures of change and the sense of its inexorability.

First World War, 1914–18

France was the traditional foe and colonial rivalries provided fresh fuel to keep fear and animosity alive. In 1898, in the Fashoda Crisis, both powers had come close to war over the Sudan. Many British commentators would have agreed with Joseph Chamberlain, Secretary of State for the Colonies, in his view that Britain and Germany were natural allies, their peoples of a similar racial 'character'.

And yet Britain and France went to war as allies in 1914. Chance played a central role in this: a major European war broke out at a moment very different to those of heightened Anglo-French and Anglo-Russian colonial tension in the late nineteenth century. Instead, fear of German intentions, and, particularly of her naval ambitions, encouraged closer British relations with France and her ally Russia from 1904. Yet, the government was divided in 1914 and the German invasion of Belgium was crucial to the decision to fight as it gave a moral imperative to the outbreak of hostilities.

The conflict is generally remembered in terms of the trench warfare of the Western Front in France and Belgium, where very large numbers fought and many died without major gains of territory. The war has been seen as the epitome of military futility and incompetence, a view traceable from war poets, such as Wilfred Owen and Siegfried Sassoon, to the savage indictments of Joan Littlewood's play *Oh What a Lovely War!* (1963) and the *Blackadder* television series, originally broadcast in 1989 and repeated on the anniversary of the war's close in 1998. The conflict was indeed horrific, a terrible experience for both an age and a generation, so many of whom served.

The London Tube and its Maps

The first underground railway in London, the Metropolitan, opened on 10 January 1863, linking Bishop's Road, Paddington (close to a major rail terminus), and Farringdon in the City. It was a 'cut and cover' tunnel near the surface and, as the trains were steam-hauled, had to tackle the underground production of smoke. Glasgow also developed an underground system, but London's was easily the largest. The system spread, with separate companies constructing individual lines. The Inner Circle (now the Circle Line) was completed in 1884. The process was helped by the replacement of 'cut and cover' by deep 'tube' tunnels excavated by special boring machines. These machines were used to construct the City & South London Railway between King William Street and Stockwell which opened in 1890, now the City branch of the Northern Line. It was the first underground electric railway in the world. This was followed by the Waterloo & City Line (1898) and the Central Line between Shepherd's Bush and the Bank (1900). The existing District & Metropolitan Railways switched to electricity.

After the First World War there was a massive expansion of the network, creating a suburbia of commuters, especially on the Northern Line north of Hampstead Heath, but also along other radial corridors. The Northern Line reached Edgware in 1924 and was followed by the Metropolitan (later Bakerloo) to Stanmore in 1932, the Piccadilly to Cockfosters in 1933, and then the Northern to High Barnet and Mill Hill East. South of the Thames, the Northern Line reached Morden in 1926. Some of the lines took over earlier steam railway routes, but most were new.

Partly as a result of the expansion of the Underground, interwar London grew to house more than one-third of the population increase of the whole of England and Wales; there was widespread migration to the capital from within England and Wales. The Second World War and Green Belt policies then slowed expansion, but, from the 1960s, new lines were built in order to improve communications in the existing built-up area. The Victoria Line, opened in 1968–9, was the first automatic underground railway in the world and was followed by the Jubilee Line, completed in 1979, the Piccadilly extension to Heathrow opened in 1977, and the Jubilee extension to Greenwich in 1999. The Docklands Light Railway opened in 1987 and was operated by London Transport until 1992. Meanwhile, other travel systems were replaced. London's last tram ran in 1952, her last trolleybus in 1962.

The Underground was important in design terms. The stations of the 1930s were built in the characteristic house style of Charles Holden and combined functionalism and a simple elegance. Design was also important to what was to become the classic Underground map. The mapping of the Underground reflected a shift in cartographic technique, as well as the ability of maps to create lasting images. The first maps produced to show all the Underground lines, as opposed to those simply for an individual company, were issued free in 1908, and depicted the lines superimposed upon a central London map. The background was dropped in the 1920s, and the 1927 Underground map designed by F.H. Stingemore recorded the expansion of the network into the suburbs. In 1931, Harry Beck, a draughtsman working for the Underground, devised a diagrammatic map that emphasised clarity, rather than a close relationship to actual directions and locations. This layout was inspired by scientific models, specifically by electrical-circuit diagrams, and depicted the lines as verticals, horizontals and 45° diagonals. The popular map shrank the apparent distance between suburbia and the inner city, and ensured that movement to places such as Morden did not appear to be a case of leaving London. Instead, the ease of travel into the centre was emphasised, a visual effect encouraged by the use of straight lines for individual Underground lines.

But the hostilities were not without military and political results. Britain and other European powers made unprecedented efforts and deployed unprecedented power, fielding integrated fighting systems and, in the end, the Germans were defeated.

By October 1914 the euphoria of the war's outbreak and the general confidence in its speedy conclusion had been followed on the Western Front by the emergence of stalemate. The concentration of large forces in a relatively small area and the defensive strength of trench positions – especially thanks to machine guns with their range and rapidity of fire, and quick-firing artillery, but, also, helped by barbed wire and concrete fortifications – ensured that, until the collapse of the German position in the last weeks of the war, the situation was essentially deadlocked. It proved very difficult to translate local superiority in numbers into decisive success. It was possible to break through opponents' trench lines, but not to exploit any advantage; as yet, aeroplanes and motor vehicles had not been effectively harnessed to help the offensive. Furthermore, once troops had advanced, it was difficult to recognise, reinforce and exploit success: until wireless communications improved in late 1917, control and communications were limited. Frontal attacks, for example by the British at Neuve-Chapelle and Loos (1915), the Somme (1916), and Arras and Passchendaele (1917), led to heavy casualties, not least when a strategy of attrition was followed, as at Passchendaele, by a veritable hell of shells and mud.

The ratio of troops and firepower to space pushed up losses. The British used 2,879 guns – one for every 9 yards of front – for their attack near Arras in April 1917. Fifty-eight per cent of British battlefield deaths in the war were from artillery and mortar shells, and just below 39 per cent from machine-gun and rifle bullets. German 150mm field howitzers could fire five rounds per minute, and air-burst shrapnel shells increased the deadly nature of artillery fire. Machine guns were especially devastating against the British troops advancing slowly and in close order on the Somme in 1916. On 1 July, the first day of the offensive, 21,000 men were killed, most of them in an hour.

The impasse of trench warfare was broken in 1918. The British blocked the last German offensive in the spring and, in July–November, with French and American support, launched a series of attacks in which they outfought the Germans, overrunning their major defensive system in September. The massed use of tanks by the British was a major shock, and on 8 August no fewer than 430 British tanks broke through the German lines near Amiens. Although they rapidly became unfit for service, tanks could be hit by rifle bullets and machine guns without suffering damage and could smash through barbed wire and cross trenches. More generally, the Germans had lost their superiority in weapons systems. In 1918, British gunnery inflicted considerable damage on German defences, and was well coordinated with infantry advances.

Remembering the War

The First World War left a deep impression on succeeding generations. Some preferred to reject the entire horrific experience with desperate scorn for war itself. A sense of the futility of war was to contribute both to the internationalism of the 1920s, represented by the League of Nations, and to the appeasement of the late 1930s. Most people, nevertheless, did not seek to avoid the process of public remembrance that rapidly became a central part of communal life. The antagonism between soldiers and civilians, so noticeable in defeated Germany, was absent in Britain. In 1919, a two-minute silence was first instituted on the anniversary of the Armistice to commemorate the dead. In 1920, the Unknown Warrior was buried in Westminster Abbey and the Cenotaph was unveiled in Whitehall. Local village memorials were rapidly built across Britain and became the focus of annual services. That at Sledmere, East Yorkshire, depicts devilish Germans confronted near Mons by honest Britons, but, in general, the memorials were plain. Parish churches carried engraved lists of war dead, while vast cemeteries in France and elsewhere marked the battlefields. It was Armistice Day, rather than Good Friday, that could fill up a parish church. Edwin Lutyens, the architect of Castle Drogo, was also responsible for the Cenotaph and for the massive Memorial to the Missing of the Somme at Thiepval in France. Built for the Imperial War Graves Commission in 1927–32, it contains sixteen piers with endless lists of names.

The National Trust holds Midsummer Hill, at the southern end of the Malvern Hills, as a memorial for the war dead. Sandham Memorial Chapel in Hampshire was built for Mr and Mrs John Louis Behrend to commemorate the latter's brother, Lieutenant Henry Willoughby Sandham, who had died in 1919 as a consequence of an illness contracted during the Salonica campaign. The walls of the chapel were decorated with paintings by Stanley Spencer. Born in 1891, Spencer was a distinguished graduate of the Slade, who had been inspired by Giotto and the early Italian painters. He spent the war as a medical orderly, first in England, and then in Macedonia. In 1918, he became an official war artist but was invalided home with malaria.

The war haunted Spencer's postwar artistic thoughts, and he responded eagerly to the Behrends' commission, modelling the work on Giotto's Arena Chapel in Padua. From 1927, until he finished in 1932, Spencer recreated his own experiences as he painted the chapel. The murals did not offer a heroic view of combat. Instead, there were hospital scenes, depicting the mundane but necessary care of the shattered, and images of everyday army life, such as *Reveille* and *Filling Water Bottles*. The scene of the front line, *Dug-out*, was one of grave-like trenches and a vegetation of barbed wire.

Spencer himself pressed on with other works, showing, in particular, a tendency towards simplified volume in his figure style. His response to the world's problems was escapist – a scheme for a temple in Cookham to universal love: 'I felt the only way to end the ghastly experience would be if everyone suddenly decided to indulge in every degree and form of sexual love.' Instead, he became an official war artist in the Second World War, painting a series of works inspired by Lithgow's shipyards in Port Glasgow.

The First World War also left a legacy in political terms. The desire never to forget those who had sacrificed their lives had a number of important consequences. There was a general feeling that to push matters to extremes would be to betray those who had died. This helped explain the relative passivity of the General Strike in May 1926. For Stanley Baldwin, Prime Minister in 1923–4, 1924–9 and 1935–7, the war reinforced his commitment to service, on a personal level and in terms of the wider nation. The fellow-feeling and camaraderie of trench life gave Harold Macmillan an insight into the lives of ordinary people which made him determined, when he began his political career in the 1920s, to find a 'middle way' between capitalism and socialism.

Successes beyond the Western Front were also important. The British retained control of their home waters, checking the German high sea fleet at the battle of Jutland in 1916, and, after very heavy losses, eventually thwarted the submarine menace, in part through the introduction of convoys in 1917. They were therefore able to avoid invasion, to retain trade links that permitted the mobilisation of British and Allied resources, and to blockade Germany. The German colonies were overrun, the Suez Canal and oil supplies in the Persian Gulf both protected from Germany's ally Turkey, and the Turks eventually driven from Palestine and Mesopotamia (Israel and Iraq), although the attempt to knock Turkey out of the war in 1915 by advancing on Constantinople had been defeated at Gallipoli.

The ability to mobilise and apply resources, especially men and munitions, was crucial to the war effort, and led to an extension of the regulatory powers of the government. The Defence of the Realm Act of 1914 greatly extended the powers of the administration. It took over control of the railways (1914), the coal mines (1917) and the flour mills (1918). A powerful Ministry of Munitions which transformed the production of battlefield materials and resources developed from 1915. Lloyd George became Prime Minister in December 1916 and created a new coalition that encompassed Conservatives and Labour, although many Liberals followed the former leader and Prime Minister, Asquith, into opposition. A War Cabinet backed by a Secretariat streamlined policymaking. New ministries were created for labour and shipping, and a food production department was established in 1917. Food rationing was introduced. County agricultural committees oversaw a 30 per cent rise in national cereal production. By the end of the war, the Royal Arsenal at Woolwich employed over 80,000 people. Other communities also registered the impact of the war. In London's northern suburbs, Edmonton gained a large military hospital, while Enfield became a major centre for munitions production.

Universal military service was seen as crucial to the war effort. Conscription was introduced in 1916, helping to push the size of the armed forces up to 4½ million in 1917–18, one in three of the male labour force. Attempts to rally public opinion included the formation of the Department of Information, which, in 1918, became the Ministry of Information. The War Office created a Cinematograph Committee.

War was a major force for social change. Traditional assumptions were questioned, and social practices altered. Female employment rose and new roles, many in industry, were played by women, although female wages were lower and in factories women were controlled by male foremen. There was also a major change in the franchise. In pre-war Britain only about 60 per cent of men had the right to vote at any one time. They could vote at twenty-one if qualified (an age that was not changed in 1918), but those qualified were restricted by a complex registration process, lengthy residence requirements (in a society where many people still moved frequently so as to live near their work), and because the right to vote was explicitly kept from non-householders, for example soldiers living in barracks and adult sons living with parents.

The December 1910 election had led to a majority of MPs in favour of women's suffrage, but the key problem was what to do with male suffrage: many would not accept a women's suffrage bill which did not include universal manhood suffrage. What changed between 1914 and 1918 was a softening of resistance to universal manhood suffrage because of the heroism shown by all classes. This led to universal male suffrage in the Representation of the People Act of 1918. On the back of that, a limited degree of women's suffrage could be tackled. The vote was extended to women of thirty and over, as long as they were householders or the wives of householders. Women most likely to have worked in factories were younger and they did not get the vote in 1918. Nevertheless, the transition from aristocracy to democracy was largely complete. There was also a major redistribution of constituencies in 1918 in order to reflect the new electorate.

Although Britain was one of the victors, the First World War had exhausted the economy, public finances and society, taking hundreds of thousands of lives and costing billions. It proved impossible to sustain postwar international ambitions, not least as an immediate economic boom rapidly gave way to a slump.

FIVE

PEACE AND WAR, 1918-45

As the population ages, so experience becomes history. When I was a boy everybody who was older had personal recollections of this period. It was their life. Many looked back to the First World War. One grandfather had fought on the Western Front, a grandmother could remember Zeppelin (airship) raids on London. The Second World War was like yesterday, whether my parents recalled the difference between German V–1s and V–2s landing on London – the soundless arrival of the latter made them seem more arbitrary and terrifying – or the impact of food rationing and the novelty of the first banana. Now the inexorable quality of time has swept this aside. To children and students, the wars are dead history, interwar events, such as the General Strike of 1926, the Slump, or the Abdication of 1936, simply the litany of schoolroom exercises.

How then to make sense of a period on the cusp between memory and ancient history? A list of ministries, of Lloyd George (1916–22), Bonar Law (1922–3), Baldwin (1923–4, 1924–9, 1935–7), MacDonald (1924, 1929–35), Chamberlain (1937–40), and Churchill (1940–5), of legislation, or controversies, such as the decision to return sterling to the Gold Standard in 1925, does not focus on the developments that now seem important. Instead, it is more appropriate to note the conflation of social and environmental changes. The most important was the growth of urban Britain, and it is still continuing. The decline in the number of those who experienced rural life, in the face of the spread of urban values and mores, owed a lot to economic developments and to the impact of new technology, especially cars and the cinema. In much of Britain, rural life was marginalised. The number of agricultural labourers in England fell by a quarter between 1921 and 1939, and other non-urban activities declined. As Britain became more urbanised, however, the countryside was increasingly idealised as an aesthetic, a culture and a place to live.

Suburbia spread into the countryside, especially around London. Designed to allow the growing middle class to realise their earning potential, to escape from the crowded, polluted and unfashionable conditions of the city, and to join in the expanding hobby of amateur gardening, new housing was both cause and consequence of a massive increase in personal transport.

National private ownership of cars increased more than tenfold, and car production rose from 116,000 in 1924 to 341,000 in 1938. 'The sound of horns and motors' of T.S. Eliot's poem 'The Waste Land' (1922) was becoming more insistent, and creating a new national culture. There were nearly 2 million cars, half a million road goods vehicles, and 53,000 buses and coaches by September 1938.

Cars were only part of the equation. Having made little progress in road building during the century of rail, Britain now embarked upon a massive programme of constructing and upgrading existing ones to provide all-weather surfaces for motor cars. Major roads that had been overshadowed during the age of rail, such as the London–Brighton route via Crawley, revived in importance. Less prominent Victorian by-roads had frequently been poorly surfaced. Greater traffic flow led to pressures to improve them. The Trunk Roads Programme was devised in 1929, both to provide employment and to ensure that road improvement schemes were pressed forward. The government agreed to meet much of the cost. Nevertheless, there was no centralised planning or overruling of local views and property rights akin to the programme for the construction of the German autobahns of the 1930s.

The new roads led to new smells and sounds and affected the visual context of life, both in towns and in the countryside. Roads created new demands for signs, lamp-posts, manhole covers and traffic lights. Roads led to new boundaries and commands, to zebra crossings and Belisha beacons, the second named after a Minister of Transport, Leslie Hore-Belisha.

As the introduction of rail a century earlier had impacted on canals and roads, so the rise of the cars was achieved at the expense of the previous transport system: rail, horse-drawn vehicles, and, less significantly, bicycles. The rail system was reorganised in 1923, when more than 120 railway companies were grouped into four: the London & North Eastern (LNER), the London, Midland & Scottish, the Great Western, and the Southern. These companies sought to provide a service that could rival road or air. The Southern improved electric services, enabling it to expand commuter services, while the others produced powerful express locomotives, most famously the LNER's *Mallard* which in 1938 set the world steam speed record of 126mph. The engine can be seen in the National Rail Museum in York.

Although the railways often pioneered feeder bus services, from the 1920s they were hit by road competition. Furthermore, freight transport fell. In the interwar period 2,409 miles of track and 350 stations were closed completely, and another 1,000 miles and 380 stations to passenger traffic. More seriously for the network as a whole, the profitability crucial to investment, for example the electrification of long-distance services, was lacking. Among the 'Big Four' railway companies, the Southern Railway was alone in paying a regular dividend to shareholders before 1948. Rail transport no longer seemed the future.

Steamship services were also hit, for roads both added a dimension to the competition from rail and filled the gaps between railheads, reducing the opportunities for coastal services. As steamship services were cut, seaside settlements lost their function as regular ports. The weekly cargo and passenger service to Barmouth provided by the Aberdovey & Barmouth Steamship Company ended in 1915.

The challenge to rail from road was very different from that to canals by rail. Both canals and rail had required major investment to create routes, and the resulting systems lacked flexibility. Furthermore, access to these forms of transport needed special facilities, such as passenger stations or freight sidings, ensuring that the growth in the rail system led to an increase in the number of horse-drawn vehicles, as people or goods were transported to these facilities. Road transport was different. It offered access at every point along a road. In addition, the vehicles were far less expensive than those required for the canal and rail systems, the majority were owned by individuals, and they did not require comparable training in their use.

At the beginning of a new millennium, we are more aware of the damage and disruption brought by road transport, not least the resulting pollution, but, for much of the twentieth century, the freedom offered made cars seductive. In the interwar years, those who could not afford cars were in the overwhelming majority, but vehicle ownership became a goal or model for many of them, creating a pent-up aspiration and ensuring that future affluence would lead to the purchase of more cars. The cinema helped to foster this romance, an aspect of the interaction of new technologies. Films, both British and their very influential American counterparts, created and disseminated lifestyles and images for those who could, and the many who could not, afford them. The availability of buses and coaches also changed the experience of travel: charabanc outings came to play a major role for many.

The impact of cars was not solely a matter of aggregate figures and national images. The local dimension was also crucial, because the car changed the landscape and was to do so far more than canal or rail had done. The impact can be readily grasped in modern Britain: ribbon developments followed the new roads. Furthermore, car transport encouraged and made possible housing of a lower density. The tightly packed terraces characteristic of the Victorian city, for middle as well as working class, were supplemented by miles of 'semis': semi-detached houses with mock-Tudor elevations, red-tiled roofs, and walls of red brick or pebble-dash, with a small front and larger back garden, each with a small drive and a garage. They were built in large numbers, not only around London, but also on routes leaving all major towns, especially in areas of prosperity, such as much of southern England. Suburbia had spread in the late nineteenth century with the railways, but development then had generally not moved far from the stations. In contrast, car transport permitted less intensive development. In advertisements, cars were pictured against backdrops of mock-Tudor suburban houses.

Building on new sites away from city centres ensured that cheap land was used. This helped reduce the cost of housing, and permitted lower housing densities than in the cities. New houses ate up land and led to attempts to protect green spaces near cities, for example by the Oxford Preservation Society founded in 1927. The majority of new homes were for owner-occupiers who commuted to work by car or train, including via the electrified lines south of London and the spreading Underground routes to the north of the city. Driving to stations magnified the impact of train services. The new transport system also helped lessen costs because lorries could move housing materials from central manufacturing sites, including large brickworks, as at Peterborough, and factories producing prefabricated doors and windows.

The semis were to be criticised as lacking in individuality, wasteful of space, and dependent on the car. 'Were Edgware on a lake, would Venice stand a chance?', the satirist Alan Coren was later to quip of an outlier of London thrown up in the 1920s. The facelessness of much of the century's housing was captured in the poet John Betjeman's description of Swindon's houses as 'brick-built breeding boxes of new souls': Swindon was designated an overspill town in 1952.

Yet, as with the car, the semi-detached house expressed freedom, a freedom to escape the constraints of living in close proximity to others, and, instead, to enjoy space. These were not landed estates, nor the suburban villas of wealthier members of the middle class, but they captured the aspirations of millions, and offered them a decent living environment. Their gardens were the humble counterpart of many of the grander gardens of the period, such as Hatchlands, Hidcote and Sissinghurst.

The car and the semi permitted a degree of spatial segregation in housing that kept social groups further apart than had generally been the case in the nineteenth century, and this accounted for much of their popularity. People were buying distance. Many, however, could not. There was much poverty in the 1920s, both in town and countryside, not least due to the pressures stemming from postwar demobilisation. Promises of a land 'fit for heroes' for the returned soldiers proved highly misleading. Instead, unemployment rose, wages did not keep pace with prices which shot up in 1920, and in 1921 industrial disputes dramatically increased, not least due to an unsuccessful miners' strike. Financial problems led to a cutback in the government housing programme in 1921. Nevertheless, slum clearance programmes resulted in the construction of large numbers of 'council houses' in the 1930s. Although expenditure per dwelling was lower, the council estates shared in the interest in greenery and low density that characterised private house building in suburbia.

The growth rate in gross national product (GNP) per head was about 1.5 per cent in the 1920s, compared to 0.4 per cent in 1900–13. This reflected the expansion of high-productivity consumer industries, rather than the traditional export industries, such as shipbuilding and cotton-textiles. Expenditure on consumer durables and transport rose.

Aside from cars, there was a growing aeroplane industry. The reach of aircraft itself rose dramatically. In 1919 Alcock and Brown made the first transatlantic flight in a British Vickers Vimy plane.

The geography of prosperity and economic opportunity was, in part, reflected in the response to the General Strike of 1926, a strike that arose from the crisis in labour relations in the coal industry. Coal exports had been hit by the development of competing sources of power, and of mining in other countries, and, as exports fell, employers tried to cut wages. The General Strike began at midnight on 3 May 1926 and about 1½–2 million workers struck, in addition to the miners who had been locked out. Not all workers were called out. The response was solid in London, most coalfield towns and a number of other cities, including Birmingham, Liverpool, Hull, Norwich and Plymouth. Support was far weaker across much of the South of England, including Portsmouth and Southampton. In Bristol, Manchester and Glasgow the situation was more mixed. The government responded by moving police, deploying troops and warships, and encouraging volunteers. The last were most numerous in London and the South-East.

The TUC ended the strike on 12 May; the miners were left on their own, and eventually had to accept the employers' terms. In 1927, the government passed the Trade Disputes Act, banning sympathetic strikes and the affiliation of Civil Service trades unions to the TUC and the Labour Party, and obliging trade unionists to 'contract in' to the political levy, a means of limiting their financial support for Labour. There was not to be another national miners' strike until 1972.

Labour governments took office in 1924 and 1929, but they were minority administrations dependent on Liberal support. Throughout the decade, the Conservatives, who had been very successful in the 1918 election, were the party with the largest percentage of the popular vote, while, until 1929, they also had most seats. Thus, although Labour twice took office, it is important not to neglect the conservatism of the 1920s, particularly among the newly enfranchised female electorate. This was also revealed in local elections, and represented a continuation of the consolidation of the propertied, especially under the spur of fear of left-wing subversion, fear that played a role in the 1924 general election with a controversy over alleged links between international communism and Labour. The Conservatives also made particular efforts to win the support of trade unionists and young voters.

The 1930s

The Great Depression of the 1930s, which began with the Slump of 1929, hit hard. World trade fell, greatly harming Britain, a major exporter. Manufacturing was badly affected – exports from the Lancashire cotton mills to the Far East and, even more, India falling badly. Heavy industry suffered most of all. The shipyards on the Tyne launched 238,000 tons of shipping in 1913, but fewer than 7,000 in 1933. That was the beginning of developments that prompted the Jarrow March of unemployed shipworkers to London in 1936, for unemployment rose greatly, from 1.6 million in 1929 to 3.4 million in 1932, about 17 per cent of the labour force. About 2.6 million jobs were created in 1933–8, but 2.2 million people were unemployed in 1938, because the numbers looking for work had risen by 1.4 million, a consequence not of immigration, but of a large expansion of the potential labour force due to the relatively high pre-war birthrate and the absence of any war in this period. Unskilled workers were especially hard hit by unemployment, managers and professionals far less so. Wages were affected by short-time working.

Global and national economic problems pressed hard on the nation's finances, leading in 1931 to a fiscal crisis for Ramsay MacDonald's Labour government, which had taken office from Stanley Baldwin's Conservatives after the 1929 general election. The government was unable both to sustain public expenditure, and thus preserve social welfare levels, and to defend the value of the pound. Poor relations between MacDonald and both the trade unions and the parliamentary Labour Party accentuated tensions.

Bitterly divided and under heavy pressure due to economic crisis, the administration resigned, leading, in a crisis atmosphere, to the creation of a 'National Government', again under MacDonald, but largely composed of Conservatives, and opposed by the bulk of the Labour Party. National government appeared necessary to keep a national emergency at bay. Formed, to 'save the pound', the new government in fact both let the value of the currency fall and cut unemployment benefits. But it at least appeared to have solutions, and won an overwhelming victory in the general election of 27 October 1931. The Conservatives, who dominated the National Government, benefited greatly from their strong support among recently enfranchised female voters, although that had not brought them victory in 1929. The National Government acted as a force for stability throughout the 1930s, and ensured that Britain avoided the political extremism which was seen in countries such as Italy and Germany.

There was a strong regional dimension to the Depression. Its effects were very pronounced in mining and heavy manufacturing areas, those that were dependent on exports, such as South Wales, North-East England and Clydeside. More than a quarter of the Scottish labour force was out of work in

1931–3, as was about one-third of Derbyshire's miners. Welsh unemployment rose to 37.5 per cent in 1932. The decline of the Cornish tin industry led to 25 per cent unemployment in Redruth in 1939.

Social welfare was less limited than in the past, and the creation of the Unemployment Assistance Board in 1934 helped, but there was still much hardship. The wives and children of the unemployed were badly affected. Much of the population did not benefit fully from interwar medical advances, which included immunisation against diphtheria and tetanus, improved blood transfusion techniques, the first sulphonamide drugs, and the use of insulin against diabetes and of gamma globulin against measles. Instead, public health was hit, and tuberculosis became a more serious problem. The provision of free or subsidised milk was one response. Aside from unemployment-related illnesses, both physical and psychological, there was also much indignity. Both the Unemployment Assistance Board and means testing were unpopular. There was significant emigration from depressed areas, such as South Wales and Cornwall.

There was also much prosperity. This may surprise readers accustomed to the notion of the 1930s as a period of terrible crisis, but there was considerable growth at this time. GNP returned to its 1929 figure in 1934, and the economy recovered more completely than those of France and the USA. It is unclear how much this owed to the protectionism that was introduced in 1932 with the Import Duties Act – the legislation certainly helped the chemical industry.

Real wages rose and prices fell. Aside from the boom in housing, which led to 3 million new homes being built that decade, there were growing industries that focused on consumer demand, a demand that was encouraged by falls in the price of imported food and, in 1932, in interest rates. The National Grid for electricity developed under the control of the Central Electricity Board that had been established under the Electricity Supply Act of 1926. Household electricity supplies expanded greatly, replacing coal, gas, candles and human effort. The percentage of homes wired for electricity rose from 31.8 in 1932 to 65.4 in 1938, and this had an impact on the consumption of power and the sales of electric cookers, irons, fridges, water heaters and vacuum cleaners. This demand helped industrial expansion.

Such expenditure reflected, and helped to define, class differences. Whereas radios, vacuum cleaners and electric irons were widely owned, in part thanks to the spread of hire purchase, electric fridges, cookers and washing machines were largely restricted to the middle class. These differences were often linked to an aspect of the major social divide between those who employed others and the employed, although, in most cases, the latter now meant not full-time domestic servants, but occasional daily help. New owner-occupied suburban houses tended to have electricity supply and appliances; working-class terraces less so.

Social differences had a regional component, with ownership of such goods, as well as of cars and telephones, and access to electricity consumption, higher in the South-East than in poorer areas, such as South Wales. Whether defined in terms of income, occupation or culture, the middle class was proportionately far more important in London and the South-East than in any other region.

Industrial expansion took place on a broad front. Electronics and light engineering were especially important, and plastics became more so. Product innovation was crucial to the new industries. Radios and telephones were produced in large numbers, as were motor cars. All three came to play a large role in the lives of many and in fiction, as in the detective novels of the period and the stories of P.G. Wodehouse. The novelist and playwright J.B. Priestley undertook most of his *English Journey* (1934) by bus. Radios and telephones also played a role in the mechanics of politics. In 1923, when the ailing Bonar Law resigned as Conservative Prime Minister, the talented, but arrogant George, Marquess Curzon, the Foreign Secretary, expected to be his successor. He was tenant of the Tudor stately home of Montacute in Somerset, then very run down, and there was no telephone at the house. Curzon's wait for the call from George V was therefore longer than it might have been as he had to be contacted by a telegram. One came, and Curzon went to London, only to find that the less imperious Stanley Baldwin had been selected.

Baldwin was to be a very effective exploiter of the possibilities of radio – his broadcasts during the General Strike resembled fireside chats rather than government propaganda. Such avuncular reassurance played a crucial part in ensuring that, in the midst of much disruption, Britain remained a society largely at ease with itself.

As in the 1920s, the economy in the 1930s modernised and responded to new demands. Growth helped to push down unemployment in 1933–7, and to lead to a rise in real wages that, in turn, supported both consumer demand and Conservative electoral fortunes: the Conservative-dominated National Government easily won the general election of 1935.

Variations in the economic geography of the country became more pronounced in the 1930s. The South-East was reasonably prosperous. Thanks to the Morris works at Cowley, Oxford had only 5 per cent unemployment in 1934. The car factories there employed 10,000 workers in 1939, producing on the American model that Morris sought to copy from Henry Ford. The availability of jobs in expanding industrial centres in the South-East and the Midlands, such as Birmingham, Coventry, Letchworth, Luton, Slough, Watford and Welwyn, led to substantial levels of migration within Britain. This also registered the lack of economic opportunities elsewhere, especially in South Wales, Clydeside, and North-East England.

Other areas had varied fortunes, growth as well as decline. In Wales, alongside the problems in the South, especially in the coal-mining areas, there was growth on Deeside. Nevertheless, emigration levels were such that the Welsh population did not return to its 1921 figure until 1961.

In the North-East of England, there were grave problems on the Tyne and the Wear, but the development of the chemical industry on the Tees at Billingham brought many jobs. In Cornwall, alongside the despair of the former tin-mining areas, tourism grew, bringing prosperity to Bude and Newquay, both of which were Conservative strongholds, while, although china clay production had fallen seriously by 1931, by 1939 it had nearly recovered its 1929 levels. In depressed areas, such as Sunderland, there was still, for many in work, good housing, a higher quality of life than hitherto, and more consumer choice. Moreover, the fall in agricultural prices cut the cost of living, easing the plight of the poor.

Suburban industrial estates benefited from the opportunities provided by road transport, and located along arterial routes. This was especially important near London, an area where economic growth encouraged much investment. The Great West Road became the site of a series of spacious factories that, with their use of electricity, were very distant from the smoke-shrouded, metal-bashing works of heavy industry. On the Great West Road, aside from large-scale factories, such as those manufacturing Smiths crisps, Gillette razors and Curry's cycles, and the Hoover factory, there was a host of smaller works on the Park Royal estate. There was also development along the North Circular Road at Colindale and Cricklewood, and major expansion in the Lea Valley to the north-east of London. Elsewhere, new industrial estates, such as the Team Valley Trading Estate south of Newcastle, also sought good road links. Rail freight, in contrast, was dominated by traditional goods, especially coal, and was thus hit by the Depression of the 1930s.

The geography of industrial production had altered. In place of a need to locate near heavy raw materials such as coal and iron, and near where workers had traditional skills, there was a focus on proximity to markets and to transport links. An instructive contrast from 1936 was that between the unemployed workers of Palmer's shipyard at Jarrow, who drew attention to their plight with a march on London, and the new Carreras cigarette factory opened at Mornington Crescent in London and employing 2,600 workers.

In 1937 Butlin's opened the first purpose-built holiday camp at Skegness on the Lincolnshire coast. This was an aspect of the major increase in leisure provision in the 1930s, which included the building of numerous cinemas. By 1939, Birmingham alone had 110. Enormous picture houses were thrown up in new London suburbs, such as Gants Hill, Becontree Heath and Hendon, and elsewhere, for example the vast Roxy at Gosport. Some cinemas, such as the Ilford Hippodrome and the Rex at

Stratford, were converted theatres. They acted as foci within towns, and also gave a new strand to the urban magnetism felt in rural areas. Country dwellers went to urban cinemas, such as the Grand in Banbury, to see the wider world, through both films and newsreels.

The British film industry was overshadowed by Hollywood, despite the Cinematograph Films Act of 1927 which forced cinemas to show a quota of British pictures. The images and characterisation in American films proved more attractive to the bulk of the audience. British films tended to marginalise the working class, but the latter made up the majority of movie-goers. Many home-grown pictures were too like drawing-room comedies or were period pieces that did not coincide with the interests or ambitions of the audience. Nevertheless, the industry was still important. The first British sound production, Alfred Hitchcock's *Blackmail* (1929), was a considerable success. Film censorship helped ensure that the cinema did not seriously challenge conventional social or political assumptions until the Second World War.

The consumption of leisure reflected the reduction in the average working week: from fifty-four hours before 1914 to forty-eight during the interwar period. Paid holidays became more common in the late 1930s, and both annual breaks and holiday camps were more popular. Butlin's at Clacton-on-Sea opened in 1938. Other aspects of the expanding world of leisure included the new Penguin imprint in 1935, which provided quality works at an inexpensive price and in a convenient paperback format. In 1936, Penguin sales exceeded 3 million and a non-fiction list, Pelican, was launched.

Yet, as with other consumer indicators of the period, rising expenditure on leisure varied by region, class, gender and age, and, within these categories, family size was very important. It had become an issue in the 1920s. In place of the somewhat shadowy C.R. Drysdale and Alice Vickery, the leading lights in the British Malthusian League, the only body in Britain advocating the use of artificial contraception, came the more dynamic Marie Stopes, who in 1921 founded the Society for Constructive Birth Control.

Interwar Culture

Fashionable circles had little time for popular writers of the period, such as Arnold Bennett (1867–1931), John Galsworthy (1867–1933), Rudyard Kipling (1865–1936), G.K. Chesterton (1874–1936), and Hilaire Belloc (1870–1953), let alone for adventure writers such as John Buchan. Chesterton and Belloc offered a Catholic critique of modern society, as well as detective fiction (Chesterton), literary biography (Chesterton), travelogue (Belloc), and poetry for children (Belloc).

Instead, the Bloomsbury Group sought to further the avant-garde in a deliberate reaction against Victorian styles and assumptions. Bloomsbury was essentially a collection of friends with similar views who saw themselves as playing a crucial role in reviving a stale literary tradition. The best known novelist in the group was Virginia Woolf (1882–1941). She had no time for what she presented as the 'materialist' writing of Bennett and Galsworthy, and, instead, sought a Modernist focus on aesthetic sensibility. In 'Mr. Bennett and Mrs Brown', an essay of 1924, Woolf distinguished between what she considered Bennett's false 'realism' of surface description and a 'modernism' that searched for true realism. In place of narrative, Woolf advocated a view of life as a 'luminous halo'. Her novels explored such ideas. In *Mrs Dalloway* (1925), she employed interior monologue and stream of consciousness to reveal character; in To *The Lighthouse* (1927), Woolf offered a pointillistic meditation on time and fulfilment; and in *The Waves* (1931) provided another experimental form, including a series of interior monologues, to reveal personality and consider the role of memory. Another such form was offered in 1923 when Façade, an innovative set of poems by Edith Sitwell, was performed with music composed by William Walton.

Woolf was scarcely alone among interwar writers in focusing on people as individuals, building up or frustrating the personalities of others (and themselves), rather than as vehicles for narrative and/or commentators on social issues. An emphasis on imagination and the emotional focus was clear in D.H. Lawrence's *Women in Love* (1920). These subjects were not incompatible with comments on wider issues, however, as E.M. Forster (1879–1970) showed in *A Passage to India* (1924), at once a novel about sensibility and a searching investigation of the psychological tensions of empire.

Modernism, however, had only a limited appeal, compared to many of the 'middle'- and 'low'-brow writers of the period, and had little airing on the radio. Although 'middle'- and 'low'-brow writers might not find favour with Bloomsbury and the reviewers of the *Times Literary Supplement*, they tended to dominate sales. They benefited from the rising disposable income of the interwar period, especially the 1920s, from the ready availability of inexpensive books, and from increased leisure. Women readers were of growing importance, as indeed were children. There are suggestions that British society was more literate in the 1920s than it was to be in the 1990s.

These markets did not necessarily see themselves as 'middle' brow. Their favoured authors were not necessarily too different in style to Kipling or Galsworthy, who had both won the Nobel Prize for Literature. In *The Herries Chronicle,* a family story set in Cumberland, Hugh Walpole (1884–1941) produced a work that was close to Galsworthy's *The Forsyte Saga* (1906–21). Popular works in Walpole's saga included *Rogue Herries* (1930). He also wrote popular school stories.

Walpole's one-time collaborator, J.B. Priestley (1894–1984), also won popularity with an accessible novel, *The Good Companions* (1929), an engaging account of a touring theatrical company. A Yorkshireman, Priestley had an interest in English character, but his distance from cosmopolitanism did not make him a provincial drudge. In his plays of the 1930s, such as *Dangerous Corner* (1932), he used time cleverly for intellectual as well as dramatic effect, a theme to which he was to return in *An Inspector Calls* (1945). Another Yorkshire writer, the feminist Winifred Holtby (1898–1935), also offered a strong sense of place in South Riding (1936). This tradition continued in much of the popular novel writing of the later twentieth century, for example the works of Catherine Cookson (1906–99) which were mostly set in her native Tyneside.

A musical equivalent can be sought in the pastoral work of Ralph Vaughan Williams, for instance his Pastoral Symphony (1921). This was criticised by the composer and critic Constant Lambert as the 'cow pat school' of British music. The music of Sir Edward Elgar (1857–1934) emphasised an elegiac tone, and remained popular in concert programmes, gramophone record sales and BBC broadcasts.

The cult of the countryside was also seen in A.A. Milne's (1882–1956) popular dramatisation in 1929 of *The Wind in the Willows* by Kenneth Grahame (1859–1932), as well as in Milne's books *Winnie-the-Pooh* (1926) and *The House at Pooh*

Corner (1928). The Scottish Renaissance writers overwhelmingly concentrated on rural themes. Similarly, many of the painters of the period produced portraits or landscapes that paid scant tribute to fashionable themes. In the interwar years, the Royal Academy Schools were characterised by a conservatism greatly at odds with Modernism. Works by painters such as Picasso could be bought in the galleries in Cork Street, but their impact on the wider world was limited. Scottish art patronage was even more conservative and most Scottish painting was conventional in subject and approach. There was only limited interest among Scottish painters in theoretic Modernism. It was only in 1945 that the Trustees of the Tate Gallery in London agreed to the opening of a small room devoted to abstract art.

'Low'-brow works of the interwar period included popular romantic stories, for example those published by Mills & Boon, as well as adventure stories and detective novels. Barbara Cartland's first novel, *Jigsaw*, appeared in 1923. On the stage, the equivalent were readily accessible domestic comedies, such as the plays of Noel Coward, for instance *Hay Fever* (1925), or Priestley's *When We Are Married* (1938). P.G. Wodehouse's comic novels about Bertie Wooster and Jeeves, characters first introduced in 1917, were successfully adapted for the stage by Ian Hay.

Despite works by architects such as Berthold Lubetkin, Modernism also had little impact in architecture. Liberty's in Regent Street, built in 1924, using Elizabethan timber, better expressed the widespread desire for a style suggesting continuity, not the new. It was matched on the screen by the success of Alexander Korda's *The Private Life of Henry VIII* (1933). The architectural Modernism that looked to continental figures, especially Le Corbusier and Walter Gropius, had only a limited impact in Scotland too. As in England, pre-war styles – both revived classicism and Arts and Crafts – remained very strong.

Much of the culture of the period was not designed to challenge established practices and the social order. Dorothy L. Sayers' Harriet Vane was an independent-minded female character among a host that reinforced stable sexual and class identities, for example Agatha Christie's Miss Marple and the heroines created by Ivy Compton-Burnett (1892–1969) and Daphne du Maurier (1907–89). This was part of a conservative disposition that was very pronounced in the 1930s. Du Maurier's novels, such as *Jamaica Inn* (1936) and *Rebecca* (1938), had a particularly strong sense of place, in her case Cornwall. The upper-middle-class satire produced by 'the Bright Young Things', such as Evelyn Waugh, did not challenge established ideas.

Alongside works that were about and/or for the affluent, there was also much that might be termed 'Condition of Britain' culture, attempts to present the life of the less fortunate. These included George Orwell's social criticism in his *Down and Out in Paris and London* (1933) and his bleak and bitter description of working-class life in northern mining communities in *The Road to Wigan Pier* (1937), as well as Walter Greenwood's depiction of the harshness of unemployment in *Love on the Dole* (1933) and Walter Brierley's *Means Test Man* (1935) on a similar theme. A Scottish equivalent was the account of Depression Clydeside offered by George Blake in *The Shipbuilders* (1935).

The fall in the size of the average family cut expenditure on food and clothing, freeing funds for consumer durables, but many households did not experience such a fall and they could be hit hard. The poor were unable to participate fully in the new leisure society. Most lacked radios and could not afford the cinema, let alone holidays. In 1936, the committee for a class in 'Economic Planning' in Stanleytown, Glamorgan, wrote to express thanks to the National Library of Wales which was circulating duplicate copies of books in the depressed South Wales minefield: 'books of this nature are hopelessly out of the reach of the members who are unemployed'.

Avoiding Revolution

Public order was maintained in the 1930s. The prosperity of much of the country and the absence of any financial collapse helped, but so too did the lack of obvious options for the many in difficulties. The Labour opposition was divided after the events of August 1931 and unwilling to abandon peaceful methods. It was also under pressure from Communism. In February 1928, Labour had been condemned by the Communist Party as social fascists, in 1931 Labour candidates were burned in effigy, and in the same year Labour and Communist gangs fought each other in Edinburgh. The Communist-run National Unemployed Workers Movement (NUWM) had launched marches and demonstrations demanding work since 1921, but support was limited – only 700 marching in 1934 – and it was concerned to remain within the bounds of the politically possible. Songs such as:

> In the N.U.W.M. we fight,
> For our Freedom and the Worker's Right,
> Marching forward on to Victory,
> Give us your help, my boys,
> We're fighting the Battle for you,

could not conceal the difficulty of the situation. The Jarrow marchers, sponsored by the Labour Party, kept away from the NUWM. Riots in 1936–7 involving striking miners at Harworth in Nottinghamshire, were ended by police action, just as the police had forcefully dispersed unofficial strikers in George Square in central Glasgow on 'Bloody Friday' on 31 January 1919.

Industrial militancy was no preparation for a situation in which employers went bankrupt. The NUWM had been intended as a body to destabilise capitalism by demanding better wages and conditions; instead, it became a type of union for the unemployed. Communism was anathema to the propertied, who were now consolidated into one strong anti-Socialist party, while the right-wing extremism of Oswald Mosley's New Party, which in 1932 became the British Union of Fascists (BUF) was unacceptable, not only to the bulk of public opinion, but also to the Conservative establishment.

Mosley had been Conservative MP for Harrow in 1918– 22, before becoming an Independent and then a Labour MP. He saw himself as a second Mussolini, but it proved easier to borrow the latter's black-shirts than to recreate the political circumstances that had permitted the fascist seizure of power in Italy. In response to Mosley, the government in December 1936 passed the Public Order Act banning political uniforms (the Act was also used to control the rioting miners of Harworth), but it did not prove necessary to repress the BUF or to encourage the development of a loyalist movement.

The existence of Mosley and the BUF helped Prime Minister Stanley Baldwin. He was able to present them as the un-English/ un-British contrast to his own policies which were based on the glories of the English countryside and the stolid common sense of the people of England. Baldwin dominated the National Government, although he did not replace MacDonald as Prime Minister until 1935. He, in turn, retired in favour of Neville Chamberlain in 1937. Chamberlain remained in power until replaced in 1940 by Churchill, who became Prime Minister in a coalition government that included Labour.

Nor was Communism so strong in the 1930s that the establishment sought to create a counter movement, either by looking to the BUF or by creating a populist organisation of its own. Communist membership had risen to 11,500 in late 1926, in the aftermath of the General Strike, as miners joined, but then fell to below 3,000 in 1930, before rising to 5,500 in 1933 and about 18,000 in December 1938. Hopes that membership would reach 100,000 were fruitless. Numbers in France and Germany were far higher. The Communist Party was discredited by its association with the USSR and the Stalinist purges. In *The Road to Wigan Pier* (1937), George Orwell referred to 'the stupid cult of Russia'. Thanks in part to the economic upturn from 1933, and to the general prosperity of the metropolitan region, the opportunities for extremism were limited. Louis Yorke suspected a 'Bolshevik Plot' at his stately home, Erddig, in 1927 when five of the staff left in one day; instead, they were fed up with low wages.

The absence of any tradition of the violent overthrow of authority was also very important. Had the unsuccessful General Strike of 1926 led to widespread violence or to a change of government, neither of which was the intention of the trade union leadership or membership, then the situation in the 1930s might have been less propitious. There was no breakdown of parliamentary democracy in 1930–1. The failure of both Mosley's New Party and the Communist Party to make any electoral headway in the October 1931 election was indicative of this.

The Empire 1902–39

The inclusion of this section may appear curious, a product of reprehensible nostalgia or an inappropriate anachronism, but, for many in the world, the experience of British control marks the importance of British history, and, for many Britons, empire provided a taproot of identity, the consequence of which included a reluctant attitude towards closer relations with Europe. It is easy to present the empire as foredoomed to failure. Already, at the start of the century, thanks in part to the diffusion within the empire of British notions of community, identity and political action and practices of politicisation, specifically nationalism and democratisation, there was opposition to imperial control, although it was relatively modest in nature and demands. In 1885, the Indian National Congress was formed; in 1897 the Egyptian National Party. The Boer War of 1899–1902, nevertheless, served to undermine the assuredness of Britain's imperial mission, not least in Britain itself. In 1902, Joseph Chamberlain, the Liberal Unionist Colonial Secretary and supporter of an empire based on cooperation, told the Colonial Conference:

> The weary Titan staggers under the too vast orb of its fate. We have borne the burden for many years. We think that it is time that our children should assist us to support it. . . . If you are prepared at any time to take any share in the burdens of Empire, we are prepared to meet you with any proposal for giving you a corresponding voice in the policy of the Empire.

Chamberlain's dream of imperial federation, to be achieved through policies of imperial preference and protection, foundered, however, upon metropolitan hostility to food import duties and residual faith in free trade.

Yet, the empire, which had only recently gained much of Africa, including Rhodesia (now Zambia and Zimbabwe) and the Sudan, continued to expand, and British troops were sent where they had never gone before. At Burmi in 1903, the army of Sokoto was heavily defeated, the Caliph and his two sons killed, and resistance in northern Nigeria came to an end. On 31 March 1904, a force under Colonel Francis Younghusband, advancing through the Himalayas towards Lhasa, opened fire at Guru on Tibetans who were unwilling to disarm. Due to their two Maxim guns, four cannon and effective rifles, the British killed nearly 700 Tibetans without any losses of their own. Younghusband then proceeded to Lhasa. Thanks to the resources of the imperial state, his advance had been supported by 16,000 draught animals and 10,000 human porters.

The empire showed its worth during the First World War. More than 800,000 Indian soldiers fought for the British, many, as well as substantial Canadian, Australian and New Zealand forces, on the Western Front. Australian and New Zealand troops tried unsuccessfully to force the Dardanelles in 1915. South African troops conquered South-West Africa. Without the empire, the British would have been unable to mount offensive operations in the Middle East, would have been largely reduced to the use of the navy against German colonies, and would have been forced to introduce conscription earlier than 1916. The use of imperial forces was helped by the absence of an enemy in Asia to deter their movement further west. The situation was to be very different in the Second World War, when Japan was a determined and initially successful opponent.

The empire reached its height with the First World War. In 1914, Cyprus was annexed and a protectorate gained over Egypt, and, after the war, League of Nation mandates were acquired over much of the German and Turkish empires, including Tanganyika, Palestine, Transjordan and Iraq. Yet this position was challenged in a general crisis of imperial overreach. Unrest in the army led to a more rapid demobilisation than had been originally intended. Intervention in the Russian Civil War was unsuccessful. Revolts in Egypt (1919) and Iraq (1920-1) led to Britain granting their partial independence, and British influence collapsed in Persia (1921). The bulk of Ireland was lost in 1921, a reversal of over 300 years of imperial control.

In 1922, Andrew Bonar Law, the Conservative Prime Minister, argued that Britain 'cannot be the policeman of the world'. It was unclear in the 1930s how successfully it could even be the policeman of the empire. There were Greek Cypriot nationalist riots in 1931, Arab violence in Palestine in 1936-9, and pressure from the non-violent Indian National Congress. Yet, there was also a considerable deployment of strength. The air force was used during the Third Afghan War in 1919, against tribesmen in Iraq in 1920, resistance in British Somaliland in 1921, and against Yemen in 1927-34. The most brutal example of British force occurred in India with the Amritsar massacre in 1919. Over 60,000 men were deployed in 1936 to crush a rising under the Faqir of Ipi on the

North-West Frontier of India; two years later, 50,000 men were employed against the Arab rising in Palestine.

Within the empire, economic links improved in the interwar period, although attempts to develop an empire trading bloc, based on a degree of imperial preference that culminated in a conference in Ottawa in 1932, were handicapped by the determination of countries such as Australia to protect their interests from British exports. Nevertheless, regular air services were developed. Empire Day was important, imperial strength was celebrated in the British Empire Exhibition held at Wembley in 1924, and the later exhibition held at Glasgow, and British power was given concrete form in the building of the official quarter in New Delhi, ordered by George V 'for all time as a monument to British art and workmanship', and a major new naval base at Singapore. At Blickling Hall, Philip, 11th Marquess of Lothian, held regular meetings of 'The Round Table', an influential body of idealists that sought a modern future for empire and Commonwealth.

The Government of India Act of 1935 was bitterly opposed by some Conservatives, including Churchill, who saw its moves towards self-government, which had been prefigured in legislation in 1919, as a step towards the abandonment of empire, but it was designed to ensure British retention of the substance of power. The government saw itself as adapting, not abandoning, the empire. The process of adaptation, from empire to Commonwealth, was enshrined in the Statute of Westminster of 1931, under which Britain, Australia, New Zealand, Canada, and South Africa enjoyed an autonomous and equal relationship, and were 'freely associated as members of the British Commonwealth of Nations'. Had there been no war in 1939, it is far from clear that the empire would have collapsed within thirty years.

Thus, Britain's political culture and social solidarity were very important in helping maintain order during the Depression. This was of scant immediate benefit to the poor and unemployed, although they would also have suffered from a breakdown of government and the economy. There was no cultural rejection of authority itself, as there had been in Ireland. The 1918 general election had led there to a decisive victory for the nationalist Sinn Féin party, and the civil war of 1919–21 had led to effective independence for the new Irish Free state which gained control of all the island bar six of the Ulster counties. In contrast, in the British general election of November 1935, held early by Baldwin in order to thwart Labour, the Conservative-dominated National Government won over 53 per cent of all votes. The remainder of the electorate overwhelmingly voted for other democratic parties that were opposed to any violent changes in society. The collapse into crisis that the supporters of the National Government feared throughout the decade did not occur.

This success was the electoral counterpart of the British films, newsreels and (later) television of the period with their optimistic emphasis on social cohesion and patriotism. D.C. Thomson and Mills & Boon, two of the most successful publishers of popular fiction, actively disseminated conservative social and moral standards: sexual energy was contained, while radicalism, social strain and moral questioning were ignored. More pointedly, the Economic League compiled blacklists of Communist militants. By the standards of today, much about Britain and its parliamentary democracy in the 1930s may appear unacceptable. In comparison with the collapse of democracy over much of continental Europe in that period, it was, if not a triumph, at least a modest success.

The Second World War, 1939–45

Twenty-one years after the 'war to end all wars', Britain again found herself involved in conflict. Initially, the British and French governments had hoped that the Nazi dictator, Adolf Hitler, would be tamed by the responsibilities and exigencies of power, or that he would restrict his energies to ruling Germany. There was also a feeling in Britain that the terms imposed on Germany by the Treaty of Versailles in 1919 had been overly harsh, and that it was understandable that Hitler should press for revision. It was anticipated that German revisionism could be accommodated, and that Hitler would be another episode in European power politics, as had been Napoleon III of

France, the mid-nineteenth century reviser of the Congress of Vienna. Furthermore, in both Britain and her leading ally, France, pacifism was strong in the 1930s, and fiscal restraint even stronger. Financial difficulties ensured that rearmament was embarked on with much hesitation.

The British government, especially from 1937 under Neville Chamberlain, thought it both necessary and possible to negotiate with Hitler. He seemed no worse than the Soviet dictator Josef Stalin, and there were hopes of cooperation in some quarters. In September 1938 at Munich, Chamberlain agreed an apparent settlement of the Czech–German crisis. The Czechs were pressured into ceding territory and the agreement was widely welcomed in Britain. Despite opposition led by Churchill, Chamberlain kept the National Government and the Conservative Party behind appeasement, in part because there seemed no acceptable alternative and in part through successful management.

It took time for the government to appreciate that negotiations were not possible and, instead, dangerous. Nevertheless, rearmament gathered pace from 1938. On 15 March 1939, when Hitler seized Bohemia and Moravia, there was a breakdown of confidence in negotiations and, instead, an attempt to create an alliance system capable of intimidating him. The Anglo-French guarantee of Poland on 31 March, however, did not deter Hitler, in large part because differences between Poland and the Soviet Union made it impossible to include the latter in the alliance. Instead, Stalin turned to Hitler, and the latter, believing that Britain and France would not fight, attacked Poland. The British declared war on 3 September, Chamberlain hoping that it would be possible either to force Hitler to negotiate or to encourage his overthrow.

After Poland was rapidly conquered by German and Soviet forces, Britain and France determined to fight on to prevent German hegemony, and this led Hitler to attack in the West in 1940. Denmark and Norway fell rapidly, the Germans using air power to counter the intervention of British amphibious and naval forces in Norway. Then the Western Front was rolled up in a German *blitzkrieg* that overran the Netherlands, Belgium

1. *A Pit Head, c.* 1775–1825, English School. Mining benefited not only from the use of steam engines in pumping and winding but also from a number of innovations including the introduction of explosives, better methods of lining shafts and supporting roofs, and improved underground transport. These changes helped to ensure a move from shallow pits to deep shafts.

2. *A Connoisseur examining a Cooper*, Hannah Humphrey, 1792. George III, fearing a revolution, peers at a portrait of Oliver Cromwell. On 30 January 1793, in the annual Martyrdom Day sermon before the House of Lords that marked the anniversary of the execution of Charles I, the Bishop of St David's urged his congregation to the religious duty of loyalty, and drew attention to the examples of the English and French revolutions.

A CONNOISSEUR examining a COOPER.

3. *The Battle of Trafalgar*, 1805, by Clarkson William Stanfield. British gunnery and seamanship prevailed, but at the cost of 1,690 dead and wounded in the close contact that such engagements entailed. The French and Spaniards lost about 14,000 sailors; many became prisoners, but 7,000 died or were wounded.

4. *The Railway Station*, 1862, by William Powell Frith. As new public spaces where different occupations and classes jostled each other, stations fascinated many painters. Here the Victorian family and the arm of the law are both in evidence.

5. *Right:* The Royal Pavilion, Brighton – royal wealth joined to the image of the Orient.

6. *Below: The Royal Exchange and the Bank of England,* 1852, by Edmund Walker. The City of London was the centre of the world's financial system and of the liberal international economic order.

7. *The Reformers' Attack on the Old Rotten Tree, or the Foul Nests of the Cormorants in Danger.* Peel and Wellington try to prop up the decayed tree, which bears a number of rotten boroughs.

DEATH'S DISPENSARY.
OPEN TO THE POOR, GRATIS, BY PERMISSION OF THE PARISH.

8. *Left:* 'Monmouth Street' by George Cruikshank from Dickens' *Scenes of London Life from 'Sketches by Boz'*. (1836–7) The young Dickens' knowledge and understanding of London, both high and low, served him well in this book. This scene shows the public life of the streets. There was also a harsh side. Gutters were major health hazards. Dickens' writings accorded with the principles he had outlined in the *Daily News*, which he edited in 1846: 'the principles of progress and improvement; of education, civil and religious liberty . . .'.

9. *Right:* 'Death's Dispensary. Open to the Poor, Gratis, by Permission of the Parish', 1860 – a bitter portrayal of the hazards of public water supplies. The jugs also indicate the heavy task of carrying water. The thin, ragged children are shoeless.

10. Nelson's Column and Trafalgar Square, a still dramatic demonstration of the impact of the Napoleonic wars on nineteenth-century consciousness. On 'Bloody Sunday' in 1887 a protest called in Trafalgar Square by the Metropolitan Radical Association against the government's failure to tackle unemployment led to a violent demonstration.

11. Interior of the House of Commons by Joseph Nash – an all-male scene. Black was the dominant colour of male attire.

12. Tower Bridge, a hybrid that at once testified to new mechanical power and to the appeal of traditional architectural motifs. The construction of this new lowest bridging point over the Thames aided the development of south-east London.

13. *The Charge of the Light Brigade*, 25 October 1854. The diseased squalor in the entrenchments outside Sevastopol was less dramatic but even more deadly. The battles of Balaclava and Inkerman arose from Russian attempts to breach the Allied supply links. Allied defensive success ensured that the siege could continue.

14. Printing the *Illustrated London News*. Hoe's American Machine is on the left and Ingram's Rotary Press is on the right. Launched in 1842, this publication dominated the illustrated news market, selling more than 60,000 copies an issue in the first year and nearly 200,000 copies an issue by 1856. This is a specialised instance of the more general move towards illustrations in the press. Its advertisement soliciting subscribers for 1855 emphasised the number of illustrations: 1,000 engravings of the Crimean War alone in 1854.

15. *News Boy*, by Sir William Nicholson (1872–1949), from *London Types* (1898). Despite mechanisation, newspaper production, like other industries, still involved much manual labour. Britain was still very hierarchical, but the structure of society was being affected by the rise of individual and collective merit as a defining characteristic of precedence at the expense of heredity.

16. Box for a motor-car-based board game, *c.* 1910. In 1896 the law that required cars to follow a man carrying a red flag was repealed and the speed limit was set at 14mph. It was raised to 20mph in 1903, but was abolished in 1930. The first full-sized British petrol motor was produced in 1895.

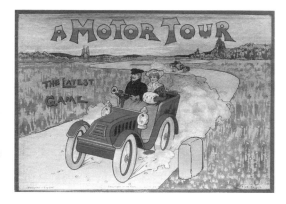

17. Advertisement for Marks & Spencer's Toyland, from the early twentieth century. Children were an important market, and one that could be reached by advertising.

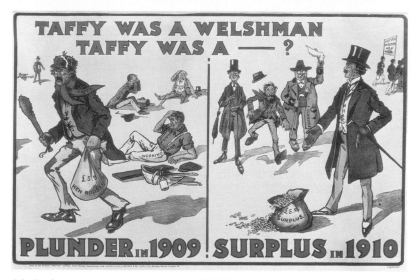

18. Budget Protest League poster of 1910 targeted against David Lloyd George. A populist by background, Lloyd George criticised the privileges of the aristocracy and landowners, but was far less critical of manufacturing wealth. His redistributive budget was designed to maintain free trade and to heal divisions within the Liberal Party at the cost of landlords.

19. Railway poster advertising the Royal National Eisteddfod at Caernarvon, 1906. With a Marine band and a work by Sir Edward Elgar, the Eisteddfod was located within the embrace of the imperial state.

20. London Underground map, *c.* 1910. The network testified to London's spread.

21. British infantrymen walk towards death, 1 July 1916. Justified revulsion at the nature of the fighting and the number of casualties has tended to make many commentators underrate the reasons for Britain's entry into the war – to prevent German domination of Europe – and also British success in defeating Germany in 1918.

22. Volunteer workers at the Labour Committee Room, Sittingbourne, Kent, during the 1918 general election campaign. Labour was no longer subordinated to the Liberals after the 1918 Representation of the People Act enfranchised more of its potential constituency. Labour gained sixty seats in the election and more votes than the Liberals. Rather than the Liberals losing support to Labour, Labour gained much from the new electorate, while the divided Liberals lost more heavily to the Conservatives.

23. County of London Electricity Supply Co. advertisement, *c.* 1935. Electricity was seen as clean and convenient, and as a way to improve the environment. Power, heat and light were increasingly dependent on electricity. The housing boom of the period meant that there were many houses that had to be equipped.

24. London Midland & Scottish Railways poster advertising Blackpool as a holiday destination, *c.* 1937. The prosperity of those in work drove an expansion in leisure in the 1930s. Seaside holidays were in part sold on sex appeal. Earlier in the century Protestant Nonconformists and early socialists had condemned Blackpool and called instead for healthy outdoor pursuits.

25. Manchester was raided by the Luftwaffe on the nights of 22/23 and 23/24 December 1940, the so-called Christmas Blitz. This picture shows burning warehouses behind Piccadilly. Between 7 September 1940 and 16 May 1941, 578 tons of bombs were dropped on Manchester.

26. Kent children being evacuated in August 1944 to protect them from V-weapon assault. Wartime evacuations were the biggest state-directed movement of civilians in British history. At the start of the war 690,000 children were evacuated from London alone. Over 1,000 V-1s landed on Kent.

27. The coronation of Elizabeth II as Queen of the United Kingdom and Commonwealth, 2 June 1953. Eldest daughter of George VI, Elizabeth became queen in 1952. The first televised Christmas broadcast followed in 1957.

28. The first edition of *TV Times*, marking the launch of ITV in 1955. In 1949 the Broadcasting Committee rejected any end to the BBC's monopoly and the introduction of advertising, but the Television Act of 1954 transformed the situation. *I Love Lucy* was an American import.

29. John Lennon, aged fifteen, playing with his skiffle band The Quarry Men at their first gig at Woolton, Liverpool, 15 June 1955. *Left to right:* Eric Griffiths, Rod Davies, John Lennon, Pete Shatton and Len Garry. Requiring only inexpensive instruments, skiffle was a forerunner of rock and roll that suited working-class teenagers.

30. Lord Fiske, Chairman of the Decimal Currency Board, 'decimal shopping' at Woolworth's in the Strand, 15 February 1971, the first day of national decimalisation. Separately, inflation put paid to coins whose purchasing power had fallen: the farthing in 1960 and the halfpenny in 1984.

31. Margaret Thatcher celebrates her 1979 election victory with her husband Denis on the steps of 10 Downing Street. The first woman Prime Minister of Britain, Thatcher had a marked preference for individual choice and market mechanisms as opposed to planning and state pricing.

32. Prime Minister John Major with Foreign Secretary Douglas Hurd, left, and President of the European Commission Jacques Delors at an EC summit in Birmingham, October 1992. The previous month the government's reputation for economic competence had been destroyed by its unsuccessful attempt to remain in the European Monetary System, although the pound's departure was to help ensure fiscal flexibility and economic growth for the rest of the decade.

33. Tony Blair during the 1997 election campaign. Labour won a large majority thanks to abstentions among Conservatives, tactical voting to secure their defeat and a degree of enthusiasm for Blair's policies. A collapse of Conservative support cost the party all its seats in Scotland and Wales. In 2001 Blair easily returned to power due to Conservative unpopularity. However, confidence in Labour's intentions and competence had been badly hit by their years in office. Image became all important under Blair, as the name New Labour suggests, and 'spin doctors' and focus groups assumed centre stage. Taxation rose without any marked improvement in public services.

34. *The Angel of the North* (1988). Situated on a hill south of Gateshead, overlooking the A1(M) and the East Coast railway line, this is seen by over 90,000 people daily, making it the most viewed piece of sculpture in Britain. The product of public patronage, the *Angel* received £791,000 from the Arts Council of England Lottery Fund.

and France, and brutally exposed the military failure of the Anglo-French alliance. The planned German invasion of Britain, Operation Sealion, was called off, however, when German air power was blunted in the Battle of Britain in 1940 by British radar, effective and growing numbers of fighter aeroplanes, able command decisions and high fighting quality.

The British gained allies in 1941 when Germany attacked the Soviet Union and declared war on the United States after her ally, Japan, had launched an assault on both the Americans and Britain. Ultimately, this widening of the war was to be decisive in the defeat of Germany and Japan, but in 1941–2 the Germans hit the Soviet Union hard and in 1942 the Japanese made major inroads into the British Empire. The surrender of Singapore with 130,000 troops shattered British prestige in Asia. The British in Malaya had outnumbered the Japanese, but the latter had the strategic initiative, air superiority and better leadership. The Japanese conquest of Burma followed.

German and Japanese offensives were blunted in late 1942, the British playing a role by pushing back the Germans from Egypt and keeping the Japanese out of India. The Allies moved over to the offensive. French North Africa was successfully invaded by Anglo-American forces in November 1942, Sicily in July 1943, Italy that September, and Normandy in June 1944. The Battle of the Atlantic against German submarines was won in early 1943, when escort carriers and long-range aeroplanes brought a decisive gain in aerial support, and radar came to play a greater role. In Burma the Japanese were outfought on the ground in 1944–5 by better trained forces able to control battles carefully, and benefiting from high unit quality and superior logistics, air power and artillery. American forces fought their way over the western Pacific, driving back the Japanese. In 1945 Anglo-American armies advanced across the Rhine, the Soviets fought their way into Berlin, and the Germans surrendered unconditionally on 8 May. As with the campaigns against Napoleon in 1812–14, Russian strength had played a crucial role, but the Anglo-American achievement had also been considerable, not least because they (particularly the Americans) bore the brunt of the war with Japan, which surrendered on 14

August 1945 after the dropping of two American atom bombs, while the British bore the brunt of the war at sea.

At the close of the war, British authority was restored in territories that had been lost, such as Hong Kong, and the British became an occupying power in parts of Germany and Austria, as well as Libya and Somaliland, former Italian territories. British forces also helped support the reimposition of Dutch and French authority in their Asian territories. Although seen as a modern event, the fighting and consequences of the Second World War were very different to subsequent British experience. In 1944–5, for example, British troops fought alongside Australian, Caribbean, Ceylonese, Egyptian, Indian, Kenyan, West African and New Zealand troops, all under British command, in a great imperial crusade to defeat the Japanese invaders of British-ruled Burma. Today, the circumstances which led to Britons fighting in the jungles of Burma have completely disappeared: Britain has no important links or influence there.

The Second World War underlined British vulnerability. The preservation of national independence had traditionally required a strong fleet, but insistent German aeroplane attacks from 1940, and, with the coming of the V–1, missiles revealed that command of the sea could no longer protect Britain from bombardment, even if it could still thwart or inhibit invasion. Although the Germans did not develop a long-distance heavy bomber force, their bombers could attack from bases in North-Western Europe, while the V–2 rockets, which could travel at up to 3,000mph, could be fired from a considerable distance. The Germans also bombarded Dover with long-range guns from the other side of the Channel. The defensive perimeter of the country was thus extended.

British industrial production was not badly damaged by aerial attack. The population was less hit than had been feared before the war, when large numbers of cardboard coffins had been prepared and there was widespread preparation for airborne gas attacks that were never mounted. London, however, suffered very heavily from air and missile attack, with 29,890 Londoners killed and 50,507 injured. Across the country as a whole, over

60,000 civilians were killed. Indiscriminate bombing, intended to destroy civilian morale, failed in its purpose although there is some evidence that spirits were lower than has been popularly thought. In Southampton, there was evidence of low morale and of a mayor and civic leaders who slept outside the town to avoid bombing, while ordinary citizens could only seek the same safety by sleeping on the common in summer. After a government report, the mayor resigned in disgrace.

There was no panic in heavily bombed London, but, aside from the immediate chaos and confusion, much of the city was devastated. This devastation and that in other heavily bombed cities, such as Coventry, Exeter, Liverpool, Plymouth and Southampton, was one of the most important long-term consequences of the bombing. The damage to the built environment was accentuated by postwar reconstruction, much of which was poor quality, although allowance has to be made for the cost of reconstruction, the massive need for new housing, and the extent of other burdens on the national finances.

Aside from the direct impact of war, there was also much disruption. For example, many houses now held by the National Trust were requisitioned. The park at Attingham Park was used for Atcham Airfield, the house first as a school for evacuees from Birmingham and then for purposes linked to the airfield. Blickling Hall was used as an RAF mess, Farnborough Hall, Warwickshire, as a military hospital, Castle Drogo as a refuge for babies made homeless by the Blitz. Penrhyn Castle was used in 1939–40 to store some of the National Gallery's evacuated paintings. It was one of the few buildings in Wales with doors large enough to admit the largest of the canvases, Van Dyck's equestrian portrait of Charles I. After the collection was moved in 1940 to underground storage in a slate mine the castle served as the headquarters of the Daimler motor company until 1945. Wartime occupation led to some damage, including a serious fire at Melford Hall, Suffolk. Blickling Hall was vandalised during its wartime occupation, as was the fictional Brideshead in Evelyn Waugh's novel *Brideshead Revisited* (1945): 'We laid the road through the trees joining it up with the main drive; unsightly but very practical; awful lot of transport comes in and out; cuts the place up, too. Look where one careless devil went smack through the box-hedge and carried away all that balustrade.'

War boosted the role of the state and the machinery of government. It was necessary to produce formidable amounts of equipment, to raise, train, clothe and equip large numbers of men, to fill their places in the workforce, and to increase the scale and flexibility of the economy. Despite war damage, production of aircraft rose from 7,940 in 1939 to 26,461 in 1944. Free trade and hitherto largely unregulated industrial production were both brought under direction. The manufacture of consumer goods was successfully cut in order to free labour and other resources for wartime goals. Conscription was introduced more rapidly than in the First World War. The experience of state intervention then ensured that it was more effective in the Second.

Conscription of men began in 1939 and of women in 1942. The size of the armed forces rose to 4.7 million men and 437,000 women by 1945. Many others joined the Home Guard and other voluntary organisations; many young women served in the Land Army. Food rationing began in January 1940, and the Ministry of Food encouraged consumption patterns and recipes that would make the best use of scarce foodstuffs; whale meat was one recommended dish. Clothes rationing followed in 1941. Government regulation became ubiquitous and the Men from the Ministry a term used to explain much. New ministries were created in 1939 for economic warfare, food, home security, information, shipping and supply. Later additions included aircraft production, fuel and power, and production. National wage negotiating machinery was established in the coal industry, and a National Coal Board was created to supervise production, but these measures did not prevent a serious miners' strike in early 1944. Of the days lost to strikes in the war, 55.7 per cent occurred in the coal industry. Government-directed import reduction policies helped lessen the impact of German submarines. The amount of land under cultivation was extended in a Dig for Victory, or at least for potatoes, campaign.

Public politics was largely suspended when a National Government under Churchill was formed in May 1940 after defeat in Norway. The need to bring Labour into the ministry and the unwillingness of the Labour leadership to serve under Chamberlain led to the change of government. There was no general election until after the war with Germany ended in 1945 (the last had been held in 1935). The Churchill government greatly expanded the hitherto limited mobilisation of national resources and state direction of the economy. This was necessary because war savaged the economy. Export markets were lost, and financial stability was hit by massive expenditure. Britain lost about 25 per cent of its national wealth during the war and its dependence upon wartime loans (mainly from the USA) made it the world's greatest debtor nation in 1945.

The war also transformed the state's relationship with society. Everything was brought under the scrutiny of government. For example, food rationing remoulded the nation's diet in accordance with nutritional science; while the hospital sector was reorganised under the Emergency Medical Service, creating, among much else, a national pathology service.

The conflict affected all sections of society. In response to the threat of bombing, there were mass evacuations of children from the major cities, 690,000 alone from London. This was the biggest state-directed move of civilians in British history, and the cause of much disruption. State control over the means of propaganda ensured that greater public access to news, through mass literacy and the ownership of radios, helped create national views largely in accordance with the intentions of the government. The BBC played a major role in supporting the war effort, not least by successfully reaching outside the middle class and encouraging a sense of common purpose. Cinema newsreels were also important in sustaining patriotism; their makers were close to the Conservative Party. As in the First World War, the press was far less critical of the government and the conduct of the war than had been the case during the French Revolutionary and Napoleonic Wars, although the left-wing *Daily Mirror* was threatened with a ban in 1942.

The war encouraged much important artistic work, ranging from the paintings of bombed townscapes, such as Somerset Place, Bath, by John Piper, to a series of classic films, notably

Brief Encounter (1945), *In Which We Serve* (1942), *Henry V* (1943) and *This Happy Breed* (1944).

The war years were very important for what came after. They closed on 26 July 1945 with an election that removed the Conservatives under the war-leader Churchill and gave Labour an increase of 10 per cent on its pre-war share of the vote and, with 393 seats (210 Conservatives, 37 others), its first clear parliamentary majority. This reflected the association of the Conservatives with interwar social and economic problems, particularly mass unemployment, but also political, social and cultural shifts during the conflict.

Socialism increasingly seemed normative. Taxation on companies, products and individuals rose during the war. Most people were brought under the demands of income tax as a consequence of the PAYE (Pay As You Earn) Scheme introduced in 1943. Belief in the necessity and value of planning rose, the cost of living was subsidised, and attitudes towards what was quintessentially British changed. The Labour Party's role in the wartime Coalition government was important to its revived standing, while trade union membership rose by 50 per cent during the war. A language of inclusiveness and sharing, and a stress on the 'home front', made social distinctions seem unacceptable. Rationing rested on a theory of equality. Thanks in part to these attitudes and to the image and prestige of the Soviet ally, Communist membership rose to 56,000 in December 1942. Labour, however, was the main political beneficiary of the war.

The war had also brought major social changes. The working population rose by about 3 million as unemployment fell and women in particular were recruited into the labour market. The number of women in the workforce rose by nearly a half, although this was not sustained after the war. The increase in purchasing power led to a greater consumption of 'leisure', especially cinema, dance halls, and theatre. There was also a relaxation of moral norms: the illegitimacy rate rose.

Although the extent to which the classes mingled during the war, for example in work and air-raid shelters, should not be exaggerated, mingling was stressed as a desirable goal and was more extensive than before the conflict. Wartime aspirations and concern about pre-war conditions were focused by the officially commissioned Beveridge Report of December 1942 that called for the use of social insurance to abolish poverty, and pressed the case for child allowances, a national health service and the end to mass unemployment. This formula for reconstruction encouraged the sense that the war had to lead to change and that it was Labour, rather than the Conservatives, who offered the best chance of change. Yet it would be wrong to assume that the people had a clear idea of what they wanted in 1945. Like other electorates fed up with a government, all they knew for sure was that they did not want the Conservatives.

SIX

FROM EMPIRE TO EUROPE, 1945–73

> . . . all that remains
> For us will be concrete and tyres.
>
> *Going, Going,* Philip Larkin (1972)

Britain in 1945 was an imperial power that had just emerged victorious from a great struggle. Less than thirty years later, the empire was gone, and Britain joined the European Economic Community, a supranational body that entailed a loss of national sovereignty. The extent of this change can be underlined by noting the degree to which the loss of empire and sovereignty did not lead to sustained popular opposition. British society appeared no longer interested in the values of earlier generations. This was part of a more widespread rejection of the past that gathered pace from the early 1960s and was an important aspect of the transformations of the era.

The changes of the 1960s are readily apparent. Different gender and youth expectations and roles command attention, and there has been a focus on sexual liberalism, abortion, the decriminalisation of homosexuality, and drug culture.

Compared to these, measures introduced in the 1940s, such as the nationalisation of the railways, or even the establishment of the National Health Service, do not appear so indicative of a sea-change in society. This is especially so if the 1950s are considered because these years were a period of conservatism and stability, even reaction, particularly, but not only, because of the long-lasting Conservative government of 1951–64. Yet it would be inappropriate to underrate the impact of the legislation passed by Clement Attlee's Labour government in 1945–51, just as it would be unwise to neglect winds of change during the Conservative ascendancy.

In 1945 there was a widespread expectation of and desire for change. As elsewhere in this book, the focus here is not on the world of politics, but the policies of the Attlee government were important. Elected with 393 MPs, Attlee benefited from a position of unprecedented strength for a Labour government. In 1929 Ramsay MacDonald had only had 288 Labour MPs to rely on.

Change certainly came. The granting of independence to the Indian subcontinent, which became the separate states of India, Pakistan, Ceylon (Sri Lanka) and Burma in 1947-8, and the end of the British Mandate in Palestine in 1948, making possible the creation of the state of Israel, were not intended to mark the end of empire. Indeed, the Labour government was committed to the development of the African territories, sent troops to maintain the British position in the economically crucial colony of Malaya in the face of a Communist insurrection (a commitment seen through to a successful close by the Conservative government), and sought to play a major role in the Middle East. Nevertheless, India had been the most populous and important part of the empire and the area that most engaged the imaginative attention of the British. Once India became independent, it was difficult to summon up much popular interest in the retention of the remainder of the empire.

If the granting of independence to India greatly altered Britain's relationship with the rest of the world, the national-isation policies of the Attlee government transformed the nature of the economy. Regional autonomies and variations, and corporate identities were eroded as the Bank of England (1946), coal (1947), railways (1948), road transport (1948), electricity supply (1948), gas (1949), and iron and steel (1951) were nationalised. This reflected the parliamentary strength of Labour and the nature of a heavily regulated economy in which state ownership could be extended easily by exchanging shares for government stock. All these moves brought more of the economy, including about 2 million workers, under direct government influence and consolidated the trend towards national control, planning, products, conditions, pricing, and wage settlements. The new British Railways employed 681,000 people in 1948. Uniformity followed. Railway nationalisation led to the gradual standardisation of carriages with the introduction of the all-steel British Railways Mark 1 in 1951. The printing of tickets was concentrated on one site.

The demobilisation of the centrally directed wartime economy was limited by state ownership, the continuation of high rates of taxation, and the crucial role of the state both in allocating raw materials until 1948 and in fixing the sterling exchange rate. Rationing continued for many goods, and was extended to include bread (1946) and potatoes (1947). Food rationing only ended in 1954, that of coal in 1958. Labour sought to use planning to ensure full employment and growth, and thus to achieve social welfare and demonstrate the value of state control. The Welfare State was seen as an aspect of the continued extension of state control over society and economy. Labour thinkers in the 1930s, such as Douglas Jay, had elaborated ideas of corporatist socialism that were now implemented. Planning reflected the collectivist tendencies of much of British society, not simply the Labour Party, and this collectivism was celebrated in the Festival of Britain in 1951. The centralised planning of the period was a response to the particular circumstances of the late 1940s; but it was to be less than successful in creating a high level of economic growth.

Self-help had gone along with the *laissez-faire* state. The comprehensive social security benefits introduced in 1948 were paid out by a National Assistance Board that was funded by taxation, not the rates. The foundation of the National Health Service (NHS) in 1948 marked another major nationalisation. The inherited variety of hospitals was brought under state control which was wielded through the Ministry of Health and new regional hospital boards. An attempted boycott by the leadership of the British Medical Association was thwarted by the Minister, Aneurin Bevan, and the General Practitioner (GP) service was organised on the basis of a capitation fee paid by the government on behalf of every patient registered with a doctor. The NHS brought many benefits, especially to working class women who had been particularly poorly served by pre-war health care. It was central to a more general attempt to ameliorate living standards. Regulation played a major role. For example, compulsory pasteurisation of milk was introduced in 1949 in the face of opposition from the agricultural lobby.

The NHS was, however, to prove far more expensive than anticipated and, in combination with the costs of anti-Soviet rearmament during the Korean War (1950–3), helped lead to the financial and political crisis of 1951. The immediate crisis was short term – charges were imposed on false teeth and spectacles, and Bevan resigned – but the long-term problem of popular expectations within a nationalised service that placed a heavy burden on the country's budget had been created.

Defence was another serious burden. The Cold War was well and truly launched by 1949, the year in which the North Atlantic Treaty Organisation (NATO) was founded. Already, on his way to the Teheran Conference at the end of 1943, Churchill had told Harold Macmillan, 'Germany is finished, though it may take some time to clean up the mess. The real problem now is Russia.' In the face of Soviet expansion, Labour was forced to take the same view after it came to office. Britain became a founder member of NATO and was also prepared to resist the spread of Communism in Malaya.

The Conservatives, who took power in late 1951 and retained office until 1964 under Churchill (1951–5), Anthony Eden (1955–7), Harold Macmillan (1957–63) and Alec Douglas-Home (1963–4), continued the Welfare State and, indeed, much of Labour policy. Only iron and steel and road haulage were returned to the private sector. A continuity of economic policy between the Labour Chancellor of the Exchequer, Hugh Gaitskell, and his Conservative replacement, Rab Butler, including a fixed exchange rate for sterling, Keynesian demand management (economic management by the state in order to tackle unemployment), and a commitment to 'full' employment, led to the phrase 'Butskellism'. There was also continuity in foreign and imperial policy. Both Labour and the Conservatives hoped that decolonisation would still leave Britain with much power, especially if former overseas possessions could be limited to self-government with Britain controlling defence and foreign policy.

National Uniformity

Within Britain, government policies, such as national public house-building programmes, helped drive the pace towards national uniformity. Other factors tending in the same direction included the economy, not least company mergers. This was true not only of products such as cars, but also of others, such as beer, that had provided a degree of local identity. Local breweries were taken over. Thus, in Portsmouth all the breweries became incorporated into Whitbreads, which, in turn, ceased brewing in the city in 1983. Local and regional newspapers and cinemas became part of national chains, and banks merged. This was not a new process – newspaper takeovers had been happening for a long time, for example, *Shields Daily News* by the Westminster Press in 1934 – but it accelerated. In 1969, Barclays and Martins, both banks that were the product of numerous amalgamations and takeovers, merged. Martins was the last national English bank to have its headquarters outside London, but, with the merger, Liverpool lost this status. More generally, nationalism and centralisation weakened the power of established regional interests and elites, not least within the Conservative Party.

The role of national marketing in the production and sale of consumer durables was an aspect of the drive for national uniformity. These goods became standard. Purchase tax on consumer durables was cut from 66.6 per cent to 50 per cent in 1953, as the Conservatives sought to replace Labour austerity with affluence, a policy that helped account for their marked lead over Labour among women voters. In 1958 25 per cent of households in the United Kingdom owned a washing machine, 50 per cent in 1964; for cars ownership reached 25 per cent in 1956 and 50 per cent in 1965, and for fridges 25 per cent in 1962 and 50 per cent in 1968. Working-class homes and lives changed accordingly. Thanks to the state provision of free or subsidised health care, education, council housing, pensions and unemployment pay, rising real incomes fed through into consumption. The increase in the sale of consumer durables helped fuel economic growth in the 1950s, especially in

1951– 5. Much of the new demand was met by a rise in domestic production, rather than by imports.

Inflation, pressure on the pound, a rise in interest rates and the Suez Crisis, however, caused contraction in late 1955 and in 1956, but, in what was termed the 'Stop–Go' cycle, growth resumed in 1957. Weak industrial productivity, inflation and an overvalued currency all remained serious problems, but unemployment was far lower than in the interwar period and growth was higher. Prosperity and Labour disunity helped the Conservatives win the elections of 1955 and 1959. After three consecutive, and successively larger, defeats in the 1950s, it looked as if Labour would never win again.

Continued problems in traditional industries ensured that unemployment was higher in areas that had been the heartbeat of the nation's economy in the nineteenth century. This was the case, not only with mining, but also with the Lancashire cotton industry. The Cotton Industry Reorganisation Act of 1959 offered compensation for the removal of now-excess capacity, and in 1959–60 about 300 mills closed and half the industry's spindles and 40 per cent of looms were laid aside. This was a major change for the economy of Lancashire as a whole and, in particular, for many of its towns.

The Age of the Automobile

The cult of the car was a classic instance of a countrywide trend. The economics of production demanded the national sale of individual models. They were marketed using countrywide advertising and pricing strategies. Car ownership fell during the Second World War, but then its rise accelerated rapidly, especially after petrol rationing ceased in 1953. In terms of thousand million passenger-kilometres, private road transport shot up from 76 in 1954 to 350 in 1974. This increase from 39 to 77 per cent of the total passenger-distance travelled in Britain, was achieved at the expense of bus, coach and rail transport. The percentage of goods traffic moved by road rose from 37 in 1952 to 58.3 in 1964, and represented a serious loss in rail business.

Cultural Developments, 1945–60

Although many commentators pretended otherwise at the time, there was life before 1964. Nevertheless, it was true that the 1960s destroyed a cultural continuity that had lasted from the Victorian period. This destruction reflected the impact of social and ideological trends, including the rise of new forms and a new agenda moulded by shifts in the understanding of gender, youth, class, place and race.

Yet to understand the earlier situation, it is important to grasp that it was neither monolithic nor static. The Second World War had provided the occasion, if not the cause, for a shift to a new seriousness on the part of many artists and their audience. George Orwell's bleak political satires, *Animal Farm* (1945) and *Nineteen Eighty-Four* (1949) made a considerable impact. Carol Reed's film *The Third Man* (1949) was set not in the future but in a corrupt and devastated present where occupied Vienna could serve to suggest similarities with austere Britain. The screenplay was by Graham Greene (1904–95). The previous year, in *The Heart of the Matter* (1948), Greene had tackled the failure to maintain moral standards in the face of a pitiless world. *Brideshead Revisited* (1945), by another Catholic convert, Evelyn Waugh (1902–66), also dealt with faith assailed and the search for some sign of divine purpose.

The music of Ralph Vaughan Williams and Sir Edward Elgar was rejected by young composers, especially Benjamin Britten and Michael Tippett. Britten's operas, the most important British ones of the century, notably *Peter Grimes* (1945), *Billy Budd* (1951) and *The Turn of the Screw* (1954), were disturbing works. The Ealing (film) comedies of the late 1940s and early 1950s, such as *Passport to Pimlico* (1949), *Kind Hearts and Coronets* (1949) and *The Lavender Hill Mob* (1951), were far less bleak, but their satire could not conceal a sense that the world was rarely benign. On radio, Britain was challenged by sinister schemes that had to be thwarted by *Dick Barton, Special Agent* (1946–51), and the character also starred in three British films (1948–50). The Boulting Brothers made *High Treason* (1951), the nearest British equivalent of the Hollywood 'red scare' films, about Communists trying to sabotage power stations.

In the visual arts of the period avant- garde ideas competed with a more conventional mainstream. The latter prevailed at the 1951 Festival of Britain. Alongside the idea that the festival was a show of the future, the dominant artistic mood was neo-Romantic. Only one abstract work was selected for display in connection with the event and that work caused a public controversy. The Director of the Tate in the 1950s, John Rothenstein, was criticised for his lack of enthusiasm about Cubism. In Scotland, the Edinburgh painters, particularly W.G. Gillies (1898–1973), William McTaggart (1903–81), Anne Redpath (1895–1965) and John Maxwell (1905–62), did not engage with theory. Far from trying to be avant-garde, they emphasised expressiveness and the use of colour in a conventional manner to produce decorative works. In contrast, other artists such as the sculptor Barbara Hepworth (1903–75) were experimenting with abstract forms. New American Painting, a big exhibition of large abstract works held in 1958, had a major impact. Looking at art and design from a different perspective, there was a shift in fine and decorative arts, graphics and industrial design from the austerity and functionalism that had characterised the late 1940s to a more affluent tone, as shown, for example, in the Coventry Cathedral exhibition of 1962.

Architecture was now dominated by Modernism. The progressive style of the 1930s became an orthodoxy that was used for the widespread postwar rebuilding, for urban development, and for the new construction made possible by the investment in hospitals, schools and new towns. A centrepiece was the first major postwar public building, the Royal Festival Hall (1951), designed for the Festival of Britain's South Bank Exhibition, by Robert Matthew, the Chief Architect to the London County Council. The Modern movement in architecture was visibly important in the transformation of British cities from the 1960s, although less so in domestic architecture.

The novelists of the 1940s had been concerned, at times despairing, but not angry. The late 1950s, in contrast, were to be the stage for the 'Angry Young Men', a group of writers who felt very much at odds with their Britain. Their problems were not those of faith in a hostile world (Greene, Waugh) or the pressure of totalitarianism (Orwell), but, rather, a sense that the postwar reforms of the Labour government and 1950s affluence had produced a vulgar materialist society that was disagreeable in itself and frustrating to them as individuals. They were impatient alike with the values of ITV and with traditionalism. In contrast to the liberal worthiness of C.P. Snow's Lewis Eliot, the protagonist of his sequence *Strangers and Brothers* (1940–70), came Charles Lumley in John Wain's novel *Hurry On Down* (1953), a graduate who flees self-advancement and becomes a window-cleaner, and Jim Dixon, the hapless protagonist in Kingsley Amis' *Lucky Jim* (1954). The latter novel also struck at the 'phoniness' of social mores in the period. Social values were lacerated in John Osborne's play *Look Back in Anger* (1956), John Braine's novel *Room at the Top* (1957), Alan Sillitoe's novel *Saturday Night and Sunday Morning* (1958), and David Storey's novel *This Sporting Life* (1960). Sillitoe's account of working-class life in his native Nottingham was an example of the 'grim up North' school that became popular in the 1950s.

More generally, this extended to a stronger interest in the 'North'. This had a number of manifestations in the early 1960s. Northern accents became fashionable; northerners, such as the dramatist Alan Bennett, 'made it' on the national stage; and northern males were said to benefit from the alleged southern preference for a bit of 'rough'. The films of Marlon Brando had revealed the limitations of the southern matinée idol. Northern men (and Welsh men, such as Richard Burton) addressed this lack; although some of the most famous 'northern' figures in the films of the period were not northern at all.

The works of the 'Angry Young Men' were a long way from the successful staples of the West End stage, the lending libraries, and the standard bookshops. In the West End, audiences flocked to see plays by Noel Coward – old, such as *Private Lives* (1930), and new, for example *Look After Lulu* (1959), alike – as well as plays by Terence Rattigan *(The Winslow Boy,* 1946) and William Douglas-Home *(The Chiltern Hundreds,* 1947, *The Manor of Northstead,* 1954). The audiences were also very large for the short stories Agatha Christie adapted for the stage: *The Mousetrap* (1952) and *Witness for the Prosecution* (1953).

The 'Angry Young Men' were not the only voices in print. There was fresh energy in Scottish and Irish writing, while in England, studies of middle age by Angus Wilson (1913–91) – *Hemlock and After* (1952), *Anglo-Saxon Attitudes* (1956), and *The Middle Age of Mrs Eliot* (1958) – enjoyed solid sales. Libraries continued to buy and lend large quantities of Christie and other secure genre writers. American popular novelists also made a greater impact than hitherto. At the cinema, Hammer's *The Curse of Frankenstein* (1957) began a series of successful horror films that made the reputation of their leading actors, Peter Cushing and Christopher Lee.

Despite the replacement of steam by diesel and electric under the 1955 Modernisation Plan, the railways lost money from the late 1950s, and *The Reshaping of British Railways* – the Beeching Report – of 1963 led to dramatic cuts in the network. The report noted 'one half of the total route mileage carries about 4 per cent of the total passenger miles . . . [and] some 5 per cent of the total freight ton miles . . . Road competition has forced down rates on good railway traffics to the point where they are quite incapable of subsidising the very costly provision of services to handle poor rail traffics.' Freight and passenger services were slashed, the workforce cut, lines taken up, and many stations became unmanned halts or were converted to other uses. Former junctions, such as Okehampton, lost all passenger services. The Beeching Report began a period of sustained construction. Railway works at major sites, such as Darlington and Swindon (1986), closed. The last pick-up of mail by a moving train was made in 1971; thereafter, mail was only brought to rail stations by road.

Rising car use led to a fall in bus services that, in turn, encouraged a further shift to cars. The number of thousand million passenger-miles by bus or coach fell from 50.3 in 1952 to 32.9 in 1976 and 25.5 in 1990. The comparable figures for rail were 24.2, 20.5 and 25.5, and by car, taxi and motorcycle the totals rose from 33.6 to 215.0 and 352.9.

The map of national and, even more, local transport routes altered radically. Assumptions about space, linkages and mobility changed, as did the experience of travel. The shift to personal road usage encouraged dispersed patterns of settlement, shopping and leisure. It also had a heavy impact on the environment, for cars and their infrastructure took up much space. The effect was both urban and rural. The national heritage was also affected, as shown by the impact on National Trust properties. The M1 speeds past Hardwick Hall, the M54 past Moseley Old Hall. The six-lane Plympton by-pass was cut through the park at Saltram in 1970, largely obliterating the eighteenth-century carriage drive. The M4 was driven through the Osterley estate in 1965, the M5 through the Killerton estate. More humble buildings have also been affected. Bredon Barn near Tewkesbury is in the noise shadow of the M5.

In towns, car parks and ring roads were constructed, frequently, as with Southampton's car parks, on the site of bomb damage. In *Anna, Where Are You?* (1953), Patricia Wentworth, like any good detective novelist, captured a sense of the changing urban fabric in even the quieter country towns:

> Ledlington has a good many points in common with other county towns. Some of it is old and picturesque, and some of it is not. In the years between the two world wars its approaches have been cluttered up with small houses of every type and shape. When these have been passed there are the tall, ugly houses of the late Victorian period with their basements, their attics, their dismal outlook upon the shrubberies which screen them from the road. Still farther on a beautiful Georgian house or two, or older still, the mellow red brick and hooded porch of Queen Anne's time – comfortable houses in their day, converted now for the most part to offices and flats. Here the road narrows to the High Street, winding among houses which were built in Elizabethan days. New fronts have been added to some, incongruous plate-glass windows front the street. A turning on one side, very competently blocked by the quite hideous monument erected under William IV [1830–7] to a former mayor, leads to the station. Nothing more inconvenient could possibly have been devised, but the answer of course is that nobody devised it. Like nearly anything else in England it just happened that way. Every few years some iconoclast on the council proposes that the monument should be removed, but nothing is ever done about it.

The fictional Ledlington also had a 'new by-pass'.

Wolverhampton's ring road was opened in stages between 1961 and 1986, clearing away established landmarks and residential districts. Carlisle's, opened in 1974, cut the castle off from the city, and was followed by the replacement of a long-established area by a shopping centre. Pressure for by-passes grew and the towns that gained them, for example Honiton in 1966, became more attractive places to live. Town and country planners struggled to contain car-driven urban growth, imposing development plans to constrain the urban environment.

Increased use of the car and the construction of more roads interacted. Trunk routes with dual carriageways were constructed, and a motorway system was created, beginning with the M6 Preston by-pass, opened in December 1958. The M1 from Watford to Birmingham was punched through the Midlands in 1959, the straight motorway making scant effort to follow the shape of the landscape or the established land-use patterns. As road usage grew, it became necessary to supplement existing routes. However, improvements to the rail system, such as the electrification of the West Coast Main Line from London, via Birmingham and Crewe, to Liverpool, Manchester and Glasgow, between 1959 and 1974 did not significantly increase rail use. By 1970, there were 12.2 million cars in Britain; the following year, car ownership rose to 224 per 1,000 people.

Greater personal mobility for the bulk of the population, but by no means all, encouraged a series of social trends. A major one was an increase in commuting, the separation of work and home. This was not restricted to the middle class. Only 42 per cent of those who worked in Newcastle in 1971 lived in the city. Most of the rest commuted by car. The rise of the supermarket in the 1950s owed much to the car; and, like the introduction of motorways, was an aspect of the Americanisation of life.

Consumer pressures, such as television advertisements, reached most of the population, but their ability to respond varied greatly. The division of the people into communities defined by differing levels of wealth, expectations and opportunity was scarcely novel, but became more pronounced. A lack of mobility was an obvious aspect of the 'underclass', but, more generally, irrespective of their access to cars, spatial segregation affected all of the population. This was related to the distribution of housing types, and the role they played in creating and sustaining neighbourhoods. In terms of their influence on quality of life, these housing differences took precedence over government attempts to create equality. Thus, despite largely free care at the point of service through the National Health Service, health indicators varied greatly, and the same was true of educational standards. Comprehensive education – the abandonment, particularly from 1965, of streaming of children by ability into different schools after eleven (twelve in Scotland) – did not introduce the planned equality of opportunity, for comprehensive schools varied greatly, often reflecting the social nature of their catchment area. Furthermore, the long-term results were unsatisfactory. According to the Moser Report of 1999, 23 per cent of the British population was 'functionally illiterate', while employers also faced problems from severe skill shortages.

Concern about the environment was fashionable in the 1960s, but, like much else in that decade, was not completely new, although it was expressed with a new intensity and in novel fashions. People as well as the environment had to be protected. Clean air was already a major issue in the 1950s, in part because of serious smogs, such as that in London in December 1952 which led to about 4,000 premature deaths. The nightmarish quality of a smog was captured in Patricia Wentworth's *Ladies' Bane* (1954):

It was rather like a slow motion picture. That was the fog of course. Nothing could really move in a fog like this. The buses would be stopped – and the cars – and the people who were abroad would crawl like beetles and wish to be at home again – and the watches and clocks would all slow down and time too.

A Clean Air Act was passed in 1956, followed by another in 1968. Most of London was designated a 'smokeless zone', and the same procedure was applied to other cities. The declining use of coal helped greatly. The Railway Modernisation Plan of 1955 noted 'many factors combine to indicate that the end of the steam era is at hand . . . the insistent demand for a reduction in air pollution by locomotives and for greater cleanliness in trains and railway stations'. Central heating replaced coal fires in many homes, electrical machinery became more important, and from the 1960s gas supplies came from the natural gas fields in the North Sea and no longer from coal. The conversion of gas production and units to natural gas was one of the many examples of nation-wide shifts in the period.

The legacy of industrialisation fatally struck home on 21 October 1966 when 111 children and 33 adults were buried beneath an unstable spoil heap at Aberfan in South Wales: the National Coal Board had failed to take care of such tips. This disaster helped encourage the rehabilitation of industrial and mining landscapes.

Anxiety about the destruction of past townscapes led to the foundation of the Victorian Society in 1958. Nevertheless, much more was torn down in the 1960s. The Doric Arch, Great Hall and Shareholders' Room were needlessly destroyed when Euston station was rebuilt. A sinister combination of developers, planners, and city councils convinced that the past should be discarded, embarked on widespread devastation and trashy rebuilding in cities such as Exeter, Leeds, Manchester and Newcastle. Losses in Manchester included the Milne Building and Cavendish Street Independent Chapel, while in Newcastle most of Eldon Square made way for a shopping centre. The Town and Country Planning Act of 1969 was less valuable in offering protection than the economic downturn that followed the massive 1973 oil price hike.

Environmental concern focused an awareness of the damage that development could produce and an uncertainty about the desirable rate of change, but its potential impact on personal lifestyles and social patterns was limited by the stronger currents of hedonism and materialism.

Concern about nuclear power and the Cold War was another movement that dated from the 1950s, not the 1960s. The Campaign for Nuclear Disarmament was launched on 17 February 1958 to press for the abandonment of nuclear weapons and a cut in defence expenditure. It achieved wide, but temporary, popularity in 1958–64 and, in response to the deployment of cruise missiles, again in the early 1980s.

Television

Television, a major feature of 1960s culture, had expanded greatly in the 1950s, hitting cinema and bingo attendance. The coronation of Elizabeth II in 1953 led many households to acquire a television for the first time. Shown live, it was probably watched by over half the adult population, and was the first time more people saw a major event than listened to it on the radio. 1953 also saw the first party political broadcast. The first royal Christmas television broadcast followed in 1957.

The launching on 22 September 1955 of ITV, a commercial channel with private programme-making companies financed by the advertisements, introduced choice and a competition that encouraged change in the BBC. That year the Post Office permitted an increase in weekly television broadcasting time from forty-one to fifty hours, with evening viewing extended to 11 p.m. The percentage of the population with regular access to a set rose from 38 in 1955 to 75 in 1959, a massive change that made television central to social life and helped lead to discussion about such problems as children watching 'the box' rather than doing their homework.

The absence of daytime and post-11 p.m. broadcasts was in part indicative of more general social attitudes towards leisure. In many respects, television helped to support class divisions. This was true both of what was depicted and of the essential divide between a BBC that catered for the middle class and an ITV for the working class. Yet, in other ways, television was a great unifier. If everyone had the same choice of channels, then, in terms of viewing habits, people became more equal. This was accentuated as certain programmes became firm favourites. The truly national appeal of such programmes as *Coronation Street* and *The Morecambe and Wise Show* confirmed that television was a medium that could transcend class barriers.

The language used on television and the images depicted became more contentious as viewing became more part of most people's day. The nation's stock of collective images, terms and memories also expanded. 'Exterminate' delivered in a metallic tone testified to the cult status of *Dr Who*, a children's series that began in 1963. The Doctor, a modern and very human white knight, travelled through time in a police telephone box and contrasted greatly with American imports such as Batman and Superman. *Six-Five Special, Oh Boy!, Juke Box Jury* and, even more, *Top of the Pops* broadcast the rise of pop music. Television popularised the satire boom of the early 1960s that helped to make the Toryism of Macmillan and Home seem dated. In contrast, the Labour leader Harold Wilson recognised the visual potential of television and used it to great effect. Even individual programmes could make a great impact. Ken Loach's powerful and bleak television film *Cathy Come Home* of 1966 led to the foundation of the charity Shelter. Colour television followed in 1968, and in 1969 television carried pictures beamed live from the Moon. Colour had many effects, some surprising, such as the popularisation of snooker.

The television was a consumer product that advertised itself. It was a powerful example of the role of design in many aspects of national life. This could also be seen in the combination of new technology and advertising in new forms of packaging, such as plastic bottles in the 1950s and polythene carrier bags in the 1960s.

The 1960s

Another aspect of the 1960s that was prefigured in the 1950s was pop art, and, more generally, a determined assault on conventional understandings of artistic content, meaning and production. *Just what makes today's homes so different, so appealing?*, a satirical collage by the influential pop art exponent, Richard Hamilton, appeared in 1959. Pop art of the 1960s included Peter Blake's collage for the album cover of The Beatles' *Sgt Pepper's Lonely Hearts Club Band* (1967), as well as The Beatles' animated film *Yellow Submarine* (1968). 'Different' art had entered the mainstream and public consciousness. This was not only the case with the visual arts. In 1966, Tom Stoppard's play *Rosencrantz and Guildenstern are Dead* wittily and successfully reinterpreted *Hamlet*, one of the greatest Shakespearian classics. Stoppard followed up

Council Houses and Pop Music:
Liverpool and the Beatles

The National Trust is generally associated with stately homes. Number 20 Forthlin Road is thus an eye-opener that reflects the Trust's wider care for the national heritage. An ordinary postwar council house, number 20 was the boyhood home of Paul McCartney who, as one of The Beatles, transformed popular music and youth culture in Britain and the world.

The state and ownership of housing had been a contentious issue since the nineteenth century. Following the 1915 Rent and Mortgage Interest Restrictions (War) Act, which owed something to the Clydeside rent strikes of that year, private landlordship became less profitable, tenant's rights more secure, and renting from local authorities, 'council housing', more important. The Housing Act of 1930 gave local authorities power to clear or improve slum (crowded and sub-standard housing) areas. Wartime damage to the housing stock, a low rate of wartime construction, and expectations of a better life after the conflict, increased pressure for housebuilding after 1945, as did a rise in the birth rate. A shortage of resources in the postwar economy, and the priority given to industrial reconstruction, ensured that, although the Attlee government built many houses, the number – under 200,000 per year in 1949–51 – was inadequate. The Conservatives saw this as an opportunity and in the election of 1951 made much of a promise to build 300,000 a year. Once elected, Churchill created a separate Ministry of Housing, and appointed to it one of his protégés, Harold Macmillan. Helped by a higher allocation of government resources and a cutting of the building standards for council houses – the majority of new houses in 1945–54 – Macmillan achieved his target in 1953.

The McCartney family was a beneficiary. After living, as many did, in a 'prefab' – a prefabricated bungalow intended as a temporary home – they moved in 1947 to a suburban council estate at Speke. In 1955 the family moved again: to the Mather Avenue estate which had been built by the council in 1949–52. This was a move up, in part because the new house, number 20 Forthlin Road, had an inside toilet.

The older son, Paul, had an interest in popular music, especially the latest American singers, with Buddy Holly being a firm favourite. In 1956, he joined John Lennon's band, the Quarry

Men, as a guitarist. Rather than performing other people's songs, the two wrote their own: in the living room at Forthlin Road. The band's musical development was soon enhanced by the tours they made to Hamburg. In the winter of 1960/1, the group, now The Beatles, established themselves as the band for Liverpool teenagers and developed the Mersey sound, one that was very different to the music of established figures such as Tommy Steele and Cliff Richard. Imitating Elvis Presley, Richard was having hits with numbers such as 'Living Doll' (1959).

To go national, The Beatles had to be repackaged. In 1961, the band abandoned their leather jackets for smart suits, and their manager, Brian Epstein, got them a recording contract with the music giant EMI (after they had been rejected by every other record company). EMI was newly responsive to the commercial possibilities of 'pop' and understood that it was no longer appropriate to expect performers to behave as they had been told to do in the 1950s. The Beatles' debut single, 'Love Me Do', written at Forthlin Road, was released in October 1962, followed in January 1963 by 'Please Please Me'. They were the sound of change. The group's producer, George Martin, led them into uncharted musical territory with a range of new sounds and instruments. As their lyrics became more complex and their arrangements more intricate, The Beatles could be said to have created a form of classical music which was representative of its age. Other Merseysiders – Cilla Black, Gerry and the Pacemakers, and the Swinging Blue Jeans – sustained the Liverpool impact on London. Yet they also left Liverpool. The Beatles became international as 'Beatlemania' spread to the USA in 1964; and 20 Forthlin Road became the home of the Jones family, who in 1981 bought it under the Conservative government's 'right-to-buy' scheme.

In film, working-class dramas set in the North of England, especially *Room at the Top* (1959) and *Saturday Night and Sunday Morning* (1960), were in vogue (and plays such as John Arden's *Serjeant Musgrave's Dance* (1959) can be seen in the same light), but they were absorbed by a more metropolitan focus. This was part of a reconfiguration of popular British youth culture towards fashionable middle-class interests. Thus, the hippies and drugs of the late 1960s reflected the affluence and ethos of middle-class South-Eastern youth, rather than their Northern working-class counterparts. The Beatles came from the latter, but took to the new culture, especially to drugs and Asian mysticism, providing it with a 'sound'. In 1969 the government gave 'youth' the vote, when the voting age was reduced from twenty-one to eighteen. The age of legal majority similarly fell the following year.

Massive open-air concerts focused the potent combination of youth culture and pop music in the 1960s, but this music and its commercialisation was in turn to be challenged in the mid-1970s by punk, a style that set out to shock and transform popular culture. Punk was a conscious reaction against the technical wizardry and excessiveness of 'glam rock'. It championed a more archaic approach where the only rule was that there were no rules. The most famous, or infamous, punk group to emerge was the Sex Pistols, whose behaviour soon attracted as much attention as their music. Yet, to reach a wider audience, punk itself had to be taken up by record companies and television, who, in the case of the record companies, then exploited it for their own financial ends. Punk was, in effect, tamed in the interests of commercial viability and, as a result, quickly lost its appeal among the record-buying public. It ultimately entered the cultural mainstream, affecting style in fashion, design, and the world of publishing. Vivienne Westwood, who first came to prominence because of her links with the Sex Pistols, was by the 1990s one of the country's leading fashion designers.

with *The Real Inspector Hound* (1968), a play that subverted theatrical conventions and the classic detective story by making the identity of its characters a mystery. Like many other innovative figures of the period who achieved fame, Stoppard, born in 1937, was young. This had been true in many periods, but youth was a particular cult of the 1960s.

In the 1960s, the rejection of the past proceeded apace. There were many symbols of change, but it would be inappropriate to see this trend only in British terms. Youth culture, feminism, the collapse of the Christian moral framework, drugs and sexual liberation were international themes, as, more generally, was anti-authoritarianism. If Harold Wilson, Labour Prime Minister 1964–70 and 1974–6, presented himself as a force for change after what he termed the 'thirteen wasted years' of Conservative government, he sought the mantle of the Democrat American

President John F. Kennedy, who had used similar language in the 1960 campaign about the replacement of Republican rule.

In some respects, change was more apparent in Britain than in the USA. Harold Macmillan, Conservative Prime Minister in 1957–63, and his successor in 1963–4, Sir Alec Douglas-Home, formerly the 14th Earl of Home, seemed to represent an anachronistic politics, one mercilessly satirised in trendy youthful forums, such as the satirical journal *Private Eye* (founded 1961) and the BBC television programme *That Was The Week That Was*, the latter itself a sign of change in a major institution. Yet the BBC was not prepared to allow the programme to be broadcast in the run-up to the 1964 election: it was taken off the air at the end of December 1963.

The electorate had become wealthier, but the percentage willing to vote Labour in 1964 was only slightly below that of 1951; and the Conservatives were hit by a modest Liberal revival. The Conservatives were again to discover in 1997 that rising real wealth under their government did not prevent a Labour victory. Under Wilson, a humanitarian politician, the death penalty was abolished and racial discrimination declared illegal in 1965, while abortion and homosexual acts between consenting adults were legalised in 1967. More generally, there was concern about those seen as disadvantaged, including women, the elderly and the disabled. The Equal Pay Act of 1970 was a response to increased disquiet about women's working conditions. It led to a rise in women's relative hourly earnings. Concern about individual rights resulted in the creation in 1967 of the Parliamentary Commissioner for Administration, the 'Ombudsman', who was empowered to investigate complaints against some, but not all, government departments.

Outside the control of government, there was a whole series of social changes, frequently involving the breaking of past taboos. Thus, the eroticised vision of marriage called for in Marie Stopes' *Married Love* (1918) was now extended to all relationships, both heterosexual and homosexual. The changes associated with the 'sexual revolution', such as increasing rates of illegitimacy and divorce, were already under way in the 1950s. In 1957, the Wolfenden Report on prostitution and homosexuality drew a distinction between sin and crime, a crucial preliminary to decriminalisation. In 1962, Penguin was unsuccessfully prosecuted for publishing an uncut edition of D.H. Lawrence's sexually explicit *Lady Chatterley's Lover*. The book sold 2 million copies in six weeks, becoming the best-selling Penguin hitherto. In 1961, the contraceptive pill was made available on the NHS, helping give women more control over their fertility. In 1963, the Brook Advisory Centre for Young People began providing contraceptives to unmarried youngsters, a major shift from the policy of the Family Planning Association. The NHS (Family Planning) Act passed in 1967 made no mention of marriage, and, in response, the Family Planning Association began to advise unmarried women, while the Brook Centres started seeing girls under sixteen. Thanks to more easily available contraception and abortion, the number of teenage mothers fell, although it again became a major issue in the 1990s and 2000s.

In rural areas the rejection of the past was marked by the continued decline of the traditional socio-economic order. The number of agricultural labourers fell, while country house life largely disappeared. Servants became a thing of the past and, thanks to the pressure of death duties and other taxes, many country houses were destroyed, abandoned, became reliant on paying visitors, or were transferred to the National Trust. Penrhyn Castle passed via the Inland Revenue to the Trust after the death of the 4th Lord Penrhyn in 1949. Death duties were responsible for the Earl of Morley surrendering Saltram to the Treasury, which handed it over to the Trust in 1957. The same year, the Treasury accepted Beningbrough Hall, North Yorkshire in part payment of death duties on the death of the Countess of Chesterfield, and handed it on to the Trust. Aristocrats also sold their town houses. One of the grandest, Londonderry House in Park Lane, the site of numerous fashionable interwar parties, was sold in 1962 and demolished.

The shock of the new age was lessened in Britain by its peacefulness. National Service had been abolished (no men were called up after 1960), and Wilson, a skilled populist then in touch with the mainstream of public opinion, refused to yield to Lyndon Johnson's pressure to match the Australasian commitment by sending British troops to help the Americans in Vietnam. As a consequence, there was no equivalent to the American anti-war movement and draft dodging, no issue that really brought government and youth culture into violent opposition.

Nor was there any agenda, issue or symbol around which conservative forces could rally. Thanks to the winner-takes-all system of British elections, it is easy to neglect the Conservatives in the 1960s, but in the general elections of 1964 and 1966 they polled more than 40 per cent of the vote, in the first case less than 1 per cent behind Labour, and in 1970 Edward Heath was to defeat Wilson. Yet the Conservative Party lacked a cause. Having established the National Economic Development Council (NEDC) in 1961, its criticisms of Labour's planning experiment sounded hollow. Having given independence to most of the empire in 1957–64, it was not in a position to criticise the abandonment of most of the rest. Having, in response to a sense of economic decline, applied, unsuccessfully, to join the European Economic Community in 1961, the Conservatives were in no position to complain about Labour's 1967 application. Both attempts were rejected by the veto of the President of France, Charles de Gaulle, who argued that Britain's claim to a European identity was compromised by her American links.

An alternative identity for the Conservatives – the populist nationalism offered by Enoch Powell, who began to attack the consequences of immigration in 1968 – was rejected by Heath, who had became party leader in 1965. He was distrustful of Powell and unwilling to associate the party with racialism. The National Front, launched in 1967, sought to unite opinion further to the right, but it lacked the necessary popularity, and split into warring factions. When the Conservative Party returned to office in 1970 it did so on the one issue upon which it had no clear policy: inflation. This was to prove the Heath government's undoing in 1973–4 as it struggled to enforce a policy of state-regulated wages which it had earlier promised not to introduce.

The Labour government had come to power in 1964 with a small majority, but with high hopes, including the use of planning to improve economic performance, harness new technology, and break the 'Stop–Go' cycle. A Department of Economic Affairs was created in 1964, and in 1965 it produced the National Plan, an optimistic blueprint for growth. The National Board for Prices and Incomes was also created in 1965, as was the Economic and Social Research Council, which was intended to be a government patron of the social sciences. A Ministry of Technology was designed to encourage new industrial processes and to promote government research and development spending on civil, rather than military, projects. A Ministry of Land and Natural Resources was also established. Prices and incomes policies were joined by active attempts at regional regeneration, including a Regional Development Fund. It was hoped that growth would fuel improved social welfare. The Labour government also abolished prescription charges and increased pensions.

The economy grew, and unemployment was kept low, its average level in the 1960s being 459,000, well below the levels in the 1980s and 1990s, but it proved impossible to sustain a successful prices and incomes policy, or to match growth rates in much of the Western world. The 'Stop–Go' cycle reasserted itself, and in 1966, when the Treasury used a balance of payments crisis to press the case for deflation, the National Plan was ditched. The Department of Economic Affairs' attempt to eclipse the Treasury had failed. Furthermore, the devaluation of sterling by 14.3 per cent in November 1967, precipitated by a further decline in the balance of payments, led to serious doubts about the quality of economic management, which were to have long-term consequences for Labour's credibility as a party of government.

More generally, Wilson came to be regarded as stronger on image than substance. The failure of his attempt to reform the trade unions in 1969 encouraged a sense of broken hopes, although it is important to note the difficulty of the situation facing the government at home and abroad. Crisis management became a serious problem for all major states in 1968, and, compared to France for instance, the situation in Britain was handled more effectively.

Harmed by poor labour relations, indifferent management and inadequate investment, Britain, nevertheless, lagged behind other leading industrial nations, such as France and Germany, in economic growth. Traditional industries continued to suffer significant problems. In Lancashire alone, 33 coal mines were closed in the 1960s with the loss of 20,000 jobs. The number of coal miners in South Wales had fallen from 112,000 in 1944 to 106,000 in 1960, but by 1970 the figure was only 60,000. In Bolton, the six Atlas Mills that, at their peak, had operated 460,000 cotton spindles and employed 2,000 people, were closed down. More seriously, there was a failure to take the lead in new areas of economic expansion. The promise of rapid economic growth through applied technology and state-directed modernisation was broken, preparing the way for Conservative reaction in the shape of the competitive features of Heath's 'Selsdon Man', a policy named after Conservative planning sessions at Selsdon Park in early 1970 that emphasised a refusal to subsidise inefficient industries.

In the 1966 election, Labour had changed the electoral geography of the country, winning many seats that it had never held before, including Brighton, Cambridge, Cardiganshire, Exeter, Hampstead, Lancaster, Oxford and York. It was now far from being a party of the old industrial areas. Labour had been re-established as a party of government. However, thereafter, Labour's popularity was hit by devaluation and the inability to reform the trade unions, and it lost numerous by-elections. Despite an upturn in the economy and in its electoral fortunes in 1970, Labour was defeated by the Conservatives under Heath that June.

Holding office in 1970–4, although by the end unable to wield or provide power, Heath pushed through change in what he saw as an attempt to modernise Britain: 'modernisation' was a buzz word in British politics long before Tony Blair began to use it. The decimalisation of the currency in 1971 discarded centuries of usage and contributed to inflation which, in turn, put paid to coins whose purchasing power had fallen: the farthing in 1960 and the halfpenny in 1984. An Industrial Relations Act in 1971, passed despite protest strikes, established an Industrial Relations

Court with extensive powers to try to limit strikes. The following year, direct rule was imposed on Northern Ireland in an attempt to improve Whitehall's control over the response to the serious Nationalist disturbances that had begun in 1969 as a result of Unionism's failure to reform itself.

Also in 1972, the Local Government Act altered the historic territorial boundaries of municipal administrations. It was based on the Royal Commission into Local Government in England under Lord Redcliffe-Maud that had been established by the Labour government in 1966 and had reported in 1969. The Greater London Council had already been formed in 1965, adding much of Kent and Surrey to the London County Council area. Coming into force on 1 April 1974, the new Act redrew the map, in order, it was hoped, to create a more efficient system that would overcome earlier unitary divisions. The recommendations, however, were not implemented in full. The top tier of Provincial Councils, for example the North-West Council, were not established. Nevertheless, new counties were created, including Avon, Cleveland and Humberside, while others, such as Rutland, were destroyed. There were also mergers, such as Huntingdonshire and Cambridgeshire, and Herefordshire and Worcestershire, major changes in the boundaries between counties, for example Berkshire and Oxfordshire, and a reorganisation of the Yorkshire ridings. In the North, Westmorland, Cumberland and the Furness region of Lancashire were merged into Cumbria.

In addition to these changes, counties were divided into new administrative districts, which were created by amalgamating the pre-1974 urban and rural district areas and redrawing boundaries. Thus, in County Durham, new regions, such as Derwentside and Teesdale, were created. Darlington was a merger of the former county borough of Darlington and the former rural district of the same name. Wear Valley fused the urban districts of Spennymoor, Crook and Willington, and Bishop Auckland, with the former rural district of Weardale. There was also extensive reorganisation in Scotland and Wales. All this was pushed through in the name of rationality. New units were generally bigger and were supposed to be the best option for the provision of services, such as education or the fire services. Little consideration was given to local views or to the value of traditional identities in providing a sense of place and belonging.

This was part of a more general displacement of customary patterns. In 1976, Al Stewart's song 'On the Border' lamented:

> the village where I grew up
> Nothing seems the same
> . . . the customs slip away
> . . . In the islands where I grew up
> Nothing seems the same
> It's just the patterns that remain
> An empty shell.

Joining the European Economic Community was part of Heath's masterplan; indeed, it lay at its heart. Membership was his focus, part of a long tradition of British leaders who had devoted attention to foreign issues at the expense of serious problems at home. But Heath fused the two. Europe, it was hoped, would provide the British economy with the dose of competition it needed to revitalise its flagging fortunes. De Gaulle had gone, and Heath was able to join on the basis of accepting the EEC's terms, which included the higher food costs of the Common Agricultural Policy with its agricultural subsidies, and the progressive prohibition of cheap food imports, especially from suppliers in the British Commonwealth, for example lamb from New Zealand. The Common Market Membership Treaty was signed on 22 January 1972, and, on 1 January 1973, the United Kingdom became a full member.

SEVEN

CONSUMERISM AND COLLAPSE?
1973–2008

'You've never had it so good', the phrase associated with Harold Macmillan, Conservative Prime Minister 1957–63, could more accurately, as far as material goods were concerned, be applied to the 1980s, 1990s and 2000s. This might appear surprising, as there was a severe economic and political crisis in the 1970s, serious recessions at the beginning of the 1980s and 1990s, and a significant portion of the population did not benefit from the economic growth of the remainder of the period. Unemployment rose above 1 million in 1976 and to over 3 million in 1982, a level it was also at for much of the early 1990s.

Nevertheless, for those in work, a growing percentage of the population, this was a period of affluence that would have amazed their predecessors. The number of employed rose from 22.5 million in 1979 to 26.9 million in 1989, in part due to the expansion of the female workforce, before falling, in the early 1990s' recession, to 25 million in 1992. Average disposable income rose by 37 per cent between 1982 and 1992. In the 1980s and 1990s a combination of rising real earnings, lower inflation and taxation, and easier credit encouraged spending. The standard rate of income tax fell from 33 per cent in 1979 to 25 per cent in 1988, and, although Margaret Thatcher's Conservative government (1979–90) found it difficult to fulfil its pledge to reduce overall taxation, there was an important increase in the spending money of many consumers. A marked fall in the birth rate that owed much to the spread in the use of the contraceptive pill, to higher levels of female employment, and to changing assumptions about marriage, and family structure and size, was also important in increasing disposable income.

Affluence can be measured in many ways. One of the most obvious in this period was the very intensity of shopping. With the end of restrictions on Sunday shopping and the availability of 24-hour stores, this became literally a round-the-clock activity. Going to the shops became a leisure pursuit for many. The rise of the hypermarket and of out-of-town retail centres in the 1980s transformed the nature of shopping and encouraged the use of cars. By 1992 16 per cent of the total retail space in Britain was made up of shopping centres, such as Brent Cross in north London, Lakeside Thurrock in Essex, the Glades in Bromley, Meadowhall in Sheffield, and the Metro Centre in Gateshead. These centres were dominated by national retailers whose ability to set market conditions appeared sufficiently monopolistic to trouble the Office of Fair Trading in 1998. It was concerned about the preponderant role in food marketing of just four retailers: Asda, Safeway, Sainsbury's and Tesco. Supermarkets hit independent retail activity. At the local level, these chains also had a powerful impact. In Exeter, where Sainsbury's had three stores, the decision in 1998 to move one from inner-city St Thomas to a suburban site at Alphington had a serious effect on traffic flow.

The percentage of the population employed in services rose, while that in manufacturing declined. This reflected investment trends, which, in the 1980s, 1990s and 2000s, focused on services, housing and the City of London. The shift also had implications for labour relations, for workers in services were less unionised and less militant. In contrast, heavily unionised sections of the workforce, such as mining and railways, lost workers. Trade union membership fell from 13 million in 1978 to 7.3 million in January 1994. This had important political consequences. Union power, with its cutting edge of miners' strikes, had played a major role in the collapse of the Conservative government led by Edward Heath (1970–4), resulting in a state of emergency, a three-day working week, and finally, in February 1974, the electoral defeat of the government, a defeat underlined that October when Harold Wilson's new minority Labour government won a parliamentary majority in a second general election.

Clothes and the Woman

The Museum of Costume in Bath Assembly Rooms offers a vivid account of changing fashion. It clearly registers the major changes of the twentieth century. Edwardian elegance had given place to less restrictive forms of female dress prior to the First World War, including higher hemlines and the end of tightly laced corsets. The war accentuated the change, leading to shorter, wider skirts. Trousers also became acceptable. The emphasis on ease of movement persisted in the 1920s, encouraging unshaped dresses and short hair. There were also more comfortable clothes for men, including easy-fitting jackets and wide trousers (Oxford Bags). The Second World War led to clothes rationing and the utility scheme that dictated the design and production of clothes. Being stylish and different was not a theme of the war years.

Postwar, there was a reaction against austerity that led in 1947 to the feminine fashions of the 'New Look': long as opposed to short skirts, softly rounded shoulders, not boxy suits, and high-heeled, rather than sensible, shoes. There was also an emphasis on consistency and completeness: shoes and handbags were expected to match; hats and gloves had to be worn.

The situation changed in the 1960s, in large part because of the impact of a newly energetic, demanding and distinctive youth culture. Skirts rose, eventually to the mini-skirt of 1965–6. Artificial fabrics were pursued more actively, leading to the use of modern plastics, such as PVC (polyvinyl chloride). More generally, synthetic fabrics became far more important after the Second World War, an aspect of the growing range and role of the chemical industry.

In the 1960s, the colours and shapes of clothes became bolder, as did jewellery. Trousers became more acceptable for women and many dressed like men in denim jeans and with similar hairstyles. Carnaby Street in London became famous for trend-setting boutiques, and designers such as Mary Quant deliberately sought to appeal to a mass young clientele.

Since 1963, the Museum of Costume has kept up to date with the annual acquisition of a dress or outfit to reflect the most influential new ideas in contemporary fashion. They record, for example, the long skirts, full sleeves, and patterned knitting of 1970, and the Armani stylishness of 1986. The annual outfits also reflect a world in which it is assumed that fashions will change rapidly, will seek the mass market of modern consumer society, and will range widely for materials; although not to include environmentally sensitive sources, such as fur animals, or tropical hardwoods for furniture. Furthermore, the dominant theme is fashion appeal, not durability, or other utilitarian goals. Looked at differently, in keeping with much of modern society, consumerism has become the utilitarian end.

Trade Unions and Consumerism

In 1974, the unions agreed a social compact with the newly elected Labour government in which moderate wage demands were to be pressed in return for an acceptable legislative programme. Inflation was brought down considerably in 1975–8, but large pay claims, particularly from public sector unions, helped to cause a crisis in the winter of 1978–9. James Callaghan, Labour Prime Minister 1976–9, proved unable to keep control of the situation or to find a new message for Labour, although neither task was easy in the aftermath of the Arab oil shock of 1973 and the impact of higher oil prices on the Western economy. Responding to the government pay limit of 5 per cent with a claim worth 49 per cent, Moss Evans, the General Secretary of the Transport & General Workers Union, declared in January 1979, 'I'm not bothered by percentages. It is not my responsibility to manage the economy. We are concerned about getting the rate for the job.' Trade Unionists showed little thought about the unemployed, and, more generally, were unwilling to accept static or even declining living standards in order to improve the chance of high employment. A 'winter of discontent' in 1978–9, with strikes by petrol tanker drivers, lorry drivers, hospital ancillary staff, ambulancemen and others, and extensive secondary picketing, helped create a sense that Britain was out of control, and aided Mrs Thatcher's electoral victory in 1979.

Public opinion polls – themselves an important aspect of the new consumerism, showed an increasing belief that unions were too powerful. Anarchic trade unionists, careless of the consequences of their actions, were central to the presentation

of Britain as a collapsing NHS hospital in Lindsay Anderson's
satirical film *Britannia Hospital* (1982).

As part of Thatcher's rejection of recent politics – both those
of Labour and the policies of the Heath government – union
rights were reduced during her period in office, encouraging
inward investment, and the government did its best to defeat
strikes in the public sector. A major steel strike in 1980 was
unsuccessful. A strike by the National Union of Mineworkers in
1984–5 was defeated due to poor and divisive leadership in the
union, the willingness of 50,000 miners to remain at work, the
determination of the government to employ all its resources,
both financial and police, and the availability of energy,
including stockpiled and imported coal. At the regional level,
divisions among the miners revealed the importance of local
circumstances. These included not only the condition of the
pit and the age of the workforce, but also attitudes to national,
regional and local union leadership, labour relations, and the
character of politicisation. After the strike, the pit closures
continued. By late 1986 there were only 13,000 miners and only
16 collieries; compared to 300 in 1947.

While many miners and others suffered privation and
unemployment, much of the population enjoyed rising living
standards. Goods and mobility are two measures of prosperity.
Ownership of telephones, washing machines, dishwashers and
video-recorders all rose in the 1980s, 1990s and 2000s. There
were 19.5 million televisions in the United Kingdom in 1986.
By 1991, 90 per cent of households had a telephone, compared
to 42 per cent in 1972; for washing machines the percentages
were 88 and 66. By the early 1990s, the majority of households
owned videos and microwave cookers. DVD-players followed
video-players.

New consumer goods became very popular. The personal
computer, computer games, the mobile telephone, the personal
stereo, and both satellite and cable television were acquired
in large numbers in the 1990s. In part, the diffusion of such
goods reflected and encouraged a growing degree of classlessness
in which many jobs ceased being so closely identified with a
specific social class, while men and women from working-class

backgrounds gained middle-class jobs. Others benefited from rising real incomes and the greater availability of credit, and shared in middle-class lifestyles. New goods also gave consumers more choice: a greater number of television channels as well as interactive computer games.

Food and drink consumption registered other changes. In 1971, food took one-fifth of the average family budget; in 1993 one-ninth, freeing disposable income for other forms of expenditure. The family food budget was also spent differently, as the national diet was affected by new ingredients and by dishes introduced from foreign countries. In P.G. Wodehouse's *Ukridge* (1924), the 'ordinary' Price family of Clapham Common are imagined having 'cold beef, baked potatoes, pickles, salad, blanc-mange, and some sort of cheese every Sunday night after Divine service'. Sixty and, even more, eighty years later, the menu and the predictability were both very different.

Appetite and fashion, rather than hunger and custom, came to dominate eating. Cheap, filling foods, especially bread and potatoes, became less important in home eating. The range of meats available in butchers changed. Out went mutton, let alone boiled sheep's head. Beef declined in popularity. In contrast, chicken became more popular.

Meal times changed, not least as more people ate their main meal later in the evening; a development that in part reflected increasing women's employment. Chinese, Indian and Italian meals came to dominate the restaurant trade, and, in the fast-food world, American-style burgers, pizzas, and fried chicken replaced traditional dishes, such as eel pies, and, although to a lesser extent, especially outside the South-East, fish and chips. Bacon and eggs fell from breakfast favour and the traditional roast was no longer the centre of many family's Sundays. Chains became more important in the sale of fish and chips, and the most successful, Harry Ramsden's, sought to cater to a more affluent population by making the dish a more up-market product. By 1998, 2 million meals were being eaten in the country's 8,000 Indian restaurants weekly: there had been only 300 Indian restaurants in 1950.

Consumerism and Drink

What the British drank changed greatly during the twentieth century and this provides an important index of the impact of consumerism and, more generally, of social changes. Foreign alcoholic drinks, and foreign types and brands of beer became more important. This process also reflected technological and retail shifts, most obviously the growing sale of canned beers and the development of supermarket sales of alcohol. The shifting pattern of alcohol consumption reflected social, gender and age shifts. The stereotypical view of drinking at the beginning of the century – with the male working class drinking beer, in some agricultural areas, cider, and in Scotland beer and whisky, and the middle and upper class drinking wine and a narrow range of spirits, especially whisky – is substantially correct. The situation changed slowly after the Second World War, with a wider drinking public for wine, but, again, the pace of change did not increase until the 1960s. Female drinking rose and encouraged major shifts in the market. As far as spirits were concerned, whisky and brandy became less important, and the white spirits – gin and, to a lesser extent, vodka – more so. Wine consumption rose, especially that of lighter white wines. From the 1980s, it became easier to purchase wine in pubs.

The greater importance of young drinkers affected sales of beer. Bitter and stout, the traditional drinks of working-class men, became less important and lagers more important. Traditional cask-conditioned or real ales became more popular from the 1980s. The prevalence of young drinkers also influenced the way in which drink was sold. Bottled beers became increasingly commonplace, particularly in nightclubs. However, sales of whisky continued to be important in Scotland. Some 45 per cent of Scottish pub orders in the 1970s were for spirits. Bitter was less common in Scotland. Instead, heavy, or beer rated by duty, was drunk.

The pace of change remained high. The 1970s and 1980s saw a further shift in the wine industry, with the rise of sales of white wine from the USA, Australia, New Zealand, Chile, Argentina and, especially after the fall of the apartheid system, South Africa. Although less markedly, red wine purchases from these areas also rose. The dominance of wine sales by French and German producers slackened. Wine growing revived in Britain, although output remained small. In 1951, 1.5 acres of vines were planted at Hambledon in Hampshire. By 1973, there were 200 acres under vines in the country, by 1998 about 2,350.

Change was not simply a matter of new and different products. The forms in which drinks were delivered altered, largely in order to maintain consistent qualities for bulk provision, a characteristic need of modern capitalism. Pressurised pumps were used to deliver beer in pubs. Wine boxes were designed to enable drinkers to drink less (or more) than one bottle without spoiling the rest. Wine bars became popular from the 1970s. Their rise forced the traditional public house to change its image in order to win back customers. Pubs ceased to be male-orientated, domino-playing, crisp-eating places to visit. Instead, the need to attract younger people led to the emergence of the 'theme pub' serving a wide range of beers and spirits to the sound of the latest chart hits. Pubs increasingly served food in a quest to make them more family-friendly. The advent of beer gardens also allowed children to accompany their parents. The possibility of near all-day drinking, with the liberalisation of licensing hours, first in Scotland after the report of the Clayson Committee in 1973, and then in England and Wales, represented a significant social change. Pubs in the 1990s opened at 11 a.m. and closed at 11 p.m. (with clubs open until at least 2 a.m.).

Coffee drinking also changed radically. In place of a situation in which there were few alternatives to 'instant', filter coffee became more popular from the 1980s. Tea had been the overwhelmingly dominant hot drink, but its relative decline was part of a major shift in the consumption of non-alcoholic drinks. This was a matter not only of the rise of coffee, which had been drunk in Britain for centuries, but also of decaffeinated hot drinks. The range of cold drinks also altered, with the increased consumption of bottled mineral water and of a wide range of fruit juices. These shifts all became pronounced from the 1980s. Even conventional products changed. Thus, in 1980, the range of teas available in supermarkets or cafés was limited, principally to Darjeeling. Earl Grey was a minority choice. Most people drank tea with milk and the majority also took sugar. In contrast, by 2001 the readily available range had expanded greatly to include Chinese and Japanese green teas, as well as fruit teas. Furthermore, the use of milk and, in particular, sugar in tea had become less widespread.

Supermarkets increasingly stocked foreign dishes. In the 1990s there was growing consumption of continental-style breads. There has also been a widening in the range of fruits available: avocados, passion fruit, star fruit, kiwi fruit and mangoes, largely unknown in Britain in the 1960s, are now widely available in supermarkets and deployed in recipes. The increased consumption of convenience foods, generally reheated rapidly by microwave cookers, has provided a major market for new dishes, such as Thai chicken, and for Indian and Chinese food sold by supermarkets. By 1998 one supermarket chain, Waitrose, alone stocked sixteen regional Indian dishes. There were regional, gender and social dimensions to shifts in food preferences. Thus, London and the South-East were at the forefront of the change, moving towards fruit, vegetables, fish and pasta, while the Scots and the poor ate the fewest vegetables. Per capita meat consumption was highest in Yorkshire. Female consumers were more ready than men to abandon meat and potatoes for fish and fresh vegetables.

An interest in foreign food and drink owed much to the massive growth in foreign tourism that was an important aspect of consumerism and mobility. Thanks to jet aircraft and widespread disposable income, the number of Britons travelling overseas rose. Between 1995 and 1998 passenger traffic through airports in the London area increased at a rate of 7 per cent a year. British tourist expenditure abroad in 1987 was £7,255.2 million. This shift was linked to a decline in the relative importance of domestic tourism, that led to a changing sense of place for many. Glaswegians who went to Majorca, rather than Largs, or Londoners who travelled to Cyprus, not Cornwall, now had a different experience of their own countries, and mental maps altered accordingly.

Transport and the Environment

Consumerism and mobility combined in the car. The number in Britain rose from 12.2 million in 1970 to 21.9 in 1990, and ownership per 1,000 people from 224 in 1971 to 380 in 1994. There were more roads. The motorway system spread.

Motorways crossed the Pennines from Leeds to Manchester (M62), provided a second route from London to Birmingham (M40), opened a new means of travelling from London to East Anglia (M11), and circled London (M25), the last becoming the busiest route in the country. There were major improvements to other routes, as roundabouts and junctions along trunk roads such as the A1 were replaced by slip roads.

Major bridges were built. There were significant engineering achievements that altered the geography of the country. The Humber Bridge, built in 1972–80 and opened in 1981, was the longest single-span bridge in the world, with an overall length of nearly 2,220 metres (about 1½ miles), and 1,410 metres (4,626 feet) between the towers. Due to its length, the two supporting towers had to be set out of alignment by 36mm (1½ inches) to allow for the curvature of the earth. The record length of the bridge was only beaten in 1998 by the Akashi–Kaikyo bridge in Japan. The Humber Bridge helped make Humberside a more viable unit by improving links within the new county. In 1997, a second road bridge crossed the Severn estuary, helping bring Bristol and Cardiff closer.

The social impact of the car has become more insistent, both for drivers, passengers and others. For example, whereas in 1971 14 per cent of junior school children were driven to school, in 1990 the percentage was 64. The marked fall in those walking or going by bus is an aspect of the declining use of 'public space', and one related to the increase in obesity and lack of fitness among children. Commuting by car has become more widespread, altering the nature of life in the countryside and eroding the boundary between rural and urban society. The number of commuters travelling into London, Birmingham and Manchester in 1981–91 increased by 7, 18 and 29 per cent respectively.

Such developments have brought major problems, although most of these are the consequences of the density and affluence of the population, as much as the car. The automobile is easily identified as the villain, but few motorists are willing to give it up: public transport is always most appropriate for others. Although there was a steady growth of passenger traffic on major rail routes in the 1990s and 2000s, train travel has become relatively more marginal as a consequence of the continued rise of the car and lorry. It did, however, avoid the dramatic cuts proposed in the Serpell Report of 1983. That would have reduced the system to 1,600 miles, essentially a few major routes. Instead, the system has stabilised at about 11,000 miles, just over half the interwar mileage. Furthermore, there have been important improvements. The InterCity 125, a high-speed diesel train capable of travelling at 125mph, was introduced in 1976 on the Paddington to Bristol and South Wales routes, and then spread to other non-electrified main lines. The tilting Advanced Passenger Train did not prove a success, but, on the East Coast Main Line from London to Edinburgh, fully electrified 225s, capable of travelling at 225km (140mph) were introduced in 1991. The Channel Tunnel was opened to rail travel in 1992. The improvement in rail services, however, did not match the convenience of cars, and in 2000 grave limitations in the reliability and safety of the network and its ability to respond to bad weather were revealed.

British Rail was privatised and split up in 1996 as part of the Conservatives' policy of widespread privatisation of publicly owned bodies. This was not reversed when Labour came to power in 1997. As a consequence, the prospect of using such bodies in order to pursue a policy of national planning disappeared.

Cars themselves are dangerous, not least because they are frequently driven too fast. By the early 1990s, 45,000 children were being hurt on the roads every year, and among those aged between five and fifteen two-thirds of deaths were the result of road accidents. In 1992, 4,681 people were killed in car accidents, compared to 499 by murder, although subsequently the number of road deaths fell. Alarmist and often lurid reports about the murders fed popular concern about crime. In contrast, deaths and injuries through road accidents were seen as personal tragedies, aroused less public interest and concern, and were treated as a fact of life, although successive Christmas 'don't drink and drive' campaigns helped focus the public mind. The danger posed by cars is rising, as their engines become more silent.

Cars also threaten animals, both domestic and wild. Large numbers of cats, dogs, rabbits, hedgehogs, birds and other animals are killed each year. For example, between 3,000 and 5,000 barn owls are killed on the roads annually.

There is also the more insidious danger from exhaust emissions. Cities that in the 1960s enjoyed far more sunshine hours from the clearer atmosphere after the declaration of smokeless zones are now noting a decline as a result of car exhausts. Lorries are particularly to blame for noxious emissions. Air quality is falling.

These are not the only problems. The assault on the environment is becoming stronger, although, thanks to afforestation, there were twice as many trees in 1995 as at the beginning of the century. Global warming may be leading to major changes in climate and, through the melting of the ice caps, to a rise in sea level that will hit vulnerable coastal areas, including much of the east and south coasts. Widespread flooding in inland areas after persistent heavy rain in 2000 and 2007, strengthened political and public concern about the issue, although it owed much to drainage policies, agricultural practices, and building in floodplains, for example near York.

Large quantities of industrial and domestic waste are deliberately dumped into the sea, especially the North Sea and, to a lesser extent, the Irish Sea and English Channel; while accidents, such as the spillage of oil on the Pembrokeshire coast in 1996 from the beached tanker Sea Empress, have done terrible damage. Industrial pollution is also responsible for 'acid rain', which has damaged much of the country's woodland and hit both rivers and lakes.

More material goods tend to mean a greater use of energy, although reliability and energy efficiency have risen. In 1990, 158 million tons of carbon dioxide were dispersed into the environment above Britain. Increased use of water, thanks in part to machines such as dishwashers, put great pressure on reserves, and led to the depletion of natural aquifers and to restrictions on water use. In 1990, hosepipe bans affected 20 million customers. There was also concern about the quality of the water, specifically of the consequences of contamination by chemical fertilisers spread on farmland and entering the water supply. Such pollutants have been linked to declining sperm counts and hormonal changes among the population, specifically the acquisition of female characteristics by men.

The consumer society produces steadily greater quantities of rubbish, much of it non-bio-degradable and most of it not recycled. The massive increase in the importation, treatment and burying of hazardous waste in the 1980s led to concern about possible health implications. The legacy of past pollution is heavy. The Millennium Dome was built in Greenwich in 1997–9 on the site of what had been Europe's largest gasworks. This made coal gas in a process that produced toxic waste, including arsenic, asbestos and cyanide. Much of the waste from the site was buried in rural dumps, while the Dome site was sealed with crushed concrete, plastic and clay, and each building had to have a gas-tight membrane underneath. Noise and light pollution were other consequences of technological development.

The impact of these changes on health is unclear. Possibly as a result of increasing car exhaust emissions, respiratory diseases, such as asthma, have definitely risen, and some others may also be increasing. Visibility has been reduced, and eye irritation become more serious. The safety of food became more of an issue, especially after the identification in 1988 of a new infectious disease, *salmonella enteritidis*, which was shown to have contaminated egg production. Food safety became an even greater concern in the mid-1990s after scientific research revealed that there was a risk of bovine spongiform encephalopathy (BSE) or 'mad cow disease' being transmitted from cattle to humans via beef products and causing variant Creutzfeldt-Jakob disease, a degenerate brain illness.

Yet there have been important advances in public health. Postwar improvements have continued. Average lifespan increased by an average of two years every decade from the 1960s. As a result, the number of pensioners rose, which made it hard for governments to contain welfare expenditure. Infant mortality fell by nearly two-thirds between 1971 and 1994. The Clean Air Act and other environmental measures, safety at work awareness, and the Health and Safety at Work Act, as well as a growing understanding of the dangers of working in smoke-filled buildings and with asbestos, all contributed to changes in health, not least to the decline of chest illnesses. The hazards of drinking to excess and, particularly, of smoking became generally appreciated and were addressed by government action, with smoking banned in pubs, restaurants and even, in an indicative restriction of liberty, private member clubs. On average people became healthier and longer-living. Nutrition improved considerably. The possibility of genetic engineering bringing a solution to hereditary diseases was advanced when the world's first patented animal, the genetically engineered 'onco-mouse' of 1989, was followed in 1997 by Dolly the sheep, the first cloned mammal.

There were, and are, also serious problems and obvious inequalities. Health care became a greater burden on state and society, and the rise in life expectancy led to a major rise in dependency. Once introduced, state welfare was seen as a right, and there was little interest in making direct personal contributions to the cost of health care or pensions. Although inflation played a major role, the cost of the NHS rose from £433 million in 1949 to £26.2 billion in 1989 and £42 billion in 1997.

Government health programmes met serious resistance in fields such as discouraging underage smoking, which rose, especially among women, in the 1990s. There were 138,000 smoking-related deaths in the United Kingdom in 1990. A Department of Health survey in 1993 suggested that half the adult population was clinically overweight or obese, helping to explain high rates of heart disease. Furthermore, the percentage of the population judged severely overweight rose, for example from 8 to 13 among men from 1986 to 1991. It continued to rise thereafter. Death rates from coronary heart disease in Scotland and Northern Ireland are among the highest in the world for both men and women, and England and Wales are close behind.

If the rise in certain illnesses was a problem, so were some of the cures. In the 1990s, concern rose about the over-prescription of antibiotics and their decreasing effectiveness. Similar concern had for long been expressed about the use of tranquillisers. This provision was itself a product of the sense that patients were entitled to treatment and a cure. This attitude led to controversy in 1999 over the government's attempts to limit the prescription of the anti-impotence pill Viagara on the NHS. At the end of the century, despite the immense advances made since 1900, some diseases still lacked cures. Most types of cancer became treatable, but few became curable.

Social Changes

Health changes were linked to social shifts. The rise in tuberculosis since 1995 has been linked to an increase in refugees and immigrants, although that was not the sole reason. There were also major regional variations in health. Blood-pressure rates are especially high in Northern England and the West Midlands. More generally, the poor have poorer health and less access to medical care. In Newcastle, a large number of doctors' surgeries and clinics continue to be located to the north and north-east of the city centre, in Heaton, Jesmond and Gosforth, a situation that bears little relationship to the overall distribution of population and to those in greatest need. The same is true in other cities.

Such social and spatial inequalities can be found in other spheres, such as housing and education. Increases in the price of property, subsidised by tax relief on mortgage interest repayments, helped to ensure that property distinguished the haves from the have-nots. The percentage of dwellings that were owner-occupied rose from 26 in 1945 to 66 in 1988, fuelling the demand for new furnishings and kitchen appliances. The privately rented sector fell from 54 to 12 per cent. Having risen due to council house building in the late 1940s and, especially, the 1950s, the percentage of publicly rented dwellings then fell in the 1980s, due to council house sales and a halt to fresh construction.

There was no comparable extension of private provision in education or health, although contributory pension schemes became far more common. In education, there was a marked increase in the control of central government. The Education Act of 1988 required that state schools conform to a national curriculum, and publish examination results. This reflected a lack of confidence in the education system and was designed to ensure national minimum standards. Test results certainly revealed marked discrepancies in attainment. More generally, there has been a failure to focus on technical education.

Higher education expanded, in part in a deliberate attempt to improve social opportunities, while meeting a developing economy's requirements for skills. In 1962, Local Education Authorities were obliged to finance all students accepted at university. The Robbins Report of 1963 called for a marked acceleration of an already expanding system. The percentage of eighteen-year-olds going on to university rose from 4.6 in 1961 to over 30 by the late 1990s, a process helped by the upgrading of polytechnics as universities in 1992, but essentially due to an expansion in provision. The proportion of eighteen-year-olds entering higher education as a whole rose from 3 per cent in 1939 and 8 per cent in 1960 to perhaps 50 per cent in 1998.

As with many other aspects of state provision, much of the benefit, however, flowed to the middle class and, indeed, the percentage of middle-class women in universities rose markedly. In contrast, the percentage of students from the unskilled working class remained low, in part possibly because of the desire and need to move directly from school to employment. The introduction of tuition fees and abolition of maintenance grants by the Blair government may also have discouraged the children of working-class parents from attending university, although there were better terms for such children.

There was also a gender dimension to changing labour patterns. Thatcher stressed traditional 'family values', but her economic policies led to rising male unemployment, while the female workforce (much of it part-time) rose. The changes challenged those family values and traditional gender stereotypes.

The Decline of Christian Britain

At the beginning of the twenty-first century, most Britons saw themselves as Christians, but, for many, their religion was not central to their life. The Church of England was hit especially hard by a strong current of secularism and scepticism in society.

During the First World War, widespread disruption affected established practices, including church-going, throughout Britain, and the hostilities sapped confidence in the divine purpose, but there seems to have been a recovery in at least nominal church attendance thereafter. In the interwar years, however, the established churches continued to find it difficult to reach out successfully to the bulk of the industrial working class. Much of this group was indifferent to, or alienated from, all churches. The Catholics were most successful. Their number rose from 2.2 million in 1910 to 3.0 million in 1940. In contrast, in the interwar period, the number of Methodists, Baptists, Congregationalists, and Welsh Presbyterians all fell, as did the number of Scottish Episcopalians after a peak in membership in about 1920. The Church of England had scant change in membership, but, given the rise of population, this was an important proportional decline.

The most influential clergyman of the interwar years, William Temple, Bishop of Manchester 1921–9, and Archbishop of York 1929–42, and of Canterbury 1942–4, sought to reverse the decline of organised religion, and to make England an Anglican nation again, and thus justify the Church of England's claim to speak for it. Temple offered a synthesis of Christianity with modern culture in works such as *Mens Creatrix* (1917), *Christus Veritas* (1924), and *Christianity and Social Order* (1942). At times, Temple, who viewed welfare as representing Christian social values, was seen as left-wing, but it was a label he would have denied. Although he strengthened the Church, he failed to give England a more clearly Christian character. Furthermore, Temple's inspiration of the already developing role of the Church as a voice of social concern and criticism led to it being seen increasingly in a secular light. This was despite major efforts to keep religion central to society and to public life.

More generally, in the interwar period church-based societies became less important, both for the young and for their elders. Poverty helped lead some to question faith; although many of the poor did find meaning and support in it. Religious ideas were important in popular moral codes, and in public traditions, even for those who lacked faith. The established churches were more successful in catering to a middle-class constituency, not least because of the important role they had in middle-class socialising and female 'voluntarism' (voluntary service).

This contrast between poor and middle-class responses to the churches remained apparent after the Second World War. Between 1939 and 1945, there was a fall in denominational membership, especially of the Church of England. The 1950s, however, were not a period of obvious crisis. Attendance ebbed, for both the Church of England and the Methodists, but not greatly, and the Catholic Church and the Church of Scotland remained strong. Elizabeth II's coronation in 1953 was very much an Anglican ceremonial, and there were signs of vitality, including the building of a new Coventry cathedral, the construction of churches in new towns and other newly built neighbourhoods, and the popularity of Billy Graham's evangelical missions and of the theological writings of C.S. Lewis, such as *The Screwtape Letters* (1942) and his spiritual autobiography, *Surprised by Joy* (1955).

From the 1960s, however, the established churches were hit by the general social currents particular to that period, especially the decline of deference, patriarchal authority, social paternalism, the nuclear family, and respect for age. Divorce reform had prefigured this shift, for the Matrimonial Causes Act of 1937 had loosened matrimonial ties and sought to make men and women equal. The permissive 'social' legislation of the 1960s and later, such as the decriminalisation of homosexual acts between consenting adults in England and Wales with the Sexual Offences Act of 1967, further changes in divorce legislation, and the granting of equal rights to illegitimate children, flew in the face of Church teachings, and left the Church confused and apparently lacking in 'relevance'. This was especially serious for an age that placed more of an emphasis on present-mindedness than on continuity with historical roots and teachings.

Belief in orthodox Christian theology, especially in the nature of Jesus, in the after-life, the Last Judgment, and the existence of Hell, lessened. Absolute and relative numbers of believers fell rapidly, especially in the Church of England, the Church of Scotland, and Methodism. The issue of relevance was raised in 1963 in *Honest to God*, a widely read book by John Robinson, Anglican Bishop of Woolwich, that sought to address the inability of the Church of England to cater for many, especially in run-down urban areas, by pressing the need for a determination to respond that would include a new liturgy. Cranmer's English in the *Book of Common Prayer* was criticised as antique and replaced by a series of new liturgies.

The Church of England did manage to reassert its moral authority, albeit momentarily, during the 1980s. The report it published in 1985 on the problems facing the inner cities, *Faith in the City*, made a considerable impact. Government policies were lambasted for laying waste to urban Britain. However, the response of the Thatcher government to the report, dismissing its supposed 'Marxist' leanings, highlighted the difficulties that the established churches had in finding a role in an increasingly secular society. The roots of Thatcherism in part lay in a Nonconformity that was hostile to an Anglicanism which was perceived as too strongly connected to 'consensus politics'. Margaret Thatcher saw the Church as wedded to consensus and conciliation. Her call for 'Victorian values' did not extend to a leading role for clerics, many of whom were disenchanted by what they saw as an excessive stress on individualism and economic gain.

This belief in a gap between Church and state was not, however, restricted to the Conservatives. It was found across the political spectrum and also reflected general social values. Furthermore, the public perception of the Church, as captured on television or in plays such as David Hare's *Racing Demon* (1990), was frequently critical. The Church of England certainly could not readily generate respect. Instead, it appeared divided and unsure of itself. Christianity was satirised too, as in the film *Monty Python's Life of Brian* (1979).

The established churches also had to confront challenges from within the world of religion. They were affected by other Christian churches, by traditional non-Christian faiths, and by new cults. In the first case, the greater success of the Catholic Church in retaining the loyalty of its flock and its greater religiosity, at least as measured by church attendance, was a particular reproach in the 1980s and early 1990s, although the Catholic hold over many communicants had been lessened by widespread hostility towards the ban on artificial methods of contraception in the 1968 papal encyclical Humanae Vitae. The Catholic population of England and Wales fell from a peak of 4.257 million in 1981 to 4.155 million in 1999, while weekly Mass attendance fell to 1.041 million. Furthermore, many Catholic clergy proved unresponsive to lay initiatives. Hopes of ecumenical rapprochement were chilled by the attitude of Pope John Paul II, who treated the Church of England as very much a lesser creed, while the decision to ordain women to the Anglican priesthood in 1992 (implemented in 1994) led some traditionalists to join the Catholic Church, which rejected female ordination.

The attitude of the traditionalists reflected long-standing tensions within the Church of England, and the difficulty of absorbing differences in a society increasingly ready to reject such accommodation. Liberal Anglican theologians fell foul both of Evangelicals and of High-Church Anglicans. In reality, the liberal tradition dates back (at least) three centuries, and emerges from time to time. In 1989, one liberal theologian, David Jenkins, became Bishop of Durham. His unorthodox views on the Virgin birth and the bodily resurrection of Jesus caused great controversy. When, that year, York Minster where he had been consecrated, was struck by lightning, this was seen by some Evangelical critics as divine judgment. It was not only the Church of England that was in serious difficulties. The Nonconformist churches were also affected by a decline in faith. The number of Baptists, for example, fell from 300,000 in 1970 to 230,000 in 1992, and the total of young believers was particularly hit.

The established churches were also challenged by the rise of 'fundamentalist' Christianity, inspired from America. This focused on a direct relationship between God and worshipper, without any necessary intervention by clerics and without much, if any, role for the sacraments. Certain aspects of this Christianity, especially its charismatic quality, epitomised by the American evangelical Billy Graham, appealed to some Anglicans, creating tensions within the Church of England.

The Christian tradition also became more diverse, as a consequence of the participatory character of worship introduced by immigrants from the West Indies. In addition, non-Trinitarian religions (that do not regard Jesus as the Son of God), such as the Christadelphians and Jehovah's Witnesses, grew in popularity in the 1980s and 1990s. The long-established Mormons had 90,000 members in Britain in 1970 and 150,000 in 1992.

The challenge to Christianity from cults was not new. Spiritualism, for example, had been popular in the late Victorian period and enjoyed a marked revival in strength and prestige during the First World War. Both 'new age' religions and Buddhism appealed from the 1960s to many who would otherwise have been active Christians. They proved better able than the churches to capture the enthusiasm of many who wished to believe in a material world where faith had become just another commodity. The popularity of cults was also a reflection of the atomisation of a society that now placed a premium on individualism and on personal responses. Such a society was peculiarly unsuited to the coherence and historical basis of doctrine, liturgy, practice and organisation that was characteristic of the churches.

This begs the question of whether the earlier decline of religious practice and belief had not itself permitted the development of just such a society, rather than the society causing religious decline. In answering such questions it is necessary to stress the diversity of the 1960s and subsequent decades, and to note our limited knowledge and understanding of popular religion and what is termed folk belief. It is unclear, for example, how best to understand the popularity of astrology, and, in particular, how far this was an aspect of a magical or non-Christian religious world view. Christianity did not collapse; it declined, and there were still many committed Christians, as well as a large number of conforming non-believers.

By the 1990s, only one in seven Britons was a member of a Christian church, and by 1999 7.7 per cent of adults attended church, although more claimed to be believers: generally over two-thirds. Both for most believers and for the less or non-religious, faith became less important not only to the fabric of life but also to many of the turning points of individual lives, especially dying. Events such as marriage ceremonies and baptisms were no longer so often occasions for displays of family and social cohesion. This was due to the simple fact that more couples were choosing to live together and more parents were choosing not to have their children baptised. A disproportionately high percentage of those who attended church were women, middle aged, and middle class.

Furthermore, it is difficult to criticise the Church of England without noting that religious observance also declined throughout the Christian world. In Eire (the Republic of Ireland), there were legal and political battles over divorce, homosexuality, abortion and contraception as the authority of the Catholic Church was contested. Yet, the decline was certainly more marked in England than in Northern Ireland or Eire, Scotland, or the USA. In the late 1990s, 10 per cent of the English population had been in a church in the last month, but the percentages for Scotland and Northern Ireland were 16 and 52 respectively. In Northern Ireland, communities were and are more tight-knit and religion is a crucial expression of community identity. This is not true of England.

This has been the case now for several decades, and is likely to continue to be so throughout the twenty-first century. The change can be perceived in different ways. It can be argued that secularism is a sign of an advanced society. Alternatively, or in addition, it can be said that it is a cause of an atomisation of social mores and practices that has destructive consequences. Good or bad, it is worth reiterating that the secularisation of society was one of the major trends from the 1960s. The failure in the 1990s of the 'Keep Sunday Special' campaign, heavily backed by the established churches, to prevent shops from opening on the sabbath, confirmed this general trend.

The Thatcher Years

Margaret Thatcher was a figure of great controversy, and, for those who remember her period as Prime Minister (1979–90), this controversy has not ebbed. She was a phenomenon, holding continuous office for longer than any other prime minister in the age of mass democracy, indeed than any since the Earl of Liverpool in 1812–27. Thatcher attracted peculiar hatred on the Left, far more so than any other Conservative prime minister in the twentieth century, and was intensely disliked by most of the intelligentsia of the country. 'Thatcherite' became a term of abuse to a degree that 'Heathite' or 'Majorite' could never match; indeed the comparison is absurd. Furthermore, within her own party, Thatcher aroused strong negative passions. Her predecessor as Conservative leader, Heath, hated her, and the 'one-nation' paternalists who had dominated the party since Churchill replaced Chamberlain in 1940, were appalled at what they saw as her divisive language and policies.

Thatcher, in her turn, had contempt for those she called the 'wets' (her critical term for one-nation paternalists whom she thought 'spineless') and a dislike of a tradition, ethos and practice of compromise and consensus that she felt had led to Britain's decline. Arguably, Thatcher had more contempt for 'wets' (who were not 'one of us') in her own party, than for her opponents in other parties. She blamed previous Conservative governments, from Macmillan to Heath, as well as the Labour governments of Wilson and Callaghan for causing Britain's problems, although Callaghan had abandoned Keynesian policies, and there was an element of continuity in fiscal policy between him and Thatcher.

She openly attacked what she termed 'the progressive consensus'. Conversely, she called for a return to what she saw as older values, for example telling to *The Times* on 10 October 1987 that children 'needed to be taught to respect traditional moral values'. Pleased to be known as the Iron Lady and promising strong leadership, Thatcher relished her determination to weather the storm. It endowed her politics with a sense of virtuous struggle. Thatcherism was just as much a moral as an economic creed. She had no time for doubt, or even debate. The Cabinet became less important and, instead, the Prime Minister relied on personal advisers, although less so than Blair was to do. As with Blair, she sought to transform the political culture and, self-consciously, to implement an ideology.

Thatcher and her supporters, such as Sir Keith Joseph and Nicholas Ridley, wanted to rewrite British history. In particular, they rejected the Keynesian analysis of the past. Thatcher referred positively to her youth in 1930s Grantham. The Thatcherites also criticised post-1945 economic management and 1960s social policies. Keynesian economics was condemned for a willingness to accept dangerous levels of inflation, and inflation itself was seen as socially disruptive, as well a threat to core Conservative constituencies. Thatcher offered an apparently straightforward solution to Britain's economic problems (control of the money supply) at a time when other politicians seemed lacking in both insight and determination. She benefited from the extent to which the views towards poverty and the poor that had contributed to the Welfare State created in the late 1940s were insecurely rooted, and, in particular, were compromised by concern about tax implications. Furthermore, Thatcher argued that, in 1945–79, both Conservative and Labour governments had failed to restrain trade union power.

In practice, as with all politicians, there was much compromise: Thatcher was not the most Thatcherite politician;

intuition and self-confidence as much as ideology and doctrine were central to her leadership. Indeed, there was to be criticism that her rhetoric of 'rolling back the state' was misleading, and that government expenditure did not fall as anticipated. In part, this was due to factors she had not anticipated, especially a major rise in unemployment during her first government (1979–83) and the consequent rise in unemployment payments.

Yet, rhetoric and policies were fused, because, although there was less unalloyed Thatcherism or indeed a consistent body of policy that could be called Thatcherism than the Prime Minister suggested, there was, nevertheless, a stated determination to persist that was different in degree and style to that of her predecessors. This aroused both widespread hostility and genuine doubt. Both owed much to the particular policies and problems of the first years of the government.

After coming into office, the government rapidly signalled its intentions with a budget on 12 June 1979 that was seen by its supporters as an attempt to provide incentives in society and the economy, and by its critics as grossly unfair. Public expenditure was cut by £4,000 million. The basic rate of income tax fell from 33 per cent to 30 per cent, and the top rate on earned income from 83 per cent to 60 per cent, while the top rate on 'unearned' income – interest from savings and other investments – was cut from 98 per cent to 75 per cent. In contrast, Value Added Tax (VAT) rose from 8 per cent to 15 per cent, although there were important exemptions.

This was a major shift from direct to indirect tax. It was criticised as regressive, in that taxes on the wealthy fell, while the poor were hard hit. However, cuts in direct taxation were popular, and helped provide Thatcherite Conservatism with both a value system and popularity. Rising prosperity and more widespread taxation had ensured that 80 per cent of households were paying direct taxation by 1975. As a result, taxation levels became more central in public awareness and public debate, and the principal factor in the response of many throughout society to government policy. Public expenditure was cut by another £1,275 million in the second budget – on 26 March 1980 – and the public sector borrowing requirement (PSBR) was restricted to £8,500 million.

Lower taxes released purchasing power. The net effect was to push up inflation: it rose to 18 per cent in 1980. Interest rates rose markedly in order to cope with inflation. Combined with the impact of North Sea oil, now being produced and exported in large quantities, high interest rates led to a rise in sterling. The combination of a high exchange rate for sterling and high interest rates hit the economy, especially export industries, while the high exchange rate also led to a fall in the price of imports. Much of the economy became uncompetitive. Company bankruptcies pushed up unemployment. Social security payments thus rose, driving up public expenditure at a time when the economic recession was hitting national income and government revenues.

The government responded, on 10 March 1981, with another budget in which spending was cut by a further £3,290 million and some taxes (not income tax) increased. This was an attempt to reduce the budget deficit as a percentage of GDP, specifically the PSBR, which had increased by 130 per cent in 1977–9. Far from following Keynesian precepts, and trying to invest and spend its way out of crisis, the government was following a deflationary policy, a course that aroused great controversy.

Unemployment rose further. By the winter of 1982/3, it had reached the unprecedented postwar figure of 3.3 million. The shrinking of the economy hit manufacturing industry particularly hard (and services far less so). In terms of public perception, these lost jobs were 'real' jobs. They were predominantly male and in traditional industrial tasks, such as 'metal-bashing'. Furthermore, many factories that were closed, such as the Consett steel works in County Durham and the Corby steel works in Northamptonshire, were crucial to entire communities. This focused the social costs of the long-term decline in heavy industry. The rapid rise in unemployment was completely out of line with recent experience and thus had a heavier impact than the comparable recession in the early 1990s. The toll was repeatedly driven home because unemployment figures were published monthly, and not, as with many other indices, quarterly.

To critics, both inside and outside government and the Conservative Party, these figures suggested policies that had failed, and a government that must change direction, as Heath had done in 1971. Far lower unemployment figures then had seemed disastrous. Thatcher's response defined her government: 'The lady's not for turning', she told the 1980 party conference, and the delegates applauded. Throughout her period as Prime Minister, Thatcher was popular with the Conservative Party conference, more so than in the Cabinet and the parliamentary party. The last was to abandon her in 1990 and show that the prime minister does not enjoy presidential power.

She remained adamant the following year, despite an outbreak of rioting not seen, outside Northern Ireland, since 1832. These were not industrial disputes involving violent secondary picketing, and thus answerable to some sort of control. Instead, from April 1981, in Brixton and Southall in London, Toxteth in Liverpool, Moss Side in Manchester, and, to a lesser extent, other centres, such as Derby, crowds rioted, looted, and fought with the police. From the perspective of today, these were small-scale disturbances, many of which reflected specific local problems, especially relations between black youth and the police, which became the focus of the report from the Scarman Inquiry that was set up after the Brixton riots. At the time, however, it was unclear how far these riots would spread and how they would stop.

Evidence of the strains on social cohesion that were the result of government policy did not lead Thatcher to change direction, and she was able to regain the initiative, thanks to an Argentinian invasion of the Falkland Islands on 2 April 1982. An expeditionary force was sent to the South Atlantic on 5 April, and the Argentinians were totally defeated. The victory raised Britain's international prestige, and won the government, and Thatcher, widespread support in Britain. It also increased her already strong sense of purpose and self-confidence, her disinclination to adapt to the views of others.

The gut patriotism released and displayed in 1982 made many commentators uncomfortable, but Thatcher knew how to respond. It helped give her leadership a dynamic reputation enjoyed by no Conservative leader since Churchill. Assisted by opposition divisions, Thatcher pressed on to win the 1983 election. Thatcherism was not to be a one-term phenomenon.

Despite serious problems in the economy, the Conservatives won the elections of 1983, 1987 (both under Thatcher) and, far more narrowly, 1992 (under John Major), in part because the Labour divisions of the early 1980s and the creation of the Social Democratic Party, which eventually merged with the Liberals, split the opposition. Parts of the Conservative programme, not least the attacks on trade unions, the battle with inflation, and the cuts in direct taxation, were popular. Thatcher's attempt to encourage people to rely on their own resources, rather than on social welfare, did not strike the same chord; while the rift with the Establishment, specifically the criticism of non-utilitarian privilege and long-held liberal sentiments, however much justified, had only limited impact.

Nevertheless, Thatcher was successful in winning and retaining considerable working-class support with her own brand of Conservative populism. They preferred her council house sales and tax cuts to the policies of the Labour Party which advanced a particularly radical agenda in the 1983 election and appeared unable to control trade union demands. Thanks to developments, such as council house sales and the spread of mortgages and banking, the 1980s 'working class' had a different interaction with the national economy than its predecessors.

The impact in the 1980s and 1990s of the Conservative policies of monetarism (the belief that the economy can be regulated by the control of the money supply), deregulation, privatisation, and the abandonment of the goal of full employment exacerbated regional economic differences. The wealthiest regions grew fastest: in England, in 1977–89, Greater London and much of southern England experienced greatest growth. Services rather than manufacturing were central to the economy of these regions.

Conversely, there were low levels of both gross domestic product per head and of economic growth in Cleveland, Merseyside, South Yorkshire and Cornwall. The coal industry continued its decline, as did steel and shipbuilding. Earlier areas of growth, such as Teesside with its chemical industry, decayed. In 1981, the car factories at Linwood in Strathclyde and Speke on Merseyside closed. This was a reversal of the decentralisation of the car industry away from the West Midlands and the South-East that had begun in the 1960s with government encouragement but by the 2000s the car industry was in serious decline in its traditional centres. This was an aspect of the overall problems of British manufacturing, problems which led to unprecedented trade deficits.

Changes in industrial location were linked to new technology and to labour relations. In the case of docks, long-established ports with militant workers, especially Hull, Liverpool, London and Southampton, lost business to those where a more flexible workforce welcomed container loads, for example Dover, Felixstowe and Harwich. Thanks in large part to the decline of employment in the car industry, the percentage of the working population in Oxford engaged in engineering manufacturing fell from 28 in 1971 to 7 in 1991, while that in professional occupations rose from 24 to 30.

Greater regional specialisation also exacerbated regional differences. Management, research and development jobs were increasingly separate from production tasks: the former concentrated in South-East England, in areas such as the M4 corridor west of London, near Cambridge, and, to a lesser extent, in 'new towns' in southern England, such as Milton Keynes and Stevenage. The Conservatives, and the 'Establishment' in general, became more focused on London, the South-East, and the world of money and services, largely to the detriment of traditional industrial interests. Conservative liberalisation of the financial system following the abandonment of exchange controls in 1979 both helped make the City of London boom, and secured the Conservatives' move away from interventionist economic planning.

Such liberalisation also helped promote foreign investment in Britain (and British investment abroad). In 1999 Britain was the largest foreign direct investor in the world and the second largest recipient of such investment. The percentage of cars manufactured in Britain that were made by Japanese firms rose from

5 in 1988 to 25 in 1995. Investing primarily within established industrial areas, such as Derbyshire, North-East England, and, in particular, South Wales, foreign firms and other investors, nevertheless, located on 'greenfield' sites. Foreign investors sought the same socio-economic policies as the government: high-skill, high-productivity plants with cooperative unions and little or no interest in traditional working practices and mores. The Conservative government of Thatcher was as opposed to corporatism as it was to collectivism.

Regional economic differences encouraged migration, leading people in general to move from the North to the South of England, although this was hindered by inflexible public housing policies and a restricted low-cost private rental sector. Employment levels and wage rates varied greatly across the country. Unemployment was highest in traditional mining and industrial areas, and they also had the highest expenditure per head on income support and the highest percentage of households with a low weekly income. In 1994, the average weekly earnings of a working man was £419.40 in South-East England, £327.80 in northern England, and £319.20 in Northern Ireland. The South-East also paid a disproportionately high percentage of taxation, and thus benefited particularly from Thatcher's major cuts in income tax. No other part of the country saw office development to compare with that in London's Docklands in the 1980s. Yet there was and is also much poverty in the South-East, not only in London, but also along the Thames estuary, and in the Medway towns, Brighton and the unappealing new town of Crawley.

Areas with high rates of unskilled labour were hit particularly hard by the economic changes of recent decades. Until the 1970s, there was a strong labour market for skilled and semi-skilled jobs, and many jobs for the unskilled; but extensive de-industrialisation since has reduced opportunities for unskilled labour, while they have also been hit hard by large-scale immigration. The real income of the bottom 10 per cent in Britain increased by 10 per cent in 1973–91, but the top 10 per cent gained 55 per cent, a reflection of the strong demand for educated labour. The bottom tenth of manual workers earned only 64 per cent of average income in 1991, and suffered, more generally, from the decline of Tory paternalism under Thatcher, a politician more interested in both social mobility and the idea of 'one of us', than in the drive for a less unequal society. The percentage of the population below half average income rose from 11 to 21 in 1971–95, although that average increased greatly, and the failure to distinguish between relative and absolute poverty is a major problem with such statistics.

Differences in disposable wealth were related to other financial indices, such as savings and house values. They were also linked to variations in consumption patterns, such as car ownership and tourism. Some of these variations were a matter not only of quality of life but also of life-safety indices. This was true not so much of health insurance as of the ability to keep homes warm, and other comparable indicators.

The same disparities were also marked at the more local level, and this provided much of the detailed fabric of social geography. Crude regional indices concealed striking variations. In the South-West, for example, the unemployment and poverty of much of Cornwall, hit badly by successive crises in tin-mining, fishing and upland farming, was very different to the situation in West Dorset. In South Devon, Dartmouth and Totnes were far more prosperous than Dawlish and Paignton. The Medway towns were and are very different from the rest of Kent. In 1987, rates of unemployment in the Newcastle wards ranged from 8.9 per cent in Westerhope to 36 per cent in West City.

These local contrasts deepened in the 1980s, 1990s and 2000s, in part because of shifts in housing. Council house sales under the 'Right to Buy' legislation of the 1980 Housing Act were widespread but skewed. The better housing in the wealthier areas sold, while the public sector increasingly became 'sink housing', rented by those who suffered relative deprivation. Thus in Newcastle, there were above average sales of council houses in the western and northern estates, and below average sales of those along the river and in the east. Other cities had similar trends. 'Sink housing' areas tended to have higher rates of crime and drug addiction. In desperation, local authorities increasingly demolished such housing from the mid-1990s.

The National Trust

The role of the National Trust throws some interesting light on modern British society. It is a striking feature of modern Britain that the National Trust, a registered charity, has more members than any political party: in 1997–8 the number rose above 2.5 million. This was testimony to the astonishing success of a body then just over a hundred years old. So also was the way in which visiting Trust properties became a part of the lives of millions, whether walking across magnificent scenery or going for tea (and visiting an accompanying stately home). The history of the Trust has not been free of differences and controversy. The balance between countryside and buildings has been, and is, a difficult one, and finances have always been tricky. This has led the Trust since 1975 to refuse any newly offered properties that come without a major cash endowment, a policy that prompted it to turn down Heveningham Hall, Suffolk. Yet, controversy is part of the flavour of British life. It would have been surprising if the Trust could have avoided dissension over issues such as hunting on its property, which was banned in 1997.

The range of properties cared for by the National Trust and the National Trust for Scotland is astonishing pressure on the environment is growing, and government has not been up to the task of protecting it. This is most clearly seen along the coastline. The Trust has played a crucial role through Enterprise Neptune, which by 1998 covered 575 miles of coast, in protecting what has been spoiled across much of Europe. In 1998, the Trust also owned 244,500 hectares (603,000 acres), making it the largest private landowner in England. Its properties are enjoyed: in 1997 there were 11.7 million visitors to the 251 properties open at a charge, an increase from 10.5 million in 1993.

The places most frequently visited reflect the popularity of gardens. In the year 1 March 1997 to 28 February 1998, the most popular was Wakehurst Place, an extensive woodland garden in the Sussex Weald to the south of London. The second, Fountains Abbey and Studley Royal, contain Georgian water gardens, and the third, Stourhead Garden, is a masterpiece of Georgian landscape gardening. Polesdon Lacey, the fourth, is a house and gardens within easy day-trip distance of London. St Michael's Mount, the next, has no grounds, but the following two – Sissinghurst Castle and Lanhydrock – are famous gardens. Other popular gardens and grounds include Nymans, Bodnant, Cliveden,

Sheffield Park, Hidcote and Claremont, while gardens and grounds provide much of the appeal of many of the popular building properties, for example Cragside and Killerton. The figures for 2000 showed Wakehurst and Fountains again first and second, but in 2001 the situation was affected by the impact of foot and mouth disease.

Aside from horticultural interest, these estates also offer orderly, managed trips into the open air. They reflect the power of the garden in the British, more particularly English, psyche, which is, in turn, an important part of the rural aesthetic. This aesthetic is amply served by the products sold in National Trust shops, not least their packaging, and is also catered for in the Trust's holiday cottages and, indeed, the menus in many of the restaurants. It is also a tamed aesthetic.

The National Trust also reflects the character of British society at the close of the twentieth century. The growing role of professionalism is striking in what was, and still, in large part, is a body reflecting the voluntarism in society. By 1998 the Trust had 38,000 volunteers.

The impact of government, legislation and litigation are readily apparent. Thus the Trust was affected in the 1990s by changing policies towards agriculture and the countryside, training and work experience for the employed, planning and regional development, minimum wages, pensions and taxable relief on donations and investment income. Tax policies have always been important to the Trust. In 1937, it was allowed to accept from donors of houses, without either side paying tax, additional property, cash and securities as income-generating endowments. Donors and their families were also allowed to continue to live in their houses as tenants, an issue that has caused controversy, and the National Trust was permitted to earn income from its properties. These tax changes were crucial to the expansion of the Trust's holdings of country houses. By 1950, it had forty-two. The Trust has the unique statutory power of declaring land inalienable – it cannot be sold, mortgaged or compulsorily purchased against the Trust's wishes without special parliamentary procedure.

The Trust is also of great interest as a NGO (non-government organisation). It is, for example, one of the largest owners of farmland in Britain.Scholars are focusing more on such bodies as they seek to appreciate their importance in modern society. NGOs frequently elicit more enthusiasm and support than government bodies.

NGOs are of great importance for modern Britain, because the nature of political change is such that the state and its government are being transformed, in large part losing functions to European bodies and also eroding as Britain is dissolved. This poses a challenge to NGOs, especially those that operate at a level above the locality or region. Not only will they soon probably have to adapt to new bodies asserting fiscal, governmental, legislative and jurisdictional powers and doing so in a different fashion to comparable bodies elsewhere: Wales and East Anglia for example. In addition, NGOs may end up within a European super-state as the prime representatives of national identity and continuity. It is unclear what the effects of this will be, but it is likely that the challenges of recent decades will pall beside those of a new world of national reconfiguration.

There were also important inequalities between ethnic groups. While some migrant groups, especially Chinese and East European Jews, did particularly well, on average 'outperforming' the 'indigenous' population, West Indians tended to suffer higher rates of unemployment and, partly as a consequence, on average, have poorer housing, education and health care. Ethnicity or 'colour' were clearly not the sole issue. Unemployment rates and social problems among Pakistanis and Bengalis, for example, were higher than those among Indians, which may be linked to Muslim attitudes toward women. The Race Relations Acts of 1965 and 1976 were probably less important in countering often vicious racialism than the ability of many from immigrant backgrounds to take advantage of economic growth, and also the success of role models in a series of high-profile activities, such as athletics, football and television.

Ethnic groups have different attitudes to integration. Muslims, in particular, are wary of many aspects of secularism. Racial tension played a major role in riots in St Paul's in Bristol in 1980, Southall and Brixton in London and Toxteth in Liverpool in 1981, Tottenham in London and Handsworth in 1985, and Brixton in 1995.

Membership of the European Union and its extension into Eastern Europe led to a large-scale immigration from the latter in the mid-2000s, especially of Poles. This greatly increased the overall immigration figures, helping ensure a serious burden on housing and public services, especially health and education. The situation was greatly exacerbated by the Labour government's failure to control immigration, not least by fulfilling its own commitments on the matter. The Eastern European migrants altered the character of overall immigration. The percentage of foreign-born workers in the labour force rose from 7.4 in 1997 to 12.5 in 2006, and by then a quarter of the babies born in Britain had a foreign parent.

Moreover, by the mid-2000s there was also a considerable (although far smaller) emigration of the indigenous population. This included emigration in search of work, particularly to America and Australia, and for retirement, especially to France and Spain.

The importance lower price of property in these two countries reflected both the growing centrality of property price movements as a definition of opportunity and relative wealth, and also the extent to which British prices had increased.

Frequent surveys and the massive amount of information available to government bodies and private-sector marketing agencies ensures that the local, regional and national geographies of the country can be better observed than ever before. There was no Victorian equivalent to *Social Trends,* an annual synthesis of official government data produced from the 1960s that was designed to bring statistics to the people. The significance of what is observed, however, is a matter for profound disagreement, as is indicated, for example, by controversy about the impact of single parenthood. Furthermore, the way in which location, space and routes are understood, the process of mental mapping, is difficult to assess and evaluate. It has probably been profoundly altered by the mass media. This change in mental mapping can be seen as a social equivalent to the increasing reconceptualisation of space as a result of the growing use of computer-related information and communication systems.

Television and Social Mores

Television use has become near universal. It succeeded radio as a central determinant of the leisure time of many, a moulder of opinions and fashions, a source of conversation and controversy, an occasion for family cohesion or dispute, a major feature of the household. A force for change, a great contributor to the making of the 'consumer society', and a 'window on the world', which demands the right to report everything, television has become increasingly a provider of common visual images and a reflector of popular taste. Thanks to television, events, such as the funeral of Diana, Princess of Wales in 1997, were accessible to people of very different social and geographical circumstances to a degree that was impossible earlier. Television was more successful in setting the tone of British society than more historic institutions, such as the established Churches. For example, it encouraged a permissiveness in language and behaviour by making such conduct appear normal. By the mid-1990s, most television and radio 'soaps' supposedly depicting normal life seemed to have their quota of one-parent families, abused children, and sympathetically presented homosexuals.

A sense of social fluidity was also captured by cartoonists. One of the best, Mark Boxer, had a braying upper-class woman declare in the *Guardian* on 1 June 1983, 'Nonsense, nanny. We're *thrilled* Emma's fiancé is self-made', and another on 3 October 1983, 'We couldn't afford to give Fiona a season; but luckily she is in a soft porn movie'. On 27 July 1983, a woman in bed in a Boxer cartoon addressed her partner: 'Will you get out of bed; I want you to be one of the 8 per cent who propose on their knees', an ironic comment on the prevalence of pre-marital cohabitation.

Divorce became more common. It was an expression of a greater experience, indeed consumption, of different lifestyles, and a facet of the growth in single parenting that concerned many commentators. Although in the mid-1990s about three-quarters of children lived in a family with both their natural parents, and three-quarters of births outside marriage were registered by both parents, both marriage and the family became less normative than earlier in the century and both took on different meanings.

It is unclear how far this was linked to a widespread breakdown in the socialisation of the young that was especially serious in the case of young males. The percentage with criminal records rose, as did recorded crime. By 1989, Britain had a higher proportion of its population in prison than any other West European country, except Luxembourg. Crime hit most in run-down neighbourhoods, further de-socialising life there. Although blamed by many on Conservative government between 1979 and 1997, crime had, in fact, increased from the 1950s. For much of this period, unemployment rates were low and the standard of living of the poor rose. Thus, an economic explanation of rising crime appears less pertinent than one that focuses on social dislocation.

Institutions adapted to social trends and thus helped to strengthen them in public culture, although there was opposition to doing so in the Conservative Party, and this was seen in its legislative programme in the 1980s. Section 28 of the 1988 Local Government Act forbade local authorities from 'promoting homosexuality' or teaching 'its acceptability . . . as a pretended family relationship'. There were, however, no prosecutions. The same year, the Education Reform Act ignored the idea of multi-culturalism. Nevertheless, it proved difficult to neglect social trends. In 1995, the General Synod of the Church of England (the governmental body established in 1969) abandoned the phrase 'living in sin', and in 1997 asserted the right of cohabiting couples, including homosexuals, to receive fertility treatment. By then Britain had a divorce rate well above that of the European Union, and this remains the case.

Television both demanded novelty and served what has been termed the heritage industry. Period dramas on television, such as *Upstairs Downstairs*, first screened in 1971, and the televised versions of Jane Austen novels frequently broadcast in the 1990s and 2000s, were very successful. Critics claimed that period dramas were a sign of dangerous escapist nostalgia, reflecting a lack of confidence in present and future. This might be so, but they were not a recent development. Galsworthy's *Forsyte Saga* had been a great success on television in 1967, and nostalgia can be found in much popular fiction of the twentieth century, such as the novels of Georgette Heyer and her many successors. Attitudes to religion, sex and the role of women in the 1970s, 1980s, 1990s and 2000s, scarcely suggested a yearning for an earlier age.

The same was true of the British film industry. The industry had been hit when quotas were abandoned in 1983. By 1992, only 4 per cent of films shown were British productions, while their American counterparts had 92.5 per cent of the market. The most successful British-produced films of the 1990s – *The Full Monty, Four Weddings and a Funeral, Mr Bean, Trainspotting and A Fish Called Wanda* – were not excursions into the world of Jane Austen. Instead, they were aspects of British success in the fields of entertainment, music and design. Success was particularly marked in the world of music. The groups Oasis and the Spice Girls were at the forefront of the Britpop explosion in the 1990s, although the 2000s have been less successful.

Film and television had a great effect on the British sense of identity, on how the British saw themselves and named each other. In 1997 and 1998, the most frequently chosen names for newborn children registered in England and Wales were Jack and Chloe, the names of the oft-discussed children of the presenters of the television programme *This Morning*. Other television- and film-linked names whose popularity rose in 1998 included Courtney, Caitlin, Phoebe and Ethan. In 1998, John, the most common name earlier in the century, was no longer in the top fifty.

The personal computer gave individuals more independence than television, although it was similarly a form of machinery and communication dependent on commercial suppliers. Like the television, the internet shrank space and overcame distance, providing near-instantaneous transmission of material. Access to this new technology is socially skewed, so that a new index of deprivation, analogous to that of limited personal mobility, is being created. Yet, despite this skewing, access overall is at a high level.

Britain and Europe

The political map, meanwhile, changed fast and is continuing to do so. This is a consequence both of deepening integration within what is now the European Union and the creation of new institutions and political bodies within the British Isles. Membership of the European Economic Community was re-examined after the Conservative government of Edward Heath was replaced in 1974 by Labour, still under Wilson, but a Wilson who now had little to offer bar not being Heath and being able to appease the unions. Wilson sought to settle divisions within the Labour Party, which had voted against entry to Europe in 1972, by holding a national referendum in 1975 on Britain's continued membership; 67.2 per cent of those who voted favoured membership, the only areas showing a majority against being the Shetlands and the Western Isles. The available evidence suggests that the voters tended to follow the advice of the moderate politicians, including the three party leaderships, who generally supported staying in, rather than the opposing voice of Enoch Powell on the nationalist right and Tony Benn on the socialist left; and that public opinion was very volatile on the EEC, implying a lack of interest and/or understanding. Benn saw the size of the opposition vote as 'some achievement considering we had absolutely no real organisation, no newspapers, nothing', but the referendum result was decisive, and relations with 'Europe' did not become as divisive a domestic political issue again until the late 1980s when they played a major role in the fall of Margaret Thatcher in 1990.

Thatcher tried to keep European integration at bay. She declared: 'We have not successfully rolled back the frontiers of the state in Britain, only to see them reimposed at a European level with a European superstate exerting a new dominance from Brussels', and watered down the European Social Charter, gaining exemption for Britain in 1989. Nevertheless, under her government, there was an important erosion of national autonomy that vindicated many of the fears expressed by critics of membership in the referendum campaign. The Single

European Act, operative by 1987, gave new powers to the European Parliament and abolished the veto rights of a single state for most issues. In October 1990, Britain joined the Exchange Rate Mechanism of the European Monetary System, a fixed exchange rate system designed to help financial movements within the European Community which the EEC had become. (It is now the European Union.) Agreement was also reached on the construction of a Channel Tunnel. Public interest in the European movement, however, remained low. The percentage turnout at elections for the European Parliament rose from only 32.6 in 1984 to 36.2 in 1989 and 36.4 in 1994, figures well below those in France and Germany.

Thatcher's Conservative replacement, John Major (1990–7), also sought, with only limited success, to slow down the movement towards European integration, which had gathered pace from 1985, and become especially strong with the end of the Cold War and the unification of West and East Germany in 1990. An alliance of France, Germany and the European Commission pushed through the Maastricht Treaty on European Union of 7 February 1992 which brought a commitment to greater integration, including political integration. The British obtained opt-out clauses over the social chapter and the single currency, but the struggle to win parliamentary endorsement for Maastricht divided the Conservative Party and badly weakened the Major government. The Conservative vote against Maastricht eventually encompassed one-fifth of the party's back-bench MPs. The House of Commons ratified the Treaty in June 1993 by a majority of only three. Denmark, France and Ireland all held referenda that year on the Treaty, but the Major government refused to do so.

The government was also discredited by the exit from the European Monetary System that was forced on the pound in September 1992 by overvalued exchange rates, the interest-rate policies of the Bundesbank, and speculators. In practice, this exit brought much benefit, enabling the country to manage its finances, and helping encourage economic growth in the mid-1990s, but, at the time, it created an abiding impression of poor, not to say inept, leadership.

The European link inflicted another blow when serious health problems with parts of the British cattle herd – bovine spongiform encephalopathy – led to a prohibition on beef sales by the European Union (EU), and a humiliating series of applications to it: the inability of the British government to regulate the situation and its subordination to European bodies were made abundantly clear. In some cases EU institutions were, at least in part, motivated by national hostilities to Britain. By the mid-1990s, the growing Euro-scepticism of the Conservative Party was such that not even Major's attitude of 'wait and see' over the single European currency could hold the party together.

After Labour came to power in 1997, the ability to defend national interests, indeed to have a sense of the national interest, declined further. The opt-out from the Social Chapter was relinquished in 1997, leading to more regulations for employers. In 2007, what was in effect a new European constitution was signed by Gordon Brown despite the major infringements on British governmental authority and power it entailed. Pressure for a referendum was rejected and understandably so because public opinion polls indicated the unpopularity of the measure.

The persistent failures of British policies within Europe were not lessened by successes elsewhere. Britain played an important role in the successful Gulf War against Iraq in 1990–1 and, thereafter, took an active military role in a number of international issues, for example both enforcing the Gulf War ceasefire on Iraq and peacekeeping in former Yugoslavia. Although referred to as showing that Britain could 'punch above her weight', this activism, like Britain's nuclear status and permanent membership of the United Nations Security Council, brought little obvious benefit to the British, and, in part, reflected a vainglorious attitude on the part of the British leaders, seen in particular in Blair's aggressive stance during the Kosovo crisis of 1999. The position he took over Iraq in 2003 was far more controversial. Issues of deceit were much discussed, although a lack of prudence proved more deadly. This was an aspect of a more general charge against Blair, that he lacked both intelligence and integrity.

Humans v Animals

Other creatures have been decimated by human activities. House-building and road-building have all had a serious impact on the size of the land base while changes in agricultural practice have radically altered the way the remaining land was farmed. This impact varied between different parts of the country – house-building, for example, was more of a problem in South-East England than Lincolnshire. Nevertheless, the general trend throughout the twentieth century was one of cumulative assaults on the environment. The possibility of animals and humans sharing territory diminished. For example, the increased use of the car in the early decades of the century led to the asphalting of former rural tracks. This was environmentally damaging in itself, and also affected the ability of animals to find food there. In the 1990s, between 3,000 and 5,000 barn owls were killed on UK roads each year, joining large numbers of rabbits, hedgehogs, badgers, deer and other animals.

The number and viability of animal species in Britain was hit. Pine martens, members of the weasel family, were reported in 1995 to have vanished from England in 1994, and to be on the brink of extinction in Wales. Pressure on animal habitats became more insistent during the century, and came to affect all animals. To take a few examples of the many that could be quoted, in the second half of the century, the numbers of stone curlew fell by 85 per cent with the fall accelerating from the 1960s. The loss of grassland was seen as particularly significant in this case, but changes in the management of this kind of habitat, especially more intensive stocking of pastures and the switch from hay to tillage, which destroys nests, were also very important. Among other birds, the number of skylarks fell by about 50 per cent in 1976–98; while that of grey partridge fell by more than half, due in large part to the destruction of nesting sites when hedgerows were grubbed up, and also to the lesser availability of winter stubble for feeding. The decline in the rook population gave cause for concern from the mid-1970s. Loss of habitats and early silage cutting on grassland helped to reduce the number of corncrake to fewer than 500 mature males by 1998. Most of the surviving birds were concentrated into a small number of areas. Bitterns were hit by a drastic reduction in wetland habitats. Drainage improvements were responsible for the fall in the number of bitterns in the Fens.

The decline in the population of black grouse was rapid and dramatic. In early Victorian times, the black grouse was common in the New Forest, Hampshire, Wiltshire, Dorset and most counties south of the Thames and was well established in the West Country. A 1924 survey reported that there were only six counties in England and Wales where it had never been recorded. Yet, by the 1990s, there were only remnant populations, probably on the verge of extinction, in the West Country, Derbyshire and North Wales. Scotland was the only part of Britain where the black grouse was still numerous. Indeed, Scotland was the last remaining stronghold of many other species. On the whole, lowland species were more seriously affected than their upland counterparts by development and agricultural changes, largely because more upland was protected and because agriculture there was less intensive. Nevertheless upland species were also affected, in part due to overgrazing as sheep density rose.

The grey partridge was the gamebird that declined most seriously. Research by the Game Conservatory suggested that its demise was caused by the shrinking number of nesting habitats, the reduction in insect food, and the increase in the level of predation. Pheasants were also affected, but the decline in the indigenous population was partly offset by increasing the number of birds reared artificially and released. Not all the damage to bird populations came as a consequence of human action. The Royal Society for the Protection of Birds (founded in 1889) estimated in the 1990s that sparrow-hawks, of which there were 34,000 pairs counted in 1991, ate between 50,000 and 100,000 British songbirds every year.

Other forms of wildlife were also badly hit by human action. The destruction of hedgerows and wetlands, ensured that more than 78 per cent of breeding colonies of the pipistrelle bat, the most numerous species, were lost between 1979 and 1998, while bats as a whole were hit by the increasing use of timber preservatives in the old buildings that were their breeding sites. The loss of habitats in sand dunes, salt marshes and heathlands largely wiped out the natterjack toad, and the filling-in of ponds, in which they bred, greatly hit the great-crested newt. The brown hare was another species in chronic decline. Reasons included changing agricultural methods, especially 'prairie farming', with its destruction of hedgerows, and an increase in fox predation. Far from being inconsequential, such changes made rarer sights and sounds that had once characterised the country. Throughout the

British Isles, pesticides were used extensively in agriculture, and entered the ground-water system. They affected wildlife as well as humans. Thus, the fall in the rook population in Surrey and elsewhere was blamed on chemicals. The diminution (and even disappearance) of the dawn chorus in several parts of the country was a particularly poignant indicator of loss to changes in land use, as well as pollution and pesticides. The spring became quieter thanks to the massive decline of common garden birds like song thrushes.

Other changes in animal cultures were more varied. Mankind had the capacity to introduce such fur-bearing animals as the muskrat and coypu, and, exceptionally in their cases, the ability to exterminate them, despite their having become feral – the muskrat in the early 1930s and the coypu in the late 1980s. The ecosystem in the Norfolk Broads altered when coypu escaped from local fur farms, and had an impact on other wildlife. Coypu also damaged the drainage system and destroyed sugar beet. The mink, rabbit and grey squirrel, however, were examples where it proved impossible to eliminate the species, even locally, once it became established. In the New Forest in 1998, 'animal rights' activists deliberately freed mink from fur farms, with unintended consequences for other local wildlife: the mink had a devastating effect on small animals, birds, and farm stock. Four North American mink that escaped from a fur farm on the Isle of Harris in the late 1960s, created a colony of abut 12,000 that attacked both rare seabirds and chicken farming.

Public concern about the fate of wildlife became more pronounced from the 1960s. It also had a powerful impact in children's literature, with works such as Richard Adams' *Watership Down* (1972).

The process of human pressure on wildlife was not all one-way. The Welsh red kite was brought back from the brink of extinction, the Cornish clough was returned to the wild in Cornwall, the population of many species in the 1990s was stable, for example of sparrow-hawks, and efforts were made to protect animals. The breeding sites of creatures such as bats and nests of hornets became protected. However, the pressure was almost all negative. The designation of particular protective areas was generally linked with a deterioration in the situation elsewhere, and was, indeed, commonly a response to it.

Dismantling Britain?

The continued existence of Britain now became a matter of debate. Under both Thatcher and Major, the Conservatives defended the constitutional system in Britain, specifically the position of Scotland and Wales. Major's defence of the union between England and Scotland was important to the party's general election campaign of 1992.

The constitutional position of Scotland and Wales had been increasingly challenged by nationalists from the 1960s. The Labour Party was powerful in both Scotland and Wales, and also dependent on its position there to counter the strength of English Conservatism, a situation accentuated by the persistent over-representation of Scotland and Wales in the House of Commons, an over-representation that challenged the democratic credentials of the Labour Party. A Scotland and Wales Bill introduced in 1976 proposed an assembly in each country with control over health, social services, education, development and local government, but with no taxation power and with the Westminster Parliament retaining the veto. Its eventual passage was only possible after the government conceded referenda, a novel constitutional development in Britain, although one which had had its supporters since the Edwardian period. Referenda on devolution in 1979 produced a majority of those voting in favour in Scotland, but not the necessary majority of the electorate, while a large majority of those voting in Wales opposed devolution.

The Conservative government elected in 1979 was no friend to devolution. Thatcher was firmly committed to a view of British identity focused on the sovereignty of the Westminster Parliament. The extent to which administrative responsibility for Scottish affairs had been transferred from Whitehall to the Scottish Office in Edinburgh helped to encourage a sense of governmental autonomy and responsibility in Scotland, but there was little real element of democratic control over the Office. The unpopularity in Scotland of Thatcher's government, with the Poll Tax being introduced there in 1989, one year earlier than in the rest of the United Kingdom, and her inability to appeal to the Scottish dimension of Britishness, helped to complete the decline of the link between the Conservative Party and working-class Scottish Protestant culture. There were no Conservative seats in Glasgow after 1982, only ten out of the seventy-two Scottish constituencies after the 1987 election, and none after that of 1997 which ended Tory government and brought Labour under Blair to power. Conservative representation also collapsed to zero in Wales in 1997. Thatcher's policies had been unpopular, particularly the Poll Tax, as had been the choice of English MPs to serve as Secretary of State for Wales.

Blair's theme was 'New Labour', a different Labour Party eager for modernisation. This entailed what he presented as a 'Third Way' between socialism and conservatism, as well as the 'Cool Britannia' of a modishly new set of cultural values. 'Modernisation' of the country became a focus of government activity, and this necessitated a protracted period of constitutional change in order, it was claimed, to bring power closer to the people. The 1997 joke 'Did you know that Tony Blair MP is an anagram of I'm Tory Plan B?' made little sense in Scotland or Wales. A large majority in a referendum in Scotland in September 1997, and a tiny one in Wales, provided the basis for the creation of assemblies with legislative powers. They first met in 1999. The Scottish Parliament was given tax-varying powers, but the Welsh Assembly was not. The over-representation of Scotland and Wales in the Commons was not tackled. The government in 1999 removed most of the hereditary peerage from the House of Lords as part of its policy of at once 'rebranding' Britain and securing Labour hegemony. The notion of an 'elective dictatorship' advanced as a criticism of Thatcher appeared to be adopted as a means of government by Blair.

Re-mapping Britain was one consequence of Blair's policies. Increasingly, policy was set with reference to the European Union, and the value of presenting Britain as a political unit independent of the continent was questionable. This was particularly apparent with the spreading impact of European legislation and judicial authority, and with the government responsive to the notion of joining the single European currency 'when the time is right'. It was unclear how far the coherence of the British state would be maintained. The proposed renewal, reconfiguration or break-up of Britain was, and is, not restricted to Scotland and Wales. Under the terms of the Good Friday Agreement of 10 April 1998, not only would a new Northern Ireland Assembly be established, ending direct rule from Westminster, but so too would a British–Irish Council. This council would include representatives from the British and Irish governments, the Northern Ireland Assembly, the Scottish Parliament, and the Welsh Assembly.

In addition, plans for the creation of new regional assemblies in England invited the possibility that any delegation of power would not be limited, but would become part of a continuous process in which new regional institutions would not only demand the transfer of power, but would also seek a more direct relationship with European Union institutions. In one respect this process seemed obvious. There are important differences between parts of England, and, also, a frequent use of geographical terms, such as East Anglia, the North-East or the West Country. In 1999, eight Regional Development Agencies began work.

However, it is unclear that there are coherent, clearly defined units to match terms such as the West Country or South-West. This area has a vague geographical existence, but, despite frequent references to it in the local media, plays no part in defining residents' sense of identity: counties remain the primary focus.

To take the region that is most frequently held to have a clear identity, the North. It is apparent that attempts to suggest that the 'North' or the 'North-East' – for there is a crucial lack of clarity here – has a separate identity that can emulate that of Scotland are deeply ahistorical. It is not simply that Scotland was a separately governed nation until 1707. Scottish identity was also expressed and sustained in a distinctive established Church, legal system, educational system, and local government. Scotland retained clear boundaries. Thus, a sense and practice of Scottish identity remained strong, at the same time as conceptions of

Britishness were advanced in Scotland. Identity is neither exclusive nor constant: a sense of collective self-awareness can include a number of levels or aspects of identification.

The situation in northern England is radically different to that in Scotland. There is no continuity with past identifications to lend historical roots and rationales to present-day demands. The North of England was absorbed by the West Saxon state in the tenth century and, since then, distinctive political structures have been essentially administrative in character, representative of the local authority of the national state, as with the palatine jurisdiction of Durham, and the Yorkist and Tudor Councils of the North. Similarly, there has been no autonomy in religious or cultural terms: the archdiocese of York was scarcely the basis of a separate identity.

Indeed, any reading of the history of the last millennium will offer cold comfort for those who wish to suggest a separate Northern or North-Eastern identity. This is also apparent if the cartography of identity is considered. If there is a North where does it begin, where does it reach to, and how far do overlapping senses of identity challenge any clear regional spatiality? This is also true of the North-East. Geographically this is more coherent, essentially because the established image of the region reflects several urban nodes from Tyneside to Cleveland centred on Newcastle, Sunderland and Middlesbrough, with sparsely populated largely rural areas to north, west and south that can seem to serve as buffer zones for the region – part of it, but unable to challenge the manner in which the urban nodes define its interests and culture.

Yet this urban 'construction' of the North-East is open to question. The extent to which the dominant image and images of the North-East can be seen as an accurate reflection of the region as a whole is open to debate. Alongside (or is it interacting with?) this world is that of a largely rural region, of isolated farmsteads, small towns and open spaces, or again another, of suburban developments, out-of-town shopping centres and 'executive' housing estates. It is a rash individual who says that one is more 'true' to a regional identity than another. If out-of-town shopping centres, most famously the

Metro Centre at Gateshead, were a novelty of the 1980s, the world of coal and heavy industry that was, and is, so important to the area's traditional identity was not an immutable feature of the region.

A sense of identity often develops, or is expressed most clearly, in hostility or opposition to other groups, and their real or imagined aims and attributes, and these groups are frequently ones with which relations are close. Indeed, the reality of overlapping senses of collective self-awareness can be very difficult. This can be seen in current discussion of Northern identity, much of which expresses a depressingly repetitive and small-minded hostility to London and national government.

If regional identity is dependent on a feeling of dispossession and alienation then it will be profoundly unattractive. If it is linked to a political platform then it will be limited and restricted, and will run the risk of typecasting alternative local views in terms of the hostile centre, rather as Scottish nationalism is prone to do. More generally, rather than thinking in terms of metropolitan versus regional, it may be more pertinent to address the issue of how best to conceptualise interacting or competing national attitudes and their local resonances. This is especially relevant as the mobility of the population remains high, adding to the sense of impermanence and fluidity.

In the case of the South-West, it is very unclear where the boundaries and centres should be, and the notion of a distinct and separate identity is questionable. In Cornwall, there is a strong sense of dissatisfaction with national government, but it is very unclear that government agencies based in Bristol, or even Plymouth or Exeter, would be more welcome. The distance from Penzance to Bristol, Swindon or Bournemouth is great, and accentuated by poor communications, and all the latter look more to London than to Devon, let alone Cornwall. In the South-West shared economic interests are limited, and there is little sense of a cultural or political consciousness that can define and unite a region.

The regional situation is even more obscure elsewhere. To take the Midlands, where two separate regions, West and

East, are often discerned, it is unclear how far counties such as Cheshire, Derbyshire and Oxfordshire should be seen as integral, or as transition zones to neighbouring regions. The East Midlands north, and even immediately south, of the Trent can be seen as part of the North, Oxford is increasingly a commuter town for London, while Cheshire is as much part of the North-West as of the West Midlands. In the South-East, there is the bagel problem: London is central to it and without London it is unclear how far the constituent parts have any identity or unity. Yet London and the South-East if established together as a distinct governmental region would be far more populous and wealthy than any other, and this might lead to an inherent instability in the process of regionalisation.

The questioning of assumptions of British nationalism came not only from 'Euro-enthusiasts', Scottish and Welsh nationalists and regionalists. In addition there was an assault on the supposed implications of this nationalism. The Commission on the Future of Multi-Ethnic Britain, which reported in 1999, declared, with no real evidence, that 'Britishness, as much as Englishness, has systematic, largely unspoken, racial connotations', and also called for a change in their historical treatment, specifically 'reimagining' to challenge racism. The accuracy of the report was a matter of debate; what is clear is its preference for social engineering and its hostile reponse to the liberal dimension of British public culture.

More generally, there is the question whether the changes currently discussed or in prospect mean the collapse of Britain, or whether the proposed reconfigurations within Europe, the British Isles and England amount to a necessary modernisation that is appropriate to the demands of the twenty-first century and, specifically, to the challenges posed by globalisation. Not only the sovereignty and cohesion of the United Kingdom, but also the character and unity of England are being recast – or is it destroyed? – in the name of modernity.

Readers will have their own views. This book has been all about change, but to claim that traditions can be and are moulded, even created, is not the same as suggesting that they are without value. Nor is it the case that this process of moulding and creation necessarily justifies the replacement of the existing practices and ideas that give people a sense of continuity, identity and value.

To conclude on a note of uncertainty and dissolution is not to offer the 'upbeat' summary of national achievements and character that popular historical works frequently proffer. Such a conclusion would be inappropriate, an insult to readers well aware that we are all in a period of unprecedented flux. Does the historian have anything to offer at this juncture? Yes, a warning. Any reading of the past leads to an understanding that change is unpredictable, the promises of politicians discarded, the hopes of future benefit often facile. It is all too easy to throw away our history, the sense of place and time that provides identity and helps maintain social values. To do so for the reasons currently offered is foolish.

SELECTED FURTHER READING

It is best to begin not with the writings of historians but with those of contemporaries. They exist in astonishing quantities: everything from cookery books to parliamentary debates. I would recommend newspapers as most accessible. Old ones are kept in the reference or local studies sections of most libraries, especially big libraries. The other contents of local studies sections are also very helpful and interesting.

Other than newspapers, diaries and correspondence are probably the best sources. Travel accounts offer much of value. Two recent editions of accounts from the start of the period are *An American Quaker in the British Isles. The Travel Journals of Jabez Maud Fisher, 1775–1779*, edited by Kenneth Morgan (New York, 1992), and *A Frenchman's year in Suffolk: French impressions of Suffolk Life in 1784*, edited by Norman Scarfe (Woodbridge, 1988). Very different travels were recounted in William Cobbett's *Rural Rides* (London, 1830), J.B. Priestley's *English Journey* (London, 1933) and George Orwell's *The Road to Wigan Pier* (London, 1937).

Another source that is often overlooked is old maps. It is instructive to consider changes in successive maps, as in *Mapping the Past. Wolverhampton 1577–1986* (Wolverhampton Libraries and Information Services, 1993). Historical atlases of particular localities are also very useful. Recent ones include D. Dymond and E. Martin, *An Historical Atlas of Suffolk* (3rd edn, Ipswich, 1999), *An Historical Atlas of County Durham* (Durham, 1992), *Newcastle's Changing Map* (Newcastle, 1992), Peter Wade-Martins (ed.), *An Historical Atlas of Norfolk* (Norwich, 1993), Stewart and Nicholas Bennett (eds), *An Historical Atlas of Lincolnshire* (Hull, 1993), Susan Neave and Stephen Ellis (eds), *An Historical Atlas of East Yorkshire* (Hull, 1996), Joan Dils (ed.), *An Historical Atlas of Berkshire* (Reading, 1998), Roger Kain and William Ravenhill (eds), *The Historical Atlas of the South West* (Exeter, 1999), and Kim Leslie and Brian Short (eds), *An Historical Atlas of Sussex* (Chichester, 1999). Valuable earlier historical maps can be found in atlases such as *Atlas of Portsmouth* (Portsmouth, 1975). Historical geography is best approached through the articles in the *Journal of Historical Geography*, for example, I.S. Black, 'Money, Information and Space: Banking in Early-Nineteenth Century England and Wales' (1995). Modern mapping can be seen in Daniel Dorling, *A New Social Atlas of Britain* (Chichester, 1995). For more specialised historical mapping, J. Langton and R.J. Morris, *The Atlas of Industrialising Britain, 1780–1914* (London, 1986), Rex Pope (ed.), *Atlas of British Social and Economic History since c. 1700* (London, 1989), Hugh Clout (ed.), *The Times London History Atlas* (London, 1991), Andrew Charlesworth et al, *An Atlas of Industrial Protest in Britain 1750–1990* (London, 1996), Robert Woods and Nicola Shelton, *An Atlas of Victorian Mortality* (Liverpool, 1997). On mapping, Katherine Barker and Roger Kain (eds), *Maps and History in South-West England* (Exeter, 1991) and Catherine Delano-Smith and Roger Kain, *English Maps. A History* (London, 1999).

Valuable introductory works covering the period include Jeremy Black, *Convergence or Divergence? Britain and the Continent* (London, 1994), *Modern British History since 1900* (London, 2000), and *Britain since the Seventies* (London, 2004), and Norman McCord and Bill Burdue, *British History 1815–1914* (2nd edition, Oxford, 2007). Tom Devine, *The Scottish Nation, 1700–2000* (London, 1999) emphasises a distinctive national history. There is much of value in Boyd Hilton's detailed study of the early nineteenth century, *A Mad, Bad, and Dangerous People* (Oxford, 2006).

For social history, recent works include Andrew Adonis and Stephen Pollard, *A Class Act: The Myth of Britain's Classless Society* (London, 1997), Simon Dentith, *Society and Cultural Forms in Nineteenth-Century England* (London, 1999), David Gladstone, *The Twentieth-Century Welfare State* (London, 1999), Harry Goulbourne, *Race Relations in Britain since 1945*

(London, 1998), David Hirst, *Welfare and Society, 1832–1991* (London, 1999), Alan Kidd, *Society and the Poor in Nineteenth-Century England* (London, 1999), Joseph McAleer, *Popular Reading and Publishing in Britain, 1914–1950* (Oxford, 1992) and *Passion's Fortune: The Story of Mills and Boon* (Oxford, 1999), Arthur McIvor, *A History of Work in Britain, 1880–1950* (London, 2001), Hugh McLeod, *Religion and Society in England, 1850–1914* (London, 1996), W.D. Stephens, *Education in Britain 1750–1914* (London, 1999), David Taylor, *Crime, Policing and Punishment in England, 1750–1914* (London, 1998), and N.L. Tranter, *British Population in the Twentieth Century* (London, 1995). For gender, Sue Bruley, *Women in Britain since 1900* (London, 1999). Other important works include W.H. Fraser, *A History of British Trade Unionism, 1700–1998* (London, 1999), and Peter Kirby and S.A. King, *British Living Standards, 1700–1870* (London, 1999).

Recent work on nineteenth-century political history, includes Rodney Barker, *Politics, Peoples and British Political Thought since the Nineteenth Century* (London, 1994), John Belchem, *Popular Radicalism in Nineteenth-Century Britain* (London, 1995), Eugenio Biagini, *Gladstone* (London, 1999), David Eastwood, *Government and Community in the English Provinces, 1700–1870* (1997), Angus Hawkins, *British Party Politics, 1852–1886* (London, 1998), Terry Jenkins, *Disraeli and Victorian Conservatism* (London, 1996), *The Liberal Ascendancy, 1830–1886* (London, 1994) and *Sir Robert Peel* (London, 1999), H.S. Jones, *Victorian Political Thought* (London, 1999), John McCaffrey, *Scotland in the Nineteenth Century* (London, 1998), Ian Machin, *The Rise of Democracy in Britain, 1830–1918* (London, 2001), and Robert Stewart, *Party and Politics, 1830–1852* (London, 1989).

For the twentieth century there are numerous memoirs, for example Denis Healey, *Time of My Life* (London, 1989), Roy Jenkins, *A Life at the Centre* (London, 1991), Margaret Thatcher, *The Downing Street Years* (London, 1993) and Roy Hattersley, *Fifty Years On: A Prejudiced History of Britain Since the War* (London, 1997). Diaries include Richard Crossman, *The Diaries of a Cabinet Minister* (3 vols, London, 1975–7).

More concise and scholarly works include C.J. Bartlett, *British Foreign Policy in the Twentieth Century* (London, 1989), D.G. Boyce, *The Irish Question and British Politics, 1868–1996* (2nd edn, London, 1996), John Charmley, *A History of Conservative Politics, 1900–1996* (London, 1996), Sean Greenwood, *Britain and the Cold War, 1945–91* (London, 1999), David Harkness, *Ireland in the Twentieth-Century: Divided Island* (London, 1995), I.G.C. Hutchison, *Scottish Politics in the Twentieth Century* (London, 1999), W. David MacIntyre, *British Decolonization 1946–1997* (London, 1998), Ritchie Ovendale, *Anglo-American Relations in the Twentieth Century* (London, 1998), Ian Packer, *Lloyd George* (London, 1998), David Powell, *The Edwardian Crisis: Britain, 1901–1914* (London, 1996), Geoffrey Searle, *The Liberal Party. Triumph and Disintegration 1886–1929* (London, 1992), I.G. Simmons, *An Environmental History of Twentieth-Century Britain* (London, 2002), Nick Smart, *The National Government 1931–40* (London, 1999), Andrew Thorpe, *A History of the British Labour Party* (2nd edn, London, 2001), Ian Wood, *Churchill* (London, 1999), John Young, *Britain and European Unity, 1945–1999* (London, 2000). For the changeable nature of national character, Robert Colls, *The Identity of England* (Oxford, 2002) and Peter Mandler, *The English National Character: The History of an Idea from Edmund Burke to Tony Blair* (New Haven, 2006).

Earlier works can be pursued through the bibliographies of the recent works that have been cited.

PICTURE SOURCES

Buckinghamshire Records & Local Studies Service 191

Colour-Rail 146

John Crook 76, 162

Dudley Archives & Local History Services 83

Electrical Trades Union 181

Stewart P. Evans 111

Fun 73

Hulton Archive 200, 206, 211, 213, 214, 227, 234, 237, 243, 251, 257

Humphrey Household Collection 7

Illustrated London News 68 (both), 87, 102 (both), 105, 107, 166

Imperial War Museum Q1142 136

Ivan Belcher Colour Picture Library 42, 86, 219

Patrick Loobey 149

Kent Messenger 174 (bottom)

Chris Makepeace 52, 88, 174 (top), 194

Mander & Mitchenson Theatre Collection 160, 188

John Marsh, from *Cumbrian Railways* by John Marsh and John Garbutt (Sutton, 1999) 50

National Library of Wales 91, 124

By permission of the National Museum of Labour History 127, 142, 151

National Trust Photographic Library 140; Michael Brown 245; Andrew Butler 58; Neil Campbell-Sharp 5; Dennis Gilbert 198

Paul Nicholls 222 (both)

Ordnance Survey © Crown Copyright 96 (both)

Photography by Graeme Peacock, reproduced courtesy of Gateshead Council 259

Robert Opie Collection 114, 118, 119, 133, 134 (both), 153, 182, 186, 196, 231

Ronald Grant Archive 157, 185, 229, 249

Royal Pavilion, Libraries & Museums, Brighton 61

RSPB Mark Hamblin 253; Andrew Hay 255

Rural History Centre, University of Reading 117

Uplands School, Leicester 204

Westcountry Publications 239

INDEX